The history of the Irish Brigade remains fascinating more than three centuries after its creation in the late seventeenth century and is regularly revived in the English-speaking world as well as in Western Europe thanks to historians, journalists, and even politicians. The military feats of these Irish troops fighting for the French kings in Italy in 1702, on the plains of Flanders, or for the Stuarts in the Scottish Highlands in 1745 still captivate people's imaginations to this day. Yet, the reality of the lives and deaths of these Irishmen is often eclipsed by nineteenth century historical myths produced in both Ireland and Great Britain for political purposes that were either different or even in complete opposition to the Brigade's raison d'être. This is not the only paradox attached to the Irish Brigade. Though successful on the battlefields of Europe, they fought other people's wars. Though remaining present in historical memories, the Brigade ultimately failed to help secure a second Stuart restoration. Though serving the Jacobite cause, they are often overshadowed by the Scottish clans of the '45. This book endeavours to explain how and why the myth surrounding the Brigade came to be by studying this military diaspora of the long eighteenth century.

This book rests on the author's ongoing forays into hitherto unused primary sources and documents and takes the reader from the heyday of the so-called 'Wild Geese' at the very end of the seventeenth century to the decline of the Brigade in the second half of the eighteenth century, using sources found in Irish, British, and French archives. The negative stereotype attached to Irish soldiers is explored in the press as well as in correspondence from French civilian and military authorities. Questions about the daily lives of officers and soldiers in the Brigade can be answered using cross-referenced information from different national and local records. The Battle of Fontenoy on 11 May 1745 represents the pinnacle of the Brigade's military identity, yet the battle also proved its undoing due to the heavy casualties suffered by the Irish on that fateful day. The rest of the century saw the Irish regiments serving the French king becoming a military tradition more than a viable asset in the ongoing wars between France and Great Britain.

Pierre Louis Coudray was born in France in 1979. After graduating from the Universities of Rennes and Caen with a degree in Irish studies, he completed a PhD in Irish and military history at the University of Lille in 2018. He is now a lecturer in British studies at the University of Le Mans. His work on the image of the Irish Brigade in the eighteenth century in France, Britain and Ireland was awarded the 2019 PhD prize from the Irish Cultural Centre in Paris. He has been published in both France and Ireland on the subject of the Irish military exiles. His interests include military history, Irish and British cultures, and visual representations of war in the English-speaking world from 1700 to 1900.

'More Furies than Men'

The Irish Brigade in the Service of France 1690-1792

Pierre-Louis Coudray

Helion & Company

Helion & Company Limited
Unit 8 Amherst Business Centre
Budbrooke Road
Warwick
CV34 5WE
England
Tel. 01926 499619
Email: info@helion.co.uk
Website: www.helion.co.uk
Twitter: @helionbooks
Visit our blog at http://blog.helion.co.uk/

Published by Helion & Company 2022
Designed and typeset by Mach 3 Solutions Ltd (www.mach3solutions.co.uk)
Cover designed by Paul Hewitt, Battlefield Design (www.battlefield-design.co.uk)

ISBN 978-1-914059-82-7

British Library Cataloguing-in-Publication Data.
A catalogue record for this book is available from the British Library.

For details of other military history titles published by Helion & Company Limited, contact the above
address, or visit our website: http://www.helion.co.uk

We always welcome receiving book proposals from prospective authors.

Contents

List of Plates   vi

List of Colour Plates   vii

Introduction: 'Les régiments irlandois' – The Irish soldiers serving France in the long eighteenth century   viii

1   'The audacity and stubbornness of the Irish' – The Irish regiments serving Louis XIV (1690-1715)   13

2   'Most of the recruits coming to us are vagrants' – Maintaining the Irish regiments in France (1700-1740)   53

3   'In Hoc Signo Vinces' – The Irish Brigade and the Battle of Fontenoy   97

4   'Our regiments are in a class of their own' – The Irish regiments at the crossroads of history (c. 1760–1815)   139

Conclusion: 'History changed by a bard'   180

Bibliography   185

Index   197

List of Plates

Louis XIV, King of France (1638-1715).   14
Detail from the Battle of Londonderry, 1689.   15
William III, king of England, Scotland, France and Ireland in 1690.   22
Anonymous, *Battle of Aughrim, 1691*.   24
James II (1633-1701), King of Great Britain.   32
Officers on a break.   55
A map of Ireland in the eighteenth century.   77
'Un Camp Volant' ('A light camp').   91
Maurice de Saxe (1696–1750).   102
A map of the Battle of Fontenoy, 11 May 1745.   103
Louis XV (1710-1774).   106
The Duke of Cumberland (1721-1765).   118
Dillon's Regiment 1750s.   141
Régiment de Lally 1757.   145
Dillon n°90 (1779).   158
Theobald Dillon's death.   161

List of Colour Plates

The Battle of the Boyne, 1 July 1690, Jan van Huchtenburg (1690-1733). i

Flag of the Clancarthy Regiment (1692-1698) held at the Invalides in Paris (6647, cote Ba 6). i

Soldiers of the Irish Brigade during the wars of Louis XIV. ii

Soldiers of the regiments of Bulkeley, Rothe, Clare, and Berwick, circa 1720. iv

Soldiers of the Irish Brigade during the wars of Louis XV. vi

Uniforms of the last years of the Irish Brigade, and of its successors. viii

A map representing the positions of the armies at the beginning of the Battle of Fontenoy, 11 May 1745, showing the position of the Irish Brigade on the French left. x

Introduction

'Les régiments irlandois' – The Irish soldiers serving France in the long eighteenth century

Let's only change leaders, and we are ready to start the battle again.[1]

In October of 1697, *Maréchal* Vauban wrote to the Marquis de Barbezieux, France's Minister for War, about the plight of Irish soldiers whose regiments were being disbanded at the end of the War of the League of Augsburg. He was urging him not to forget those exiles that had 'served well in this war', writing they were 'very brave troops and poor people driven from their country because of their religion and because of the loyalty due to their King', who were 'worthy of compassion'.[2] Though Vauban's request only concerned the immediate needs of the Irish, the notion of remembrance surrounding the role played by these exiles in French military history, as well as their living conditions in Ancien Régime France, has actually shaped most of the narratives produced about them ever since the seventeenth century. The ever-growing presence of these Jacobite refugees in the histories of Ireland, France and Britain has sparked a renewed interest for the topic over the last twenty years among both academics and military history enthusiasts. Far from being forgotten, they have become ubiquitous.

By the end of the seventeenth century, the presence of Irish soldiers in French armies was not a new phenomenon. Ever since the Middle Ages, Irish mercenaries and soldiers acquired a fearsome reputation that the Elizabethan conquest of Ireland made even more patent. After their defeat at the Battle of Kinsale in 1601 and the Flight of the Earls of 1607, even greater numbers of Irish Catholics left for the continent in order to serve Spain before choosing Louis XIII as their new sponsor in the 1650s. The *Hibernois*[3] regiments then created were poorly regarded as their ranks were filled with men better suited to be beggars than soldiers. Nevertheless, in spite of many instances of difficult relationships between those men and the French local population, France's royal authorities showed a growing

---

1   Jacques Lacombe, *Encyclopediana, ou Dictionnaire Encyclopédique des Ana* (Paris: Panckouke, 1791), p.280.

2   Pádraig Lenihan, 'The 'Irish Brigade' 1690–1715', *Eighteenth–Century Ireland / Iris an Dá Chultúr*, vol.31, 2016, pp. 47–74.

3   An old French term for Hibernian or Irish.

interest in recruiting more Irishmen. Around 15,000 of them are said to have served the Bourbons from the 1630s to the mid-1660s.[4] With Louis XIV's ambitions spurred on by his quest for *la Gloire* (military glory), France needed a large army to fight its numerous wars, with as many as 20 per cent of the rank and file being foreign mercenaries. Recruiting men from other countries, especially from nominally enemy territories, served two purposes: it meant that Frenchmen could be employed in the fields to feed the largest population of Western Europe while the French king could use foreigners with military experience and personal networks to his advantage. This was perfectly illustrated by the Irish Brigade, at least until 1746 when the hopes of a Jacobite restoration finally waned. Ironically, the more that Irish soldiers were praised, either by the French or by the British, the less likely an Irishman was to join the ranks of the Jacobite Brigade as other professional opportunities arose, both at home and abroad. Only the officer corps rested firmly in the hands of the Irish diaspora still living in France. However, once the French Revolution started, faithful service to both the Bourbons and the Stuarts meant that the Brigade could not survive as a military unit serving the French nation. Having been stripped of all its Irish and Stuart symbols still visible in its uniforms and flags, the Brigade was finally disbanded in the Summer of 1791 by an official decree from the *Assemblée Nationale*.[5]

On the other side of the Channel, the insurrections and massacres of the 1640s and 1650s had already reinforced the image of barbaric Irish soldiers in the English public imagination. The crowning of James II in 1685 and his desire for a standing army partially filled with Catholics fuelled those very fears. This led to the so-called 'Irish Fright' of 1688 when a rumour spread that the Irish troops brought to Britain to fight against William of Orange were indiscriminately slaughtering civilians in the southern counties of England. The Jacobite threat was serious enough for William of Orange – who had become William III – and his successors to justify maintaining a standing army even after the signing of the Treaty of Limerick in 1691. England's subsequent involvement in European wars in the late seventeenth and early eighteenth centuries meant a general increase of its military capacity, with units garrisoned in Scotland and Ireland to counter any Jacobite attempt. In Ireland itself, the Penal Laws adopted in the late 1690s strengthened the Protestant Ascendancy by prohibiting any Catholic from owning a weapon or serving as a soldier. However, the constant menace of an invasion backed by a Catholic power meant that finding suitable men to fill up the ranks of the army proved difficult for British recruiting parties. The Stuart expeditions of the first half of the eighteenth century focused on Scotland while Ireland remained mostly at peace, yet young Catholic Irish noblemen who wished to serve as officers were banned from entering British regiments and had to go into exile all over Europe to fulfil their martial dreams. Only the looming danger of a French invasion forced Great Britain to change its recruiting policy to improve its military capabilities, first by covertly enlisting Irish Catholics and then doing so officially after 1793. The Irish Brigade and its members, once London's fearsome enemies, were swiftly turned into fellow nationals whose past exploits suddenly became worthy of notice.

---

4   Pierre Gouhier, 'Mercenaires irlandais au service de la France (1635–1664)', *Revue d'Histoire Moderne et Contemporaine*, 1968, n°15–4, pp.672–690.

5   21 July 1791. See M. Arnoult, *Collection des décrets de l'Assemblée Nationale Législative* (Dijon: Causse, 1792), vol.3, p.307.

This is why the story of the Irish Brigade has grown with the telling, turning it into a military legend that few would now dare question as it was adopted on both sides of the Channel. That narrative always follows the same pattern: After the Jacobite defeat of 1691 in Ireland, Irish regiments were allowed to leave for France with their families after the signing of the Treaty of Limerick, hoping to restore a Catholic king from the Stuart family on the English throne with the help of the Catholic powers. The Irish Brigade, as it soon became known, quickly gained the esteem of Louis XIV and his French subjects due to their fighting abilities displayed during the wars of the League of Augsburg (1688–1697) and of the Spanish Succession (1701–1714). As faithful servants of the exiled Stuarts, the Irish successfully integrated into French society. Their military reputation, already bolstered by the Battle of Cremona in 1702, reached its peak thanks to their victorious charge against British and allied forces at the Battle of Fontenoy in 1745 in which they saved both the French army and Louis XV. Their troops were also present to defend French possessions in India and participated in the War of American Independence on the French side, serving the Bourbon kings loyally even after the French Revolution. Literary and iconographic representations of the Irish Brigade always insist on the imposing number of Irish soldiers serving France and the Jacobite cause, their martial prowess and their nickname, the 'Wild Geese', a poetic reminder of their hope of imitating those migratory birds and one day returning to Ireland.

Though everything mentioned in the previous paragraph is based on historically accurate facts, one should keep in mind that this epic story is also the result of several centuries of effective rewritings of the Irish Brigade military past. Today, even daring to question their belonging to a form of military elite provokes an outcry as mentioning the Irish regiments in a positive light has become a permanent feature in most military history books devoted to eighteenth century warfare. To begin with, the actual numerical strength of the Brigade must be put into perspective, as well as the idea of peaceful coexistence between the Irish and the French. The push-and-pull factors urging Irishmen to leave their native island for the European continent throughout this period remain difficult to identify: was it purely out of loyalty for the Stuarts, or mere expediency borne out of military and financial interests? Finally, even their nickname 'Wild Geese' divides specialists as to its origin and first adoption.

Consequently, myth making, historical reconstructions and repeated narratives have changed the historical reality of eighteenth-century Irish regiments fighting abroad. Though the first elements of these little alterations of the historical experience of the Irish Brigade can be traced back to the eighteenth century, nineteenth century authors such as Matthew O'Conor and John Cornelius O'Callaghan are the ones who actually shaped these martial narratives. [6] They managed to give the Irish Brigade an aura of respectability and invincibility that it did not necessarily possess when it was fighting on the battlefields of Europe during the long eighteenth century. They are still used today as reference, but their books – although respectable owing to the impressive collections of documents accumulated to write them – were literary means to a political end. Their Irish military history was meant to

---

6   Matthew O'Conor, *Military History of the Irish Nation* (Dublin: Hodges & Smith, 1845); John Cornelius O'Callaghan, *History of the Irish Brigades in the Service of France* (Glasgow: Cameron and Ferguson, 1870).

foreshadow an independent future for the whole island. This peculiar situation has rendered any attempt at a comprehensive and reasoned version of the Brigade's long career extremely difficult, as writing about these warring exiles cannot simply rely on previous studies but requires a major overhaul founded on archival research.

Luckily for anyone wishing to go back to the sources, French archives have kept many traces of the Irish regiments fighting under the flags of the Ancien Régime. From the second half of the seventeenth century onwards, military matters forced French authorities to dramatically expand their official administration in order to better supervise the largest army in Western Europe, leading to vast quantities of documents being deposited in both local and national archives all around France. Rosters, bills and eyewitness accounts abound, and the French army went as far as effectively creating the first national identification system to monitor its soldiers after 1716. This state of affairs has helped many historians over the past 50 years delve into the history of French military units with relative ease, though the sheer amount of information means that such an undertaking remains a daunting task.

The Irish regiments are no exception to the rule and a careful inspection of such records usually yields interesting results, with many documents challenging the ubiquitous version of the history of the Brigade, as this book will show. The first chapter will deal with the beginnings of the Irish regiments serving under the Sun King and how they were first viewed as mediocre troops before being accepted as reliable units within the French army. The second one will focus on the first half of the eighteenth century, on life and death in the Brigade with day-to-day questions relating to recruitment, payment, desertion and motivation among the officer corps and the rank-and-file. The third one will be entirely devoted to Fontenoy and the rewriting of the history of that particular battle in the Irish community exiled in France. The fourth and final chapter will observe the slow decline of the Irish Brigade up to its official disbandment in the early 1790s before turning to its dual rebirth in the service of Britain and in Napoléon's *Grande Armée* with the Légion Irlandaise.

1

'The audacity and stubbornness of the Irish'[1] – The Irish regiments serving Louis XIV (1690-1715)

The peoples of this country are so bent on being soldiers and serving [James II] that instead of the current 50,000 men one way or another on foot, he could have three hundred thousand if he had enough to arm and maintain them.[2]

After the Glorious Revolution had swept aside the Stuart monarchy in England, the Catholic Lord Lieutenant of Ireland, Richard Talbot, Duke of Tyrconnel, remained loyal to James II and hastily raised regiments to defend his cause. This Jacobite army lacked proper training, weapons and discipline, which quickly indicated to Louis XIV that James II's attempt to continue the fight over there would merely be a diversion. The Sun King's assistance was relatively limited in scope, and shipping war supplies, regular troops,[3] and high-ranking officers, such as the experienced *Maréchal* de Rosen, could hardly compensate for the lack of military resources actually available in Ireland. Yet the few convoys from Brest, and Irish resistance, allowed Louis XIV to prevent the newly crowned William III from adding England's full military might to the League of Augsburg. As long as Ireland remained in open rebellion, the *Stadtholder* could not peaceably leave London for fear of a foreign intervention in the sister island. The local Catholic population, which at first had warmly welcomed the Stuart king and his supporters, quickly became disillusioned as the war became a protracted affair devastating homes and livelihoods. This situation combined with the chronically indecisive nature of the exiled monarch transformed the entire operation into a logistical quagmire. This became even more apparent after the early encounters with Protestant forces at the siege of Londonderry (18 April to 1 August 1689) or at the Battle of Newtownbutler (31 July 1689), two defeats that immediately cast a shadow on a swift Stuart victory. But although the correspondence between the French court and Louis XIV's representatives in Ireland

---

1   Eléazar de Mauvillon, *Histoire du Prince Eugène de Savoie* (Amsterdam: Arkstee & Merkus, 1740), vol.2, p.33.

2   Archives du Ministère des Affaires Etrangères (AMAE), letter from de Gravel [French envoy to Ireland], 27 March 1689, *Suppléments Correspondance politique Documents Divers, 1676-1696*.

3   The Regiment of Berwick, that was supposed to be comprised of 40 companies of 100 men each, was to be organised in January of 1689.

Louis XIV, King of France (1638-1715). Louis XIV fought two coalition wars at the end of his long reign in which Ireland played a more significant role than generally realised. Engraving by Bernard Picart (1673-1733). (Leichtenstein-Hauslab Collection, Anne S.K. Brown collection)

clearly showed that the Jacobite war effort did not match the strategic resolve required for a successful campaign, it also displayed a growing interest in repatriating Irish soldiers back to France as their military potential became more noticeable.

'It is a chaos akin to that of the Genesis':[4] French Views of the Irish during the Williamite War

The French officers sent to help at the onset of the war openly despised their Irish counterparts, who did not all hail from noble families and had very little experience in modern warfare techniques, most notably siegecraft. Also, the reputation of reckless courage marred by ill-discipline acquired by the Irish when fighting for France in the earlier decades of the

---

4   Lauzun on the Irish campaign as quoted in François Guizot, *L'histoire d'Angleterre* (Paris: Hachette, 1877), vol. 2, p.376.

Detail from the Battle of Londonderry, 1689, Dutch print, Romeyn de Hooghe, 1689. (Rijksmuseum, Amsterdam)

seventeenth century was confirmed during the Irish campaign. Such difficulties, combined with the scarcity of resources in Ireland and James II's vacillation, rapidly led to tensions between the French and their Jacobite allies. This explains why senior French officers were extremely critical of their Irish counterparts. Conrad de Rosen often wrote about them in his correspondence with Versailles:

> There are only 25 cannonballs that can be used, and yet it is only for one artillery piece, and of all the musket balls only a third is of the right calibre, and the mould that had been brought was broken before being able to be of any use, so we only have 1,000 or 1,200 rounds left to fire. All this is due to the negligence of Makary [sic] who did not check them when they were put back in. Nor did he bother to make a single visit to the arsenal … I am obliged to tell you, My Lord, that these kinds of people are in no way fit to serve on land.[5]

One of the first Frenchmen who realised the promising military capabilities of Irish soldiers was the Comte d'Avaux, an experienced diplomat sent by Louis XIV to help James II. Even if he rapidly realised the parlous state of the Jacobite forces, he reported back to both minister of war the Marquis de Louvois and Louis XIV on the impressive physique and stamina of the local men. Though he encountered many complications in his daily managerial tasks and was faced with high desertion rates among the Jacobite forces, he thought that 8,000 Irishmen could easily be sent in exchange for 5,000 French infantrymen. Fairly soon, as James II and his entourage consistently ignored his pieces of advice, d'Avaux' attention focused solely on the possibility of getting the best Irish troops out of the island and back to France. A proposal was made to the Stuart king to have 5-6,000 chosen men sent to the continent in exchange for the same number of infantrymen from France, so that Louis XIV would not find himself short of soldiers while facing the combined forces of the League of Augsburg. One of the best officers in James II's army, Justin MacCarthy, Viscount Mountcashel, offered to lead this brigade consisting of five regiments numbering a total of 5,371 men. They were respectively O'Brien's (1,588 men), Dillon's (805), Butler's (657), Fielding's (791) and Mountcashel's own unit, named after himself (1,530).[6]

As a veteran of French wars, Mountcashel had managed to arrange the same type of contract – called in French a *capitulation* – as the one that had existed between Irish regiments and the French crown in the previous decades of the seventeenth century. This agreement specified that the Irish would be put on a higher footing than their French colleagues, earning one extra *sou* every day, and would have a separate military judicial system attached to each and every regiment. Louvois had given a specific number of companies per regiment to be recruited and required all officers to be noblemen of experience. Although the chronic disorganisation that plagued the Jacobite army delayed the efforts to assemble the necessary manpower, the scheme was finally agreed upon and in March 1690 a French fleet brought

5   Sheila Mulloy (ed.), *Franco–Irish correspondence, December 1688–February 1692* (Dublin: Irish Manuscript Commission, 1983), 'addition to the ammunition inventory of MacCarthy' (misspelled as 'Makary' by Rosen), vol.1, p.110.
6   Patrick Clarke de Dromantin, *Les réfugiés jacobites dans la France du XVIIIe siècle* (Bordeaux: Presses Universitaires de Bordeaux, 2005), p.183.

six regiments to Kinsale led by the Duc de Lauzun, France's new envoy, and left Ireland with Mountcashel's men. D'Avaux and de Rosen embarked on those very ships bound for Brest, openly relieved to leave behind this endless logistical nightmare.

Alongside the regiments sent by Louis XIV, Lauzun arrived in Ireland accompanied by René Jouenne d'Esgrigny, an *intendant,* Alexandre de Rainier de Droue, Marquis de Boisseleau, who acted as his *major général* and Charles Fortin de La Hoguette as his *maréchal de camp.* This general staff was completed by three *brigadiers* and three infantry colonels.[7] Once on land, Lauzun also vainly tried to convince James II that his army was in dire need of restructuring if it were to resist Williamite forces in the field. He was ultimately proven right at the Battle of the Boyne on the 1 July 1690 when James was defeated by his son-in-law. The Jacobite defeat, often considered as a turning point in the war, illustrated how the Irish troops simply could not compete with regular regiments. Many of the Irish wielded war scythes or iron-tipped wooden spears when Williamite veterans had muskets and pikes. Though the Jacobite cavalry did threaten the Williamite advance during the early stages of the battle, the tactical error made by James II of leading two thirds of his army away from the main action to secure a ford made defeat inevitable. The aggressive assault led by William III on the weakest point in the Jacobite line condemned the Irish army to a hasty retreat which the French regiments and the Irish cavalry, serving as an effective rear guard, prevented from turning into a rout. Madame de Sévigné, a French courtier, letter-writer and commentator on French seventeenth century society, received a message from her son Charles who took part in the battle alongside Lauzun. He did not mince his words regarding his opinion of the Irish: 'These Irishmen are strange people; let no one trust them; they are traitors. All I could do was to save the King, M. de Lauzun and the vast majority of our troops did not ask more from me'.[8]

As the fighting continued in Ireland, Mountcashel's brigade started its career fighting for France. Most Irish military histories refer to the existence of these units as the founding elements of the Brigade, but usually only mention the three regiments that actually joined the French war effort in mainland Europe, that is Mountcashel's, Dillon's and O'Brien's (soon to become Clare's). They generally downplay the fact that these units were actually fighting for Louis XIV and not James II and fail to explain the fates of Butler's and Fielding's regiments. French correspondence during the months leading up to the departure of the Irish and in French local depositories once the soldiers landed in Brittany allow us to understand what actually happened. Most of the men picked to leave Ireland in 1690 had been deemed less than worthy by the French emissaries because James II and his partisans showed little enthusiasm in letting their best infantrymen leave Ireland, while the lack of officers actually belonging to the aristocracy among the regiments fuelled Louvois' suspicions about the quality of the troops about to be exchanged. James II had long resisted against a provision in the contract that allowed the French to dismiss any officer they did not consider sufficiently suitable, before finally relenting.

---

7   Bibliothèque Nationale de France (BNF), Département des Manuscrits, réf. Français 7666, Louis de Courcillon, abbé de Dangeau, *Journal des bienfaits du Roi,* vol.9, February 1690, p.169.

8   Madame de Sévigné, *Lettres de Madame de Sévigné: de sa famille et de ses amis* (Paris: Hachette, 1863), vol.7, p.259.

When the five units actually landed and were sent on their way to the front, the French discovered that an inordinate number of men had died due to the rough sea voyage, a situation that was worsened once on French soil by the Breton climate and the lack of resources to clothe and equip them. In the Spring of 1690, rosters from hospitals and death certificates in western France were soon filled with the names of these newcomers. The local scribes often struggled to spell them correctly, sometimes making it hard for historians to track down Irishmen in French archives:

> ... there are five hundred sick people in hospital, whereas in normal times there are only thirty ... most of the houses where *Irois* [old French for Irish] soldiers have been put are infected with the stench and vileness due to their illnesses and infirmities ...[9]

Louvois knew of their situation and tried to remedy it:

> I see there is a lot of sickness among the Irish, that you need to help them as much as you can, and instruct the commissariat to force the officers to get them cleaned from the vermin infesting them, and to take as much care of them as possible.[10]

The winnowing of the Irishmen by French authorities before and after their arrival at Brest, and the losses due to disease, eventually led to the merging of these five units into three, each regiment being composed of three smaller battalions. First gathered in Nantes, the units were sent to Bourges in central France and officially entered Louis XIV's service on 18 June 1690. Their uniform was the same as that of French units, an off-white coat adorned with different coloured facings, but their flags reflected their allegiance to the Stuart cause. They belonged to *Maréchal* Catinat's army and served under the Marquis de Saint Rhue (or Saint Ruth), who was later sent to Ireland to replace Lauzun. In June 1690, the French courtier and diarist Philippe Courcillon, Marquis de Dangeau, wrote about them:

> In Versailles, it is said that the 6,000 Irishmen who disembarked in Brittany are marching in Berry where they will be clothed and armed and in two months' time they will be sent to Italy in M. de Catinat's army. Their commander, Milord Montcassel [sic], has been made *lieutenant général* by the King. The King gave him a 4,000 *écu* pension and another 4,000 *écus* to get equipped.[11] Besides the pension, the King gave him one *sou* for every *livre* out of the pay given to the Irish.[12]

Right from the start, finding recruits to keep the regiments ethnically Irish proved difficult, a problem the Irish Brigade subsequently faced throughout its entire history. While

9   Patricia Dagier, *Les réfugiés irlandais au dix–septième siècle en Finistère* (Quimper: Généalogie Cornouaille, 1999), p.17.
10   Service Historique de la Défense (SHD), Louvois to Bouridal, 11 May 1690, D.G. (Dépôt de la Guerre) n°960.
11   Another source gives 12,000 *livres* for his pension and his personal equipment.
12   Philippe de Courcillon de Dangeau, *Journal du Marquis de Dangeau* (Paris: Firmin Didot Frères, 1854), vol.3, pp.143–144.

Louvois insisted on getting more men from Ireland in the spring of 1690 regardless of James II's reluctance, Louis XIV had to issue orders in December 1690 to get Irishmen already serving in his French or foreign regiments to fill in the ranks. Units like the *Gardes Suisses* were called upon to relinquish any Irishman serving in their ranks, forcing them to join Mountcashel's regiments. As for their military records, to claim that Mountcashel's brigade was immediately considered as an elite group of regiments would be overestimating its first trial by combat under the golden lilies. To begin with, although it is often designated as a brigade, the regiments were separated from each other and sent on garrison duty to replace regular troops in southeast France where they were trained. They were then sent to northern Italy which at the time was a relatively minor theatre of operations compared to the campaigns of Flanders and western Germany:

> His most Christian King ... pressed on with his conquests in Flanders and on the Rhine, won battles and took strongholds under the leadership of the Marshals of Luxembourg and Lorge, to whom he sent all his elite troops, whereas he only gave M. de Catinat inexperienced militias or Irish troops, because he was confident and did not need more to maintain the war in Italy, which moreover provided him with very substantial advantages.[13]

Soon the Irish were fighting in the mountainous terrain of northern Italy against the Vaudois and the barbets, light infantrymen used by the Duke of Savoy to wreak havoc in the region. One description of the type of combat they faced gives us an idea of the difficulties they encountered and overcame:

> The enemies fired upon them but in spite of their resistance, the rock was forced & those who guarded it were put to flight. They fled to the highest peaks of the mountains, where our people, who pursued them vigorously, killed more than one hundred and fifty of them. ... this first advantage cost us only three Irish killed & two wounded. Milord Montcassel [sic] was wounded in the left breast, but only slightly ... It was a very narrow gorge, ... However, M. de Lée [sic] colonel of the Aubrehenne [O'Brien] regiment climbed up to the height of the mountain on his left, and went around in places so impassable that one could hardly have imagined it. He went straight down into the entrenchments of the enemies who were fortified behind several ditches as wide as they were deep. They fled as soon as they saw him ... we found in their camp bread and wine which M. de St Ruth gave to the Irish who were allowed to go into the mountains to take the herds that were thought to be grazing there. ... Not a single man was killed in this last action.[14]

Yet their fighting abilities were still questionable, at least if an officer from the Holy Roman Empire who faced them during the siege of Carmagnole in 1691 is to be believed. In his

13   Anon., *Mémoires de Mr D.F.L. touchant ce qui s'est passé en Italie entre Victor Amédée II Duc de Savoye et le Roy T. C.* (Aachen: Anthoine Steenhuysen, 1697), p.81.
14   Marquis de Quincy, *Histoire militaire du règne de Louis Le Grand* (Paris: Denis Mariette, 1726), vol.2, pp.304–306.

memoirs, the Irish were described as fleeing an ambush after a rainy night that precluded the use of muskets by Austrian troops. The Austrians resorted to swords after spending hours in water-drenched trenches:

> We waited to be five steps away from the enemy in an ominous silence, as I had ordered, we fired from behind the raised earthworks, but most muskets did not give fire, and instantly everyone ran at the enemy with their swords in their hands, fury painted in their eyes. The Irish who expected to meet half-drowned people in the trench were so shocked by this welcome that they turned tail, most of them without firing a shot. We chased them at sword point … we killed more than two hundred of them and made seventy prisoners. I only lost seven soldiers in this action. The continuous rate of fire from the ramparts forced us to quickly withdraw from the trench with our prisoners.[15]

The Irish also took part in the siege of Montmélian, the last Savoyard stronghold, which cost them dearly. One of the inhabitants of that town, a Monsieur de Chamousset, left a diary in 1692 in which he referred to the presence of Irishmen fighting for the French:

> The next day, the same party returned to the same place; they met an Irish captain named Bermingan, who came from Chambéry … a sergeant and ten men escorted him. Ours charged them; they killed three of them, wounded the officer, whom they took prisoner, and put the rest to flight. … On the 18th [of October], ten soldiers of the garrison, among whom was a Savoyard gentleman named de Lalle, who had been in the vineyards between Arbin and Cruet, faced a party of eighty Irishmen, and after skirmishing for part of the day with them, they pursued them to the last houses of this village.

The author also noted the outstanding bravery of one of the Irish officers:

> … the enemies fled and our people killed five soldiers and a lieutenant of the regiment of Montcastel [sic], which was generally regretted. He also deserved it; for having recognised that he could not avoid being caught, he charged with those willing to follow him into one of our guardhouses, put as many as he could to the sword, and withdrew to the *Marches* pierced by 12 blows, of which he died the same morning. I am quite irate that I did not get to know the name of such a brave man.[16]

One source specified that the Irish still used war scythes to assault the enemy as they had done in Ireland.[17] Nevertheless, the news of Mountcashel's and his men's exploits were

---

15   Abbé André Cavard, *Mémoires du comte de Vordac, général des armées de l'Empereur* (Paris: Veuve de Jean Cochart, 1702), p.265.

16   Léon Ménabréa, Mémoires de la société royale académique de Savoie (Chambéry: F.R. Plattet, 1841), vol.10, pp.528–529, 532.

17   Joseph Perreau, 'Catinat et la défense du Dauphiné en 1692', *Bibliothèque des Souvenirs et Récits Militaires*, n°48 (Paris: Henri Gautier, 1897), p.19.

echoed in France and its reputation improved, as proved by Roger de Bussy Rabutin's opinion of them: as a former senior officer in the French army and a cousin to Madame de Sévigné, he wrote in 1692 that 'the Irish [had] turned into Caesars'.[18]

Meanwhile, the situation in Ireland did not improve, and though the Jacobites managed to foil William III's attempt to take Limerick in the summer of 1690, the internal strife among the French and Irish officers led to disastrous strategic choices, though individual successes like the destruction of the Williamite siege artillery at Ballyneety by Patrick Sarsfield, one of the most popular Jacobite leaders, proved that the Irish army was still a force to be reckoned with when the right circumstances materialised. Yet if 1691 started off with a more promising prospect for the Jacobite side, it proved a false dawn as Aughrim and the surrender of Galway in July of that year sealed the fate of the Stuart cause. The French still provided the Irish with war supplies to support their diversion against William III, but Versailles recognised that Saint Ruth's death actually put an end to any hope of a Jacobite recovery. According to French archives, officers sent by Louis XIV like the Marquis d'Usson and the Chevalier de Tessé were left behind after Aughrim to 'gather up what remained [of the Irish forces]' and continue the fight.[19] After a final show of resistance at the end of the summer, the Irish were accused by the French of using defeatist language and were even under suspicion of secretly parleying with the enemy.[20] In a besieged Limerick, Tyrconnel and Sarsfield represented two opposing sides in the Jacobite camp. The former advocated a firm resistance hoping for more French help, while the latter was open to a relatively quick surrender. After Tyrconnel's natural death in August 1691, which provoked many murmurs about a possible assassination to weaken any idea of resistance in Ireland, Sarsfield remained as the main Irish negotiator. Though the Irish are often depicted in subsequent narratives as eager to continue the fight by going over to France, d'Usson and de Tessé, in one of their letters to Versailles, left a very different account of their attitudes during the last stages of the war in the island:

> They [the Irish] would have assuredly surrendered without our [the French] partic-ipation, and not one of them would have thought to ask the liberty of sending troops in France, most are so opposed to it that we would not dare recount to His Majesty the difficulties that are made about it every day, those staying being afraid the enemy might blame them for letting the troops go [to France]. ... We would not be able to give Your Majesty an exact account of the number of troops that we will send because we need to gather those who come from Selego [Sligo] which capitulated without our participation and those that are in the counties of Clare and Kerry. We hope to lead the entire garrison of Limerick but it has diminished so much that we had to reduce it to two brigades from the four it had at the beginning of the siege.[21]

---

18   Ludovic Lalanne (ed.), *Correspondance de Bussy Rabutin* (Paris: Charpentier librairie éditeur, 1859), vol.6, p.376.
19   National Library of Ireland, (NLI), positive microfilm n°143.
20   NLI, positive microfilm n°143.
21   NLI, positive microfilm n°143. Letter to Versailles, 19 October 1691.

On the Williamite side, General Ginkel had been urged by William III to end the war as quickly as possible to allow his troops to join the fray in Flanders. William's attempts at ending the conflict had so far foundered on the difficult choice between crushing the Jacobites, which could unite them in their desperation, prolong the war and weaken the United Provinces; and negotiating with them, which could alienate the Protestant Irish community on the island, increase the cost of the war and let Jacobite forces live to fight another day.[22]

William III, king of England, Scotland, France and Ireland in 1690. Pieter Schenck (1660-1719). Fiercely hostile to Louis XIV, William III won the decisive Battle of the Boyne but had to rely on General Ginkel to win the war. (Leichtenstein-Hauslab Collection, Anne S K Brown collection)

The French had planned to send 15,000 Irish troops to France to form new regiments there with enough extra men to replace the casualties suffered by Mountcashel's brigade. An agreement between the Jacobites and Ginkel was finally reached on 3 October 1691. The Treaty of Limerick, as it came to be known, contained two parts, one relating to the military and one to the civilians remaining in Ireland. The controversy surrounding the civilian articles, which were not respected and subsequently led to the creation of the Penal Laws against the Catholic population and the advent of the Irish Protestant Ascendancy, still echoes to this day. Nevertheless, the fact remains that the military side of the treaty was scrupulously complied with and unintentionally gave birth to the Irish Brigade. In the end, Ginkel allowed the Jacobite forces to retire to France with their families using both French and English ships. In spite of contradictory rumours, he noted how eager the Irish were of embarking for Brest.[23]

The officers originating from Irish families who had lost any hope of recovering forfeited lands obviously encouraged their comrades in arms to leave Ireland and join the French in the hope of one day returning home with a victorious army. Those who still owned property expected to see service in William's army or at least to keep their estates and return to a more peaceful existence. As for the French, they were adamant

---

22 See J.G. Simms, *War and Politics in Ireland*, 1649–1730 (London: Hambleton Press, 1986), chapters 15 and 16, pp.181–225.
23 Public Records of Northern Ireland (PRONI), D638/12/115, letter from Ginkel, 29 December 1691.

about sending as many Irish units back to France as possible.[24] Eventually, Sarsfield was the one who persuaded a large number of soldiers and officers to join him in exile across the seas, hoping to lead a major army in France and make a name for himself there. One of his war companions, Gerald O'Connor, left a description of the ceremony during which the men chose between leaving for France, joining William III's forces or staying in Ireland:

> On the sixth of October 1691, our whole forces, perhaps 15,000 strong, marched out of Limerick under arms, and with their standards flying. Hundreds of the soldiers were in rags and unshod; but all bore themselves well, and had a dauntless aspect. It had been agreed that the men who were to take service in France were to defile beyond an appointed spot; those who were willing to remain were to turn away. The choice of the immense majority was soon seen; some 11,000 passed beyond the selected point; some 2,000 went quietly to their homes. Scarcely 1,000 threw in their lot with Ginkel. Sarsfield looked on with pride at the spectacle exhibiting the noble spirit of our race. "These men," he said, "are leaving all that is most dear in life for a strange land, in which they will have to endure much, to serve in an army that hardly knows our people; but they are true to Ireland and have still hopes for her cause; we will make another Ireland in the armies of the great king of France."[25]

Only a minority picked the Williamite side but were then sent to Ostend to join the Austrians in their wars against the Ottoman Turks in Eastern Europe.

According to the French military archives in Vincennes, 9,258 men were supposed to be headed for France in October of 1691.[26] The *Gazette*, the quasi-official newspaper of the Bourbon monarchy published in Paris, had a more optimistic assessment of the situation as well as a higher computation of the number of troops embarked:

> Six thousand six hundred and sixty Irishmen have sailed on His Majesty's ships; two thousand eight hundred on some other vessels, & four thousand five hundred on those which were in Cork. A fairly large number are still expected, who preferred to get to France rather than accept the amnesty. In the latter group are several wives & children of those who came.[27]

The nineteenth century imagery of families desperately clinging to ships and sometimes drowning in the process was not a romantic exaggeration. It was actually based on French officers' personal accounts describing harrowing scenes of wives and children begging to be accepted on board of the already overcrowded ships:

---

24 Ministère de la Guerre, *Inventaire sommaire des archives Historiques* (Paris: Imprimerie Nationale, 1898), vol.1, A1 1065.
25 William O'Connor Morris, *Memoirs of Gerald O'Connor of the Princely House of the O'Connors of Offaly in the Kingdom of Ireland* (London: Digby, Long & Co, 1903), pp.96–97.
26 SHD, A1 1081, Letters from the war commissaries, page n°174.
27 *Gazette* (Paris: Galeries du Louvre, 15 December 1691), p.716.

Anonymous, *Battle of Aughrim, 1691*. (Amsterdam: Laurens Scherm,1695).
(FMH 2695-IV/VII, Rijksmuseum, Amsterdam)

In Brest, 2 December 1691 at nine o'clock in the evening:

> M. le Vicomte de Coëtlogon has just arrived with the frigate *La Badine* under his command. He reports that M. de Chateaurenault [the French admiral responsible for evacuating the Irish] left the river Limerick on the sixteenth of last month with … about 6,000 people and he estimates that there are about 4,000 soldiers or officers … At the end of the letter De Coëtlogon again told me that it is a pitiful thing to see the people of this country throwing themselves into the sea to embark and that if there [had been] ships near Cork and Quinsale [Kinsale] we would [have embarked] as many as we would have liked.

The Arrival of the Irish Exiles in France (1691–1692)

The Irish landed in France in less than auspicious circumstances. Brest received on 3 December a very large proportion of the exiles, but other western harbours also took their share of Jacobite refugees, with some arriving on private vessels as far south as Rochefort, near Bordeaux. Arrivals took place several weeks after the signing of the Treaty, and there is evidence from a contemporary source that a future colonel of the Irish regiments brought at his expense 150 Jacobite officers who arrived at Calais, quite far away from

Brest.[28] This is the reason why authors writing about their arrival can never agree on the precise number of Irish people disembarking in Western France, since contemporary French authorities themselves could not get precise figures. A document produced in Brest by Monsieur de Fumeron, a war commissary, on 7 December 1691 counted 4,750 Irishmen in the Breton harbour, divided into 3,100 infantrymen, 1,350 cavalrymen, and 300 dragoons, officers included.[29] To add confusion to these estimates, a letter written around the same time proves that many French soldiers left behind in Ireland had joined the Irish, causing Versailles to demand their immediate removal from the disembarked units.[30] As for the non-combatants that had accompanied the Irish troops, the French civilian authorities were soon told that 'Irish passengers' were also to be taken care of, even though nothing had been properly planned for them since neither the French army nor the French navy were aware of their existence.[31] The total number of Irish military men actually present in western France between December of 1691 and January of 1692 vary from 12,000 for the most cautious appraisals of the Jacobite exile to 30,000 for the most enthusiastic supporters of a large Irish military community in France.

With occasional exceptions, Brest remained the principal port of entry for the Irish, yet Brittany was ill-prepared to welcome such a large body of troops accompanied by families and servants. Local cities, towns and villages were soon overflowing with men, women and children that the municipal authorities could not properly feed, clothe and care for all at once, even though Brittany's governor had been forewarned. Western France, contrary to other French regions, was not used to large garrisons remaining for a prolonged period of time and, strangely enough, relatively few documents have survived about the Irish passing through the province. Only hospital ledgers, graveyard registers and some craftsmen's bills allow us to document the arrival of Irish refugees in Breton parishes. This is because Irish units, like their Swiss counterparts, benefited from a legal regimen peculiar to foreign troops serving France in which crimes and misdemeanours were punished within the regiment itself rather than through civilian courts. This explains the very few traces left by the Irish in non-military archives kept in France. Unfortunately, if numerous documents about the Irish troops are probably still left dormant in some local French records, many are lost to us because of destruction during the bombing campaigns of the Second World War or even because of negligence and theft over time.

The main commissary in charge of organising the arrival of the Irish in Brittany, a nobleman called Jean-Baptiste Bachelier de Bouridal, noted that no fewer than 1,800 of those about to arrive were already sick because of the food distributed during their journey on board cramped warships. Those who were deemed too weak to be soldiers were given a small stipend to survive, while many Irish officers defrauded their own men by keeping

---

28   BNF, Département des Manuscrits. réf. Français 22710, Louis de Courcillon, abbé de Dangeau, *Collection de l'abbé Dangeau sur l'état de la France au temps de Louis XIV*. Series CLXX foreign regiments – Irish regiments 1690–1704, p.98.

29   NLI, positive microfilm n°146, n°98, *Etat des troupes irlandoises qui ont débarqué à Brest les 5,6 et 7 décembre 1691*.

30   NLI, positive microfilm n°143, letter from Versailles to d'Usson and de Tessé, 17 December 1691.

31   NLI, positive microfilm n°146, n°95, letter by the *Maréchal* d'Estrées from Nantes to Versailles, 7 December 1691.

the money they had been given to support their units. Most of the horses that were to cross over to France also suffered from diseases and few actually made it to the coast, which had consequences in the type of troops the Irish eventually formed in the French army. D'Usson and de Tessé had had orders to bring back as many horsemen and dragoons as possible but discovered that most refused to leave Ireland as they had no guarantee to serve on the same footing in France under native noble officers of their choosing. Relatively few of these high-ranking aristocrats served in the infantry, which precluded them from appealing to the loyalty of their kinsmen and followers to recruit new soldiers. This is the reason why the Irish mainly mustered infantrymen once they arrived in Brest, even though their cavalry had proven itself worthy between 1689 and 1691.

Keeping order among these refugees was a problem addressed by royal authorities who issued warnings that no breach of military discipline would be tolerated, though the local justices of the peace could do little in case of infractions. Village and towns in Brittany were to prepare beds and lodgings for the arrival of the Irish, and bare essentials, such as shoes and shirts, were to be provided by local artisans. The families brought to the continent, though by then acknowledged in official correspondences, were not supposed to receive anything. Orders were given to make sure the Irish would leave as soon as possible in order not to be a financial and human burden on the local Breton communities. Despite these precautions, the Bretons had to provide for the Irish, in spite of having themselves very few resources to spare. For instance, the hospital at Lesneven, near Brest, was only meant to care for 12 indigent patients. Yet it was ordered in November of 1691 to receive 60 Irishmen. The local authorities were hesitant about dealing with so many men and their chapel, though still too small, was used to house 45 sick soldiers, while Bouridal requested blankets and beds from the local religious communities and those exempted from billeting soldiers due to their social status, in order to expand the city's sanitary facilities. Around the same time, the inhabitants of Lesneven also had to deal with 60 to 70 penniless Irish officers who regularly harassed them for sustenance.

On the subject of Irish officers, Bouridal commented on their inordinate number roaming the Breton countryside: 'I have never seen so many colonels, deputy colonels, lieutenant colonels, majors, captains, and there are as many officers as there are soldiers in many regiments'.[32] It seems the commissary was not exaggerating the ratio of officers who took refuge in France in the winter of 1691. Another document from the French military archives shows the list of soldiers on board French ships departing from Limerick. Out of a total of 6,660 men, 4,199 were soldiers and 846 officers, with no fewer than 23 colonels and 21 lieutenant colonels. This first tally also included 234 servants, 442 women and 266 children.[33] French authorities discovered that there were so few non-commissioned officers among the Irish troops that they decided to give 10 extra *sols* to each and every sergeant available, probably as an incitement to get more men serving in that capacity. The French navy had to lend sails to provide makeshift tents for the refugees, but numerous cases of typhus and dysentery decimated the Irish in and around Brest. Lack of funds also created problems as the Irish contingent of 1691 did not enjoy the same status as the 1690 one. Unlike Mountcashel's

---

32   NLI, Positive microfilm n°146, folio n°100.
33   NLI, Positive microfilm n°146, folio n°87.

brigade, the troops of 1691 were paid on the same footing as their French counterparts and the pay for each soldier could not cover the costs of an exiled household. Local French archives confirm that entire families did cross the sea, with both joyous events, such as births on board the warships or in the harbours, and tragedies with whole families getting sick before being buried in local cemeteries. Either designated as *Hybernois, Hirois* or even *Irois*, the Irish were very often medically treated or laid to rest anonymously. Sometimes members of the Irish community who had settled in western France before the 1690s might be present, such as clergymen or merchants, who then served as interpreters and witnesses, leaving us with a few details about the deceased.

Even though the Irish and the French were allies, there were concerns about the arrival of so many foreigners in Brest as shown in this letter sent from Versailles to Bouridal:

> Sir, the King has just received news of the arrival of the Irish in Brest … as it is better not to let such people in Brest, his Majesty told me to send you this letter to tell you that even without any appearance that you may mistrust them nor that the King gave you any order, you should not let them stay in Brest where if they had some ill intent in mind, they could seize it thanks to their superior numbers and that you should lodge them 3 or 4 miles away from the shore so that the diseases they could have amongst them will not infect the air around the city.[34]

The Irish troops in Brest were described as *libertines*, a French expression referring to their unruly behaviour. French authorities were clearly afraid they might 'ruin the countryside' if left to their own devices and advocated a firm hand in handling them until they were better accustomed to French military discipline.[35] Survival soon became the sole purpose of these refugees. Irish or English Protestant officers and soldiers who had decided to side with the Jacobites usually converted to Catholicism once they had arrived in France in order to benefit from the advantages offered by the French authorities, most notably the *Invalides* hospital in Paris which excluded Protestants from its premises. Irish soldiers and Breton people soon quarrelled about food and shelter with several examples of abuses committed by Irish Jacobites on the local population. Even the military equipment given to these men was often sold to peasants in exchange for food or even simply discarded, with officers reported as being even more difficult to handle than privates. Most men suffered from a form of melancholy which got worse when the battalions were reorganised by the French in Rennes.

Once assembled in Brest, the Irish contingent was inspected by Colonel Andrew Lee at the beginning of December 1691 before being officially divided into nine infantry regiments of two battalions each, two regiments of foot dragoons, two cavalry regiments, two companies of royal lifeguards and three independent companies of foot. Dominick Sheldon, a colonel of one of the new regiments, was designated to organise the troops while Versailles reprimanded officers of the French navy who had hired Irish sailors to serve on their men-of-war as the Jacobite regiments were being organised.[36] The two royal lifeguard companies were commanded by the Duke of Berwick, one of the natural sons of James II and

---

34 NLI, Positive microfilm n°143, Letter to Bouridal, 8 December 1691.
35 NLI, Positive microfilm n°143, letter to Bouridal 14 December 1691.
36 NLI, Positive microfilm n°143, letter from Versailles to Pontchartrain, 17 December 1691.

future *Maréchal de France*, and by Patrick Sarsfield, who had become the Earl of Lucan at the end of the Irish campaign. Most regiments had 12 companies of foot soldiers, each numbering around 50 infantrymen, and one elite company consisting of grenadiers. Some senior officers who had participated in the war in Ireland were ordered to give up their units to other officers deemed more politically influent, resulting in resignations and resentment, as was the case for Colonel Richard Bellew.[37] Some units were almost entirely composed of former officers and noblemen.[38]

In France's official military records, there is evidence of a *capitulation*, an old word for contract, initially drawn up between James II and Louis XIV that would have truly made of these regiments an Irish army on French soil:

> A form of a contract designed by his Most Christian Majesty covering the troops belonging to His Britannic Majesty currently awaited from Ireland as well as the troops that were sent from that country to France in 1690 and for any and all of his subjects who are presently or will in the future be employed in the service of His Most Christian Majesty. 1) that all the said troops will serve in the same corps under the command of the king of England and that all the … officers who will be needed … will have commissions from his Britannic Majesty and that the officers and soldiers will only be subjected to the laws and disciplines that His Majesty will find appropriate. … that the king of Great Britain will have the right to lead them all or parts of these troops in his lands whenever it will be deemed appropriate.[39]

The contract also included the addition of an artillery corps attached to the regiments as well as a precise description of the number of officers, non-commissioned officers, soldiers, priests and even preachers to be included in each unit. It is then immediately followed by a French counter proposition with a reduced number of companies per battalion, the disappearance altogether of the preachers and a few paragraphs which drastically changed the immediate future of the Irish regiments disembarked at Brest in 1691:

> … when it comes to the said Irish, the King [Louis XIV] will be master of where he sees them fit to serve, either in a corps or in small or great detachments, depending on what his Majesty will deem appropriate to his service. … the Irish will not be designated as the troops of the king of England nor will have commissions from His Britannic Majesty, but will be treated either on campaign or in garrison as French troops presently serving and will execute everything written on regulations delivered until now by His Majesty and in the future.

In the end, though nominally appointed by James II, the Jacobite officers and their men did actually fight for Louis XIV. Each regiment was meant to have two battalions made up of eight companies, each numbering 100 men. Typically, these units were characterised by

---

37   Michael McNally, *Saint Ruth's Fatal Gamble* (Warwick: Helion, 2018), pp.199–200.
38   Bada Dujardain, *Apologie du Sieur Bada Dujardain imprimée par ordre de Philippe de Hesse, son maître* (The Hague: Gillis Van Limburg, 1702), p.10.
39   NLI, positive microfilm n°143.

a larger number of officers within each company than in most troops in the French army. Many of them had had to accept to be reduced to the rank of foot soldiers in the hopes of getting their commissions back once the Jacobites returned to the British Isles, a prospect that laid by then in an unspecified future. Though captains and lieutenants had proven difficult to manage in western France, their presence in the ranks definitely reinforced the *esprit de corps* as well as the fighting spirit of the Irish regiments. The regiments' pay, which should have been on an equal footing with the one given to Mountcashel's brigade, was also reduced by James II himself in order to fund his court in Saint-Germain-en-Laye. The arrears were to be paid once a Stuart restoration had been secured. Belonging to a noble family in Ireland, or at least claiming to have such a social background, did not guarantee Irish officers a commission in these regiments, which usually fuelled jealousies among peers. Plus, the French were quite uneducated when it came to distinguishing the Old Irish community from the Old English one, sometimes even merging together Irish and English, an attitude which inevitably led to bitterness and even sometimes violence in the host country.

The reputation of these new troops suffered accordingly, especially when compared with that which Mountcashel's brigade was beginning to enjoy around the same time period:

> As I have got to know the newly arrived Irish better than I did before, I find that there are several subalterns who are hardly worthy of being officers, since they themselves lead their soldiers on marauding trips and share with them the booty they have made there; they say that it is extreme necessity that forces them to this indignity; they have no authority over their soldiers, who are without any discipline; they are more like bandits and robbers than soldiers. They leave not only the battalions but also their detachment to go marauding, I have told the principal officers several times to make examples, they have promised to do so, but have not yet complied. They seem, however, inclined to do their duty; they [were] told in writing that in order to count and discipline their soldiers, a harsh and constant severity and frequent and rigorous examples were necessary. They agree and have said that they will follow my advice, the colonel of the regiment of Charlemont has just told me that he has arrested two officers who had been on marauding duty with the soldiers if they carry out what he told them they will be able to suppress in time the licentiousness of their soldiers, but there is much to be done before they are on the same footing as the regiment of Montcassel [sic].[40]

Barbezieux, Louvois' son and heir, advised Bouridal to gather the Irish in battalions to give them stern speeches and threats of severe punishment on account of their misconduct. The French Minister for War later even went as far as advocating hangings to bring back order among the troops while stopping any payment to Irish officers, giving them only what they owed to their own soldiers. There are no obvious traces of death sentences actually being executed, but the officers did seem to vehemently protest the decisions made by the French,[41]

---

40   SHD, microfilm n°1236 series A1 11 October 1692 Des Alleurs, administrateur des troupes, 1692–May 1693.

41   NLI, positive microfilm n°143, letter from Versailles to the *Maréchal* d'Estrées, 14 February 1692.

and Bouridal had indeed very difficult relationships with them, writing that he 'thought on several occasions that the Irish officers would stone me to death about their pay'.[42]

The absence of any military records from these first units forces us to recreate the path followed by the Irish regiments using only French local sources. As we are confined to a series of anecdotes, the risk of amplifying what could have been the exception rather than the rule is real. Nevertheless, French authorities and documents written by local observers did mention several incidents involving the Irish whether during their stay in Brittany or when they were stationed in Normandy for the planned invasion of Britain in the Spring of 1692. The *sénéchaussée* [seneschal's court] of Gourin in Southern Brittany gives an example of one such incident in early 1692 between Bretons and Irish soldiers, with the local population fighting back:

> Noel Cohic, a horseman in Sir Callaghan's company [was helped by] an interpreter called Der[mott ?] Callaghan major from the Port Gallois [Galloway ?] regiment in Ireland – 22 years of age – born in the village of Monedeguy[43] in Ireland – billeted in Le Faouët. A fortnight ago at Le Faouët he saw two soldiers arresting a peasant to send him to the gaols – he helped the soldiers but the rabble mistreated them and forced them to abandon the peasant. He signs Neal Coqrige (?) [sic]. Statement confirmed by two Breton witnesses.[44]

Other occurrences illustrate the problems caused by the Irish. A murder in eastern Brittany,[45] an attempted rape near Angers,[46] and a desecrated church with murdered parishioners in Tours,[47] all conspire to give a negative image of the Irish in France in the early 1690s.

That said, the local inhabitants of Normandy did notice the impressive physique of the Irish soldiers in 1692, while also observing the absence of any fighting spirit among them. Mirroring the misgivings of French authorities about their presence in Brest a year earlier, the Normans went so far as to accuse the Jacobites of being willing to surrender the French coast to the enemy. French officials did perceive the 1692 expedition as a real opportunity to get the Stuarts back on the English throne, but also saw the Irish regiments involved as a potential liability. A French abbot wrote a report about the attempt and noted that penniless Irish officers living in France were willing to participate in a Stuart restoration, but also warned his readers that the Irish were not to be trusted:

> … if those of that nation [the Irish], who wish to re-establish it, were to lose all hope, then maybe we might not expect any great help from them and there would be no reason to trust them. For it is certain that, though they serve well, they only

---

42 NLI, Positive microfilm n°146.
43 The name does not correspond to any actual village in Ireland. French clerks almost always misspelled Irish place names.
44 Archives Départementales d'Ille et Vilaine (ADIV), Fonds Bourde de la Rogerie.
45 ADIV, Fonds Bourde de la Rogerie.
46 Archives Municipales d'Angers (AMA), BB99, folio 70.
47 Archives Départementales d'Indre et Loire (ADIL), archives civiles, Canton d'Azay–le–Rideau, series E suppl. 5 (GG.5).

do it with a mind to serve their master and, as soon as they believe [we the French] no longer have his best interests at heart, we won't be able to rely on them.[48]

These tensions between the Jacobites and the French did not go unnoticed by Louis XIV's enemies who wrote about how the Irish had not learnt anything from the incessant drill imposed on them in Normandy by James II, except 'plundering the local inhabitants'.[49]

On 24 May 1692, the royal fleet that had been prepared for an invasion of Southern England saw its ships either scattered or destroyed by the combined English and Dutch men-of-war at La Hogue. According to a poem published in England, the French defeat left the 'Teagues mortified at the Havre de Grace' and James II 'with his dear twin Saints, *Monsieur* and *Teague*, joined in a more than Holy Triple League'.[50] The suspicions between the Irish and the French were not completely lifted and yet, there are traces of how the French started to view the Irish as *troupes réglées*, or regular troops. The Irish were actually given their new red uniforms in the Spring of 1692, alongside new Stuart flags. One Norman aristocrat noted the presence of 12,000 Irishmen camped around Ozeville and Réville in the Cotentin Peninsula and witnessed them marching out of the camp '750 at a time' in an orderly way once the expedition was abandoned and the regiments were needed elsewhere.[51]

'Our Irishmen distinguished themselves':[52] The Irish Regiments in Louis XIV's Last Wars

The Irish on the Battlefields of the War of the League of Augsburg
Even a few years after their initial landing at Brest, the Irish regiments still proved difficult to handle. Their bravery in the field was only matched by their inability to properly finance their regiments, as for example in 1695 when 100,000 French *livres* were stolen putting the future of an entire battalion in serious jeopardy.[53] The Stuart cause also proved difficult to support when yet another attempt at a restoration failed. Troops and equipment were gathered in and around Calais for a purported invasion of the British Isles in 1696 under the Marquis d'Harcourt, but the expedition had to be postponed due to indiscretions:

---

48   Francois–Albert Duffo (ed.), *Lettres inédites de l'abbé Renaudot au ministre Jean–Baptiste Colbert (1692–1706)* (Paris: Lethielleux, 1931), p.34.
49   Anon., *Mémoires concernant la Campagne de trois rois faite en l'année 1692* (Cologne: Pierre Marteau, 1693), p.17.
50   Anon., *Advice to a painter being a satyr upon the French King* (London: Randall Taylor, 1692), pp.4 and 18.
51   Léopold Delisle (ed.), *Les mémoires de Pierre Mangon, vicomte de Valognes* (Saint–Lô: Imprimerie Le Tual, 1891), pp.27–28.
52   Louis de Rouvroy, duc de Saint Simon, *Mémoires inédits du Duc de Saint Simon* (Paris: Marchands de nouveauté, 1838), p.108.
53   Nathalie Genet–Rouffiac, 'The Irish jacobite Regiments and the French Army: A Way to Integration', in Paul Monod, Murray Pittock, Daniel Szechi (eds.), *Loyalty and Identity: Jacobites at Home and Abroad* (London: Palgrave Macmillan, 2010), p.213. This was twice the amount of money given every month to James II by Louis XIV as a pension.

The king of England left Saint-Germain-en-Laye on the 28th of February [1696] and arrived at Calais on the second of March, but the enemy, having been made aware of the design by people who had feigned to serve the King's interests, sent from the Downs 35 large men-o'-war and several light frigates that stationed in front of Calais' harbour and made the whole attempt fail. The Prince of Orange had twenty thousand men recalled from Flanders back to London and the king of England, after having waited for some time in Calais, Dunkirk and Boulogne for the effect of the English promises he thought were on his side was forced to return [to Saint-Germain-en-Laye] on 5 May [1696].[54]

Jacobus Secundus Dei Gratia. Angliæ, Scotiæ, Franciæ, et Hiberniæ Rex.) &ct

James II (1633-1701), King of Great Britain. Though he heavily relied on the Irish as an exile monarch, the English king showed little sympathy towards his Hibernian subjects. (Yale Center for British Art)

Eventually, Louis XIV recognised William III as King of England. As for the Irish, even when sent to fight on the war's many fronts, they still retained a negative image, most notably in the campaign against Catalonia in the late 1690s as explained by Captain Peter Drake in his memoirs. Himself an English Jacobite, he served under many flags between the late seventeenth and the early eighteenth centuries:

> About the latter end of Christmas, in consequence of the peace of Ryswick, we quitted Barcelona, when the aversion of the inhabitants was so strong that they poured scalding water on us as we marched through the streets, which irritated the soldiery to such a degree that they fired on them, and wounded several. From thence we marched for Perpignan; and for the three first nights we were so alarmed at the resentment of the peasants, that we lay several nights under arms, notwithstanding the severity of the weather.[55]

---

54 BNF, Département des Manuscrits, réf. Français 7666, Louis de Courcillon, abbé de Dangeau, *Journal des bienfaits du Roi*, vol.12, February 1696, p.10.

55 Sidney Burrell (ed.), *Amiable Renegade, the Memoirs of Peter Drake* (Palo Alto: Stanford University Press, 1960), p.15.

According to a French source, Colonel Dillon, while leading an assault against the defences of Barcelona, fell into a trench and supposedly 'swore in Irish'. One of his opponents, a kinsman fighting for Spain, recognised him and refused to harm him, killing one of the colonel's captains instead.[56] Once the city was taken, Arthur Dillon became a *maréchal de camp*. Though the anecdote is questionable (Dillon would probably have spoken English rather than Gaelic), this goes to show that the Irish military diaspora and its family ties were beginning to spread throughout Europe.

The Irish joined the French army which by the 1690s had grown to an unprecedented scale, with no fewer than 21 percent of its manpower made up of foreigners serving the Sun King.[57] The Irish regiments fought on all the main fronts of the War of the League of Augsburg, as part of the army on the Meuse and the one fighting in Flanders, as well as in the French armies involved in Italy and Spain. At the Battle of Neerwinden, in July 1693, the Irish fought on the French side against William III's forces. Patrick Sarsfield famously lost his life while charging at the head of Irish cavalry units. According to Gerald O'Connor, his last words were devoted to Ireland and to the fight against England: 'I am dying the most glorious of deaths. We have seen the backs of the Tyrants of our race. May you … live to behold other such days; but let Ireland be always uppermost in your thoughts'.[58]

The Irish were also present at the Battle of Marsaglia in Northern Italy where Colonel Daniel O'Brien, Viscount Clare, died of his wounds alongside four other Jacobite officers. He was replaced by his lieutenant colonel, Andrew Lee, who back in 1690 had brought hundreds of Irish volunteers from Greder's Regiment, a German unit fighting for France, to join Mountcashel's brigade.[59] A contemporary source, a manuscript left by l'Abbé Louis Courcillon de Dangeau, brother to the diarist mentioned above, detailed the fates of senior officers within French and foreign units involved in Louis XIV's wars. The document plainly shows the impressive number of Irish officers killed in action, especially compared to their Swiss counterparts who, though considered as elite troops, suffered far fewer casualties. This is a clear indicator that the Irish troops usually found themselves in the thick of the fighting as officers had to lead from the front.[60] *Maréchal* Catinat noted that the Irish had intervened at Marsaglia using the butts of their muskets and their swords more than their fire power, earning his respect in the process.

The French orders of battle from that time period indicate that Irish regiments first appeared in the second or third line, the least prestigious position, before reaching the first line by the end of the War of the League of Augsburg. They usually were in the centre of the

---

56   BNF, Département des Manuscrits. réf. Français 22710, Louis de Courcillon, abbé de Dangeau, *Collection de l'abbé Dangeau sur l'état de la France au temps de Louis XIV*. Series CLXX foreign regiments – Irish regiments 1690–1704, p.3.

57   Guy Rowlands, 'Foreign Service in the Age of Absolute Monarchy: Louis XIV and His "Forces Étrangères"', *War in History*, vol.17, n°2 (April 2010), p.146.

58   O'Connor Morris, *Memoirs of Gerald O'Connor*, p.83. This quote was changed in the nineteenth century to become 'Would this [death] be for Ireland'.

59   BNF, Département des Manuscrits. Réf. Français 7666, Louis de Courcillon, abbé de Dangeau, *Journal des bienfaits du Roi*, vol.10, November 1693, p.117.

60   BNF, Département des Manuscrits. réf. Français 22710, Louis de Courcillon, abbé de Dangeau, *Collection de l'abbé Dangeau sur l'état de la France au temps de Louis XIV*. Series CLXX foreign regiments – Irish regiments 1690–1704 (fol. 1–128).

firing line, since the privilege of fighting on the right-hand side of an army was still a privilege reserved to senior French units. The Irish continued to fight as separate units across
multiple armies rather than as part of a brigade. Louis XIV's troops fighting in present-day
Belgium had the 'Guards of King James'. The army of the Meuse under Maréchal Boufflers
in 1697 included Clare's three battalions in the front line under Labadie, while at the same
time in Flanders under Maréchal de Villeroy the 'Royal Guards of England' were mixed
with three French regiments in the second line. In Germany, under Choiseul, the Dublin
Irlandois was joined with the Régiment Royal-Vaisseaux in the front line under Brigadier
Charmasel, but was still placed in the centre of the order of battle. Finally, Vendôme in
Catalonia had placed in Chemerault's brigade the regiments of Sourches, Solre and Dillon,
all composed of only one battalion and all placed in the front line. As Irish units started
to appear more formidable to the enemy and more serviceable to the French, Irish officers
also benefited from the system. Irish and Jacobite officers thus gained distinguished positions within Louis XIV's army, becoming brigadiers d'infanterie like William Dorrington
in 1695, Simon Luttrell in 1696 and Andrew Lee in 1697,[61] or brigadiers de cavalerie like
Pierce Butler, 3rd Viscount Galmoy and Dominick Sheldon, or even lieutenants généraux
like Mountcashel in the Spring of 1691.

With the end of hostilities in 1697, Louis XIV had to officially recognise William III
as King of England. The enormous French army was reduced to relieve the kingdom's
finances. Commissions for the Irish regiments were no longer delivered by James II but by
Louis XIV himself, which dramatically changed the administrative and personal relationships existing between the units, the Stuart court and the French royal authorities. Many
Irish regiments, already depleted by heavy casualties, had to be disbanded. Several thousand Irishmen were no longer needed as soldiers. The number of companies per battalion
were reduced, as well as the number of soldiers within each of these companies. This led
to personal tragedies as officers on half-pay and former soldiers became destitute. Some
turned to their former French brothers-in-arms for help. The Irish were taken in while
French soldiers, who could more easily return to a civilian life, were dismissed. Louis XIV
maintained some of the Irish regiments while 'reforming' – in other words disbanding
– French units that had seniority over them. Ex-Jacobite soldiers who could not get into
these Stuart regiments were sent to French or other foreign battalions and the Sun King
gave orders to provincial officials to assist Irish families as best they could.[62] The Invalides
had to accept more Irish soldiers, regardless of the institution's strict rule regarding 20
years of effective service in the French army to benefit from its facilities. Another solution
was to join the armies of foreign powers, a possibility offered by the Duchy of Lorraine or
the Kingdom of Naples. Yet in spite of these generous gestures and career opportunities,
Saint-Germain-en-Laye was soon plagued by the presence of disbanded Irish military men
accompanied by their families who either lived in houses paid for by the Stuart family –
who sold their valuables to assist their supporters – or the French Catholic Church. Some
even resorted to highway robbery in order to survive.

---

61   BNF, Département des Manuscrits, réf. Français 7666, Louis de Courcillon, abbé de Dangeau, Journal
     des bienfaits du Roi, vol.13, January 1696, p.5 and April 1697, p.15.
62   Simon Reboulet, Histoire du règne de Louis XIV (Avignon: François Girard, 1744), vol.3, pp.19–20.

The Surprise of Cremona

Peace time only lasted for a few years as simmering tensions between France and the rest of Europe led to another war in 1701. Right before his death without issue that year, Charles II, King of Spain, had chosen one of Louis XIV's grandsons as his heir. This fuelled fears in many countries of a Bourbon domination over all of Europe. The Irish units serving France were reorganised using veteran officers and soldiers from the previous war – allowing supplementary battalions to be re-established – and sent to fight on the frontiers. Very quickly, the military campaign in Northern Italy became a major concern for the French since Prince Eugene of Savoy, arguably one of the best generals of his age, started to put a dent in France's reputation of invincibility. He defeated the armies of Louis XIV at the battles of Carpi and Chiari during the Summer of 1701 where two Irish colonels lost their lives alongside more than 300 Irish casualties. They also lost one of their regimental flags that was subsequently dropped in the river Po by a member of the Guttenstein Regiment serving Austria.[63]

The French then wintered in the city of Cremona. Two Irish regiments, Bourke's and Dillon's, numbering about 600 men, were garrisoned alongside seven other French infantry units.[64] Eugene, eager to strike a decisive blow, attempted to take the city by surprise. With the help of a local priest, the Austrian general snuck a party of grenadiers accompanied by workers in the sewers of Cremona in order to open its doors to the Austrian cuirassiers waiting outside.[65] Taken aback, the French were quickly overrun and their general, the Duc de Villeroy, was captured by an Irish officer serving the Holy Roman Empire named Magdonel (or MacDonnell, depending on the sources). Villeroy tried to convince his captor to set him free by offering him to serve in the French army at the head of a brand-new cavalry regiment with a pension worth 2000 écus, but Magdonel refused, stating that he 'had been a loyal servant to the Emperor for a long time' and that 'he preferred his honour to his prosperity'.[66] Villeroy vainly raised his offer up to 10,000 pistols. The French senior officer, in a letter written to Cardinal d'Estrées sometime after the battle, confirmed the story and described Magdonel as wearing a 'red jerkin'. According to him, the Irishman did refuse the 'considerable offers' that would have brought him 'more benefits than he could have hoped to achieve from the war'.[67]

In the meantime, the French infantry managed to set up barricades in the narrow streets of the Italian town and two gates, the one leading to the citadel and the one opening onto the Po, witnessed the fiercest fighting. The French resisted successfully and were supported in their efforts by the Irish regiments:

> The Irish from Bourke's & Dillon's regiments, who were lodged nearby, came running at this noise, led by Messieurs O'Mahoni & de Wacob. They arrived on the

---

63   Anon., *La vie du Prince Eugène de Savoie* (The Hague: Adrian Moetjens, 1702), p.446.

64   Quincy, *Histoire militaire*, vol.3, p.613.

65   Anon., *Du Quartier Général à Luzarra de l'Armée Impériale, Relation de l'action arrivée à Crémone, entre les troupes de sa majesté impériale & celles des alliés*, le 1 Février 1702 (The Hague: Publisher unknown, 1702), p.4.

66   Eléazar de Mauvillon, *Histoire du Prince Eugène de Savoie* (Amsterdam: Arkstee & Merkus, 1740), vol.2, p.20.

67   'Lettre du Maréchal de Villeroi au Cardinal d'Estrées après la surprise de Crémone en 1702', in M.D.L.P., *Pièces intéressantes et peu connues*, (Maestricht: J. P. Roux, 1790), vol.8, pp.62–63.

rampart, just as the Comte de Merci[68] had seized a battery of seven 24-pound pieces intended for the defence of the bridge. They attacked him in flank by the rampart & by the streets which lead to the gate. The Imperial infantry was charged with such fury & fire, that at first it lost much ground. Merci brought forward his cavalry to support his infantry; but the latter was driven in so quickly that it fell back onto the cavalry, which was itself attacked and pushed towards the main body of the troops, where it tried to rally.[69]

Depending on the source, the Irish were either already drawn up for inspection wearing their red uniform ready for a parade or rushed out of their lodgings with barely a shirt on their backs. Either way, they retook the artillery battery the Austrians had seized near the Po gate and used the guns against them. One of their officers, Captain Daniel O'Mahony, was a supernumerary officer who acted as the regimental major in Dillon's Regiment. He was to play a pivotal role in the affair and later noted that '... we went at them with bayonets, firing & pressing them so hard that we got the better of their kettledrums & many of their officers & soldiers ...'[70]

Francophone newspapers printed in the United Provinces remarked that '... [the Irish] fired terribly at all who came too close to them'.[71] Faced with unexpected resistance, Prince Eugene sent Magdonel to try and persuade the Irish regiments to join the Austrian side. The speech Magdonel supposedly gave then was reproduced in a book detailing Prince Eugene's career in the early eighteenth century:

My fellow countrymen, His grace Lord and Prince Eugene of Savoy sends me to tell you that if you change party and go over to the Emperor's, he promises you a higher pay and more considerable pensions than the one from France. The affection I have for all the people from my nation in general and for you, gentlemen, in particular, forces me to exhort you to accept these offers given to you by the Emperor's general for should you refuse, I do not see how you could escape a certain loss. We own the city with the exception of this post, this is why his highness only waits for my return to attack you with the great majority of his forces and to cut you to pieces if you reject his offers.

The book also provided O'Mahony's answer:

Sir, if his highness only waits for your return to attack us and cut us to pieces, it seems it will not happen for a long time, for we will make sure you will not come back any time soon. To that effect, you are now my prisoner and I no longer consider

---

68   Sometimes spelled Mercy.
69   Eléazar de Mauvillon, *Histoire du Prince Eugène de Savoie* (Amsterdam: Arkstee & Merkus, 1740), vol.2, p.26.
70   Anon., *Relation de la journée de Crémone, et de la défaite des troupes impériales avec la suite des affaires d'Italie*, in the *Mercure Galant* (Paris: Michel Brunet, 1702), pp.162–163.
71   *Lettres Historiques contenant ce qui se passe de plus important en Europe* (The Hague: Adrian Moetjens, March 1702), vol.21, p.260.

you the envoy of a great general, but a mere suborner and it is with this behaviour that we hope to merit the esteem of the Prince who sent you and not by an act of cowardice and a treason unworthy of honourable persons.[72]

Magdonel was escorted out of the fighting back to the citadel as a prisoner under a French escort as the 'Irish wanted him dead for being a traitor'. Although outnumbered, the Irish successfully repulsed Eugene's attacks. Consequently, both Bourke's and Dillon's lost many men:

[Bourke's regiment] had seven officers and forty-two soldiers killed, and nine officers and fifty soldiers wounded in this action. Dillon's regiment had one officer and forty-nine soldiers killed; twelve officers and seventy-three soldiers wounded. The enemy had four times as many.[73]

As the fighting drew to a close, the Irish destroyed the bridge that could have allowed the Austrians to reinforce their positions within the city.[74] Although they seemed more disciplined than before, the Irish still retained a reputation for unbridled ferocity as they had to be persuaded by a French officer not to pursue the Austrian cavalry outside of Cremona. Abandoning the defensive position reconquered next to the Po gate earlier during the battle could have led to an offensive return of the enemy.[75]

As expected, Louis XIV's official newspapers extolled French bravery during the battle, but they did not ignore the efforts of the Irish. The *Gazette* as well as the *Mercure Galant* unreservedly paid tribute to their courage:

The two Irish regiments were the first ones to charge the cuirassiers arranged in battle on the rampart with the utmost gallantry ... They defeated them and pushed them onwards, still killing, towards the square where they regained the cannons. ... The Imperials were overthrown on both sides, notwithstanding the great resistance of the cuirassiers, from whom the Irish won a pair of kettledrums, and the gates were retaken with great loss to the enemy ...[76]

Louis XIV himself now recognised the value of his Irish regiments as he issued orders to favour them when exchanging prisoners with the enemy in Italy. Similarly, news of the victory at Cremona reached other parts of France where the daring attacks of the Irish were deemed praiseworthy. 250 miles away from the Italian city, a Jesuit school in Southern France gave a ballet in September 1702 honouring both French and Irish soldiers who were portrayed by its schoolboys.[77]

---

72   Mauvillon, *Histoire du Prince Eugène de Savoie*, vol.2, pp.31–32.
73   Anon., *Relation de la journée de Crémone*, p.163.
74   Alessandro Marquis Maffei, *Mémoires du marquis Maffei, lieutenant général des troupes de l'Electeur de Bavière* (The Hague: Jean Neaulme, 1740), vol.1, p.98.
75   Joseph Barre, *Histoire générale d'Allemagne* (Paris: Charles J.B. Delespine, 1748), vol.10, p.411–412.
76   *Recueil des gazettes, nouvelles ordinaires et extraordinaires de l'année 1702* (Paris: Galeries du Louvre, 1702), p.82.
77   *Le Travail récompensé, ballet dansé par les écoliers du Collège de la Compagnie de Jésus* (Avignon: François Mallard, 1702).

Yet if subsequent narratives of this feat of arms have inevitably insisted on how the loyalty of the Irish towards France had ultimately won the day, contemporary sources were not solely focused on them. Documents produced in the Austrian camp and quoted by the French newspaper *Mercure Galant* in 1702 clearly stated that the reason why the battle was ultimately a French success was because Prince Eugene's forces were exhausted after hours of gruelling combat in the streets of the city and had ultimately run out of ammunition, while the French could muster troops stationed elsewhere in the Italian province.[78] The Irish were barely cited. One former French officer, who had had to join Prince Eugene's army after a duel, wrote an anonymous account of the surprise of Cremona. His praises for his former comrades-in-arms published in 1703 did not mention the Irish at all.[79] Yet even books written in honour of Prince Eugene almost immediately after the event did praise the Irish as specifically brave:

> ... the garrison took to arms and gathered at the Po gate ... all the troops resolved to perish or throw out the Imperials ... the two Irish regiments were the first ones to charge with an extreme valour the Emperor's cuirassiers, [they were] lined up in battle on the rampart and the streets near St Pierre's square after having arrested an officer of their nation who had been sent by Prince Eugene to offer them a surrender under any condition they wished, but these [Irishmen] were extremely animated against the cuirassiers, defeated them and pushed them out, still killing them down to the square where they recaptured the cannons.[80]

Another source from the Imperial side was less sympathetic towards the French and the Irish, reminding its readers that 'the enemy gathered in the greatest confusion imaginable, the Irish towards the Po gate, the French towards the castle gate, barricading themselves in the streets, the houses and the convents. However, our people did wonders, killing or capturing all the French and the Irish they met'. However, the author did recognise that Cremona had been well defended: '... we would certainly have kept the city if we had had more troops and if the French and Irish garrison had not made us decamp'.[81] A biography of Prince Eugene published in the 1740s gave more information about the dialogue between the Irish officer serving the Austrians and his countrymen. During a lull in the fighting, 400 men from Bourke's and Dillon's were facing 1,200 Austrians and Prince Eugene thought the only way to disengage his forces was to 'test the loyalty of the two Irish regiments guarding the Po gate'. The text, quoting a German life of Prince Eugene, described the Irishmen putting their weapons down before taking them up again, with 'soldiers threatening [their] officers with death should they decide to opt for that unworthy agreement'.[82]

---

78   Anon., *Du Quartier Général à Luzarra de l'Armée Impériale*, p.8.
79   Anon., *La Guerre d'Italie, ou Mémoires du comte d**** (Cologne: Pierre Marteau, 1703), p.393.
80   Anon., *La vie ou l'Histoire du Prince Eugene de Savoie* (Amsterdam: Henry Desbordes, 1703), p.287.
81   M. d'Artanville, *Mémoires Pour Servir à L'Histoire du Prince Eugène de Savoie* (The Hague: Etienne Foulque, 1710), vol.2, p.208.
82   Eléazar de Mauvillon, *Histoire du prince François Eugene de Savoie* (Amsterdam: Arkstee & Merkus, 1740), vol.2, pp.32.

From the French perspective, Monsieur d'Arène, one of Villeroy's officers, claimed he was the one who had inspired the Irish in retaking the guns and occupying a church overlooking the Po gate from which they could snipe at the Austrians.[83] O'Mahony and Wauchope were not mentioned as instrumental, the French being the ones leading the counter charges. Memoirs depicting the war in Italy published in 1728 described a nameless French officer organising the Irish resistance after the incident with Magdonel:

> As soon as he had talked to the main officers, he had *eau de vie* taken from a nearby hospital distributed to the soldiers and took in his purse fifty *Louis d'or* that he gave to the Majors to be shared among the privates, the officers of the two battalions, full of zeal and valour, put them in battle array as best as the terrain allowed and they advanced on the rampart after sending a hundred men to reinforce the Po gate where only ten men remained. At that moment, the Prince of Commercy [an Austrian commander] appeared at the head of the cavalry pushing in front of him six grenadier companies who were all beaten and thrown back onto the cavalry which could not stand our musketry fire.[84]

The same author, who remains unfortunately anonymous, accused O'Mahony of being a liar as well as the puppet of another French officer who used Cremona to further his own ambitions:

> On the third of February, the Comte de Revel wrote to the King and gave him a well-informed relation of the preceding day. Quite unexpectedly, he chose Mr Mahony, a captain on half-pay in the Irish regiments, to carry the news back to court, even though he had not gotten out of his bedroom because of a supposed illness. He was highly recommended by Madame de Broglio, Revel's sister in law. Anybody else would have sent a Frenchman capable of detailing the action and who would have taken part in it, which means that the courier left for Versailles with his head filled with the all the fictions one wanted to impose onto him, which he shamelessly repeated using the witness accounts of others since he had not seen anything for himself.[85]

Gerald O'Connor, already mentioned above, described the Irish as the main protagonists, with O'Mahony as the figurehead. That officer had after all been chosen to bring the good news of Eugene's defeat back to Louis XIV himself,[86] as proven by the contemporary memoirs of a French officer.[87] As the Sun King was surprised not to hear his Irish troops

---

83   François Eugène de Vault, Jean Jacques Germain Baron Pelet, *Mémoires militaires relatifs à la Succession d'Espagne sous Louis XIV: 1702* (Paris: Imprimerie Nationale, 1836), pp.661–662.

84   Monsieur D***, *Mémoires de la dernière guerre d'Italie, avec des remarques critiques & militaires* (Cologne: Aux dépens de l'Autheur, 1728), pp.40–41.

85   Monsieur D***, *Mémoires de la dernière guerre d'Italie*, p.48.

86   O'Connor Morris, *Memoirs of Gerald O'Connor* (London: Digby, Long & Co, 1903), p.159.

87   Philippe de Gentils, marquis de Langallerie, *Mémoires du marquis de Langallery: lieutenant–général des armées de France* (The Hague: Daniel Aillaud, 1743), p.318.

being mentioned in the Irish officer's report, O'Mahony supposedly replied that they 'had followed the example of his Majesty's subjects', an anecdote that kept appearing in books collecting *bons mots* and miscellanies from Ancien Régime France up until the nineteenth century.

Officers from Bourke's and Dillon's were rewarded for their efforts:

> Mr Mahoni was made colonel and received a pension of one hundred pistols. Mr. Wacob [sic] lieutenant colonel of Bourck [sic] and Mr Connock lieutenant colonel reformed in the same regiment were made colonels, and Mr Mar-Auline [sic] lieutenant in Bourke's grenadiers has received on the companies left vacant.[88]

O'Mahony subsequently served in Spain where he became a *brigadier*. He steadily rose in the Bourbon military hierarchy as Philip V needed experienced officers to reorganise his own army. His cavalry regiment played a major part in the Bourbon victory of Almanza in 1707. Arthur Dillon was made a *brigadier* after the victory at Cremona, became a *lieutenant-général* in 1706 and then served alongside the Duke of Berwick in Spain.

The wounds sustained by Irish soldiers on that day prove how violent the assaults had been, as evidenced by the *Invalides* records.[89] This institution welcomed these veterans and this extract from the hospital's registers illustrates the dire consequences of the battle:

> Received at the *Hotel* on 28 July 1702. Theodore Conel, Irish, 40 years of age, Native from County Cork, Soldier in Sir St Jean's company, Dillon's regiment, where he served for 12 years, as stated in his certificate. Had his left wrist cut off from a sabre slash he received at the Battle of Cremona, he is Catholic. Soldier. Died 17 February 1703.[90]

Dillon's and Bourke's regiments each received a pay rise when other Irish units were still waiting to get the *haute paye*, which created tensions among Irish recruiting officers later during the war. Red uniforms started to become associated with Irish courage, which allowed O'Mahony to evoke the exploit of an anonymous member of his battalion during his exclusive interview with Louis XIV:

> ... a young man dressed in red had killed more than thirty men; but he did not know his name. H.M., who always tries to reward the courage of those who do not ask for anything and even of those whose names are not known, said it was necessary to enquire as to who that was and that he would give orders to make this happen.[91]

---

88   Anon., *Relation de la journée de Crémone*, p.435.
89   Eoghan Ó hAnnracháin 'Irish Involvement in the "surprise of Cremona", 1702', in Thomas O'Connor, Mary Ann Lyons (eds), *Irish Communities in early–modern Europe* (Dublin: Four Courts Press Ltd, 2006), p.453.
90   SHD, reference: GR/2Xy14, Act n°013098.
91   Anon, *Relation de la journée de Crémone*, p.405.

The perception of Cremona as an all-Irish affair started quite early. The Marquis de Quincy, a famous French military historian from the early eighteenth century, wrote about the defence of Cremona, detailing how the Irish used 'frequent musketry fire' and pursued the Austrian heavy cavalry 'with fixed bayonets while shooting at them'.[92] Close inspection of his work proves that he actually used O'Mahony's own report to describe the battle. Other French authors tried to remind their readers of the part played by their countrymen at Cremona, as did the Chevalier de Folard, a celebrated French officer who penned several essays on military history and tactical theory in the first half of the eighteenth century. Even if his narrative of the battle insisted on the pivotal role played by the Irish, his praise for the men from Bourke's and Dillon's regiments were more restrained when drawing conclusions on the whole affair:

> The Irish were extremely praised, and with good reason, by Messieurs de Revel and Praslin [two leading French officers] for it must be admitted that their resistance at the Po gate and their obstinacy in defending it saved Cremona; but after this action, which brought them so much honour, and a small battle which took place on the ground between the Po gate and that of Mouze, the Irish did nothing more, and had no part in the fighting that happened in other places and continued well into the night. The French troops had every right to see their valour and conduct exalted, for they fought all day, dislodged and drove the enemies from all their positions and finally threw them out after an infinite number of battles and skirmishes that seemed endless.[93]

French military archives also provide evidence that the Irish officers on half-pay attached to each regiment tried to benefit from the victory at Cremona. Versailles thus received several requests for permanent positions and pensions in the following months.

The Irish on Campaign 1701-1713

Whether in the press or in personal memoirs and correspondence, Jacobite regiments were not always named as both French and foreign sources often simply designated them as 'the Irish'. However, orders of battle published in memoirs or recorded in archives show that individual Irish regiments were spread across the frontiers and mixed with other French units, as had been the case in the previous war. The Irish thus fought at the Battle of Luzzara in Northern Italy in September 1702 under Vendôme, Villeroy's replacement, who included four Irish battalions in his army. The battle itself is now considered a draw, but the Irish were cited in Dutch newspapers alongside the *Carabiniers*, an elite French cavalry unit, as the most aggressive and effective French troops involved in that action, a piece of information confirmed by a French manuscript held in the British Museum,[94] and a document produced

---

92 Quincy, *Histoire militaire*, vol.3, p.624.
93 Dom Vincent Thuillier, *Histoire de Polybe, avec un commentaire ou corps de science militaire par M. de Folard* (Paris: Pierre Gandouin & Cie, 1729), vol.5, pp.118–119.
94 Gustave Masson (ed.) 'Extraits d'un Journal Manuscrit: Conservé au British Museum: (Fonds Egerton, n°1915 & 1916), 1700–1706', *Annuaire–Bulletin de la Société de l'histoire de France* (Paris: Librairie Renouard, 1868), vol.6, n°2, pp.5–85.

in favour of Philip V's claim on his Italian possessions.[95] Richard Talbot, the son of Lord Tyrconnel, was killed during the fighting. He had lost the command of his own unit, which was given to Clare back in 1696, for having insulted James II. By 1702, he was serving as a mere volunteer in Dillon's Regiment. Ullick (William) Bourke, '*lieutenant colonel réformé du régiment d'Albermale*', died of his wounds after the battle. Ultimately, the Irish were repulsed by the enemy with the loss of two flags.[96] Incidentally, Captain Magdonel, who had been released to return to Prince Eugene's army, was also killed during that battle.

The German campaign also saw Irish troops distinguishing themselves under the golden lilies. At the First Battle of Höchstädt in September 1703, the Irish participated with the Régiment d'Artois and some French grenadiers in the routing of the Austrian rear guard.[97] The report from the *Gazette* for that particular Franco-Bavarian victory mentioned how the Irish 'led by Mylord Clare occupied a village with a promptness and an enthusiasm for fighting that cannot be praised high enough', while the initiatives of de Lee at the head of the Brigade du Dauphin – and his subsequent head wound – proved that Irish officers were leading from the front and had reached some of the highest ranks of the French army a decade after their arrival in France. Between 1702 and 1704, Berwick, James II's natural born son, led an army in the Spanish peninsula in order to secure the Spanish throne for its French claimant, where many Irish soldiers and officers found employment after having deserted from the British Army. Irish regiments also served on the other fronts of the war, as illustrated by the career of Clare's Regiment in the early eighteenth century. It first fought in Alsace in 1701 before joining the Armée de la Moselle in 1705 and that of Flanders in 1706.

The Irish were also present during the major French defeats of 1704, 1706 and 1708. After almost 50 years of uninterrupted successes, the armies of Louis XIV were soundly defeated in Germany, Flanders and Northern Italy, and all the territories acquired by the new alliance between France and Spain were subsequently lost. In the early eighteenth century, pitched battles were not the prime objective of generals, since a campaign could be successfully resolved just by blocking the opponent's moves. Battles, unlike sieges, had unpredictable results and the French tended to avoid the former to favour the latter. This was because French high-ranking officers knew that their men were usually ill-prepared to sustain the stress of musketry fire which required intense and regular training. French infantrymen usually fired their weapons too soon, too high and too far away from the enemy, leaving them exposed to counter attacks from more disciplined troops such as the English or the Dutch. The French preferred using the impetus of a bayonet charge which was better suited to their national temperament for élan and aggressiveness. The Irish similarly privileged the use of bladed weapons and the orders of Battle of the War of the Spanish Succession reveal that the French recognised their martial potential by regularly placing them in the front line for just that purpose.

95   Antonio Bulifon, *Journal du voyage d'Italie de l'invincible & glorieux monarque Philippe V, roy d'Espagne et de Naples* (Naples: Nicolas Buliton, 1704), p.310.

96   Henri Basnage de Beauval, *Lettres historiques (et politiques) contenant ce qui se passe de plus important en Europe; et les reflexions necessaires sur ce sujet* (The Hague: Adrian Moetjens, 1702), vol.22, pp.295 and 308–311.

97   *Recueil des Gazettes, Nouvelles ordinaires et extraordinaires de l'année 1703* (Lyon: François Barbier, 20 October 1703), vol.76, p.183.

At the Second Battle of Höchstädt, a Franco-Bavarian army led by *Maréchaux* Tallard and Marsin was faced with the combined forces of Austria and Britain. The French and their allies had fortified the villages of Blindheim (now better known as Blenheim) and Oberglau which gave them the advantage during Marlborough and Prince Eugene's initial assaults, but also rendered them unable to manoeuvre out of these bastioned positions. The situation became dire for the French when 12,000 of their men were blocked within the narrow streets of Blenheim, where Marlborough had lured them, and were no longer available when a massive frontal assault shattered the French centre. The Irish under the command of de Blainville held the village of Oberglau and, though abandoned by their French comrades, continued to fight there against Marlborough's main thrust:

> The Irish acted like they did at Cremona. Milord Clare was at the head of his regiment and advanced towards an English regiment that had dared him not to fire a shot. He had his men walk with the musket on the shoulder and the English who ended up firing 20 steps from them were routed by the Irish at the tip of the Bayonet, not four of them escaped.[98]

Lee's lieutenant colonel, a man from the Cosgrafe family, died, while his own son remained on half-pay attached to that regiment. Alongside *Maréchal* Tallard himself, four Irish battalions became prisoners of war.[99]

At the end of that campaign, Irish officers requested to be promoted based on their behaviour during the battle. A contemporary letter from de Marsin to de Chamillart, Louis XIV's Minister for War, documented their demands regarding promotions. It focused on Lord Clare who complained about not being present on the list of beneficiaries:

> Milord Clare is one of these, who certainly would not have been a disgrace to the list of *maréchaux*. It is true that he would not be entitled to claim it due to his seniority as a brigadier, but he has been a colonel for 14 years, he is a foreigner of the highest quality in his country, where he has left a considerable property, he has done several distinctive actions and most recently at the last Battle of Hochstett [sic], where he did all that can be expected of one of the bravest men and best officers there is. Mr Rooth, an Irishman, a reformed colonel in the d'Oringthon regiment [sic], a man of great merit and an excellent officer, is also very mortified at not being one of the Brigadiers, having been in France for 13 years with a commission as colonel to the king commanding his regiment of Guards, and is by all accounts a very good subject ... [100]

---

98   State Archives Bavaria (SAB), 50, fol. 86r–90r, "Extrait d'une lettre écrite de Dutlingen du 23e aoust par une personne de confiance", s.l.n.d., quoted in Clément Oury, *Les défaites françaises de la guerre de Succession d'Espagne, 1704–1708* (Paris: PhD from the Université Paris–Sorbonne, 2011), p.720.

99   Bavarian State Library (BSL), Liste, Aller den 13. Augusti 1704, gefangenen fürnehmen Frantzösischen Officiers, Battaillons und Esquadrons, date and origin unknown, 40.2383#Beibd.1.

100 Anon., *Campagne de monsieur le Marechal de Marsin en Allemagne l'an 1704* (Amsterdam: Marc Michel Rey, 1762), vol.2, p.243.

In 1705, at the Battle of Cassano in Northern Italy, the Irish were once again praised for their exploits during the fighting of this contested encounter, generally considered a French victory. The *Gazette* mentioned that 'Sir Dillon, Mylord Galmoy and the officers of the Irish regiments have withstood the enemy's greatest efforts extremely valiantly'[101] but also noted that the 'Irish have suffered quite a bit',[102] while the Marquis de Dangeau, mentioned above, recorded that Vendôme wanted 'MM. du Bourg, Irishman, a major general, and Caroll, Irishman, a lieutenant colonel in Berwick's' to be particularly distinguished in the reports sent to Louis XIV.[103]

On 23 May 1706, the French were defeated at Ramillies, 12 miles north of the city of Namur in what is now Belgium, again at the hands of the Duke of Marlborough. The scenario was almost the same as in Blenheim, with a central attack following diversionary actions on the flanks of the French army. The Irish managed to resist inside Ramillies itself and beat an orderly retreat while the rest of the army melted away. The Irish fought against both the Scots Brigade in the service of the Dutch and Prince George of Denmark's own regiment. The latter was to be numbered as the 3rd Regiment of Foot in the English army and actually belonged to Charles Churchill, Marlborough's younger brother. Charles, Viscount Clare, lost his life in the confused mêlée as all these troops wore red uniforms. Clare's, Lee's and Dorrington's suffered heavy casualties as mentioned by Peter Drake in his memoirs. He clearly depicted the Irish as having saved the honour of the French army on that day:

> In short they [the French] all left the field with infinite disgrace, except Lord Clare's, which engaged with a Scotch regiment in the Dutch service, between whom there was great slaughter, that nobleman [Lord Clare] having lost two hundred and eighty-nine private Centinels, twenty-two commissioned Officers, and fourteen Sergeants; yet they not only saved their Colours, but gained a Pair from the Enemy, which we may suppose the Scotch did not fare much better than the Irish.[104]

Though the Irish are said to have captured the colours of their Scottish enemies, a rare trophy in the midst of a general defeat,[105] there is evidence that the flag actually belonged to Prince George of Denmark's Regiment.[106] Either way, this standard was preserved in an Irish convent in Ypres[107] and Clare's Regiment was given to the late colonel's son, a boy of eight, on the orders of Louis XIV.

---

101 *Gazette de Lyon*, 'Relation de la bataille de Cassano', 18 September 1705, vols. 72–77, p.152.

102 *Mercure Galant*, August 1705, pp.341–342 and 345.

103 Philippe de Courcillon, Marquis de Dangeau, *Journal du marquis de Dangeau*, 1704–1705 (Paris: Firmin Didot frères, 1857), p.399.

104 Burrell (ed.), *Amiable Renegade*, p.83.

105 Michael McNally, *Ramillies, 1706* (Oxford: Osprey Publishing, 2014), p.72. The flag is now held at Kylemore Abbey, county Connemara.

106 See Niall MacKenzie, 'The Flag in Ypres's Choir', in Demmy Verbeke, David Money, Tom Deneire (eds.), *Ramillies, A commemoration in prose and verse of the 300th anniversary of the Battle of Ramillies, 1706*, (Cambridge: Bringfield's Head Press, 2006), pp.45–56.

107 F. H. Skrine Esq., 'The Irish Brigade in the Service of France, 1691–1701', *Journal of Royal United Services Institution*, No.58, 1914, p.484.

In parallel, writings in French about the Irish became more positive. A French geographer, M. La Forest de Bourgon, described the Irish population in 1706 in terms that mixed criticism and praise, echoing their exploits on the field of battle:

> The Irish are handsome, well-built, rugged, nimble, but not very industrious, so that those who have no income find it more to their taste to beg for alms or to steal than to acquire bread by their work. … it may be said of the whole nation in general that it can go toe to toe with the bravest in Europe, it is no less estimable due to the loyalty it has shown to its legitimate sovereign James II, than to its bravery, of which it has given so many signs in these last two wars.[108]

The reputation of the Irish regiments immensely improved, but at a terrible cost. They lost an inordinate number of men which made recruiting to keep every unit at battle strength all the more difficult. Their involvement in the operations that took place in Spain or the engagements on the northern frontiers of France reduced the number of soldiers in all of their regiments, including those raised for the service of Spain by Philip V. Recruitment in the peninsula often relied on Irish deserters from the British army. The Battle of Almanza in 1707 perfectly illustrated the fact that Irishmen often fought their fellow countrymen during the early eighteenth century. The Duke of Berwick, leading the Bourbon forces, reorganised his battle line when he discovered the tactical error made by his opposing number, the Earl of Galway, a French Protestant serving the English crown. To the right of the Bourbon army, French and Irish troops were directly facing English and Dutch regiments. During the fighting, Berwick's own regiment, consisting of two battalions, was about to attack an English unit that had become separated from the rest of the army when it stopped to receive a cavalry charge from English squadrons sent to help their comrades in arms. According to a diary of the war in Spain written in 1707, French squadrons and Irish firepower 'demolished' the English cavalry unit, but not before the Irish pleaded with the enemy not to charge, for fear of killing friends and kinsmen:

> It was very remarkable that while the two squadrons of Harvey's were coming up to charge the Duke of Berwick's battalion, they did not fire a shot but called out, both officer and soldier, to Harvey's Horse, calling them by their names, for they knew them all, great many being Irish deserters from us, asking them if they were mad to sacrifice themselves in this way and told them to note the squadrons on their flank and that they would give them good quarter, but they still went into the battalion and rode over three or four platoons on the right, but with the fire of the infantry and the French Horse attacking them in their rear at the same time they were raised and then sauve qui peut and there was an end of the whole affair.[109]

---

108 M. La Forest de Bourgon, *Géographie historique, ou Description de l'univers* (Paris: Pierre Witte, 1706), pp.168–169.
109 C. T. Atkinson, 'More Light On Almanza: From The Hawley Papers', *Journal of the Society for Army Historical Research*, vol.25, n°104 (Winter, 1947), pp.144–161.

North of France, Louis XIV's forces once again faced their enemies in 1709 at Malplaquet. The Irish occupied a vital part of the defensive perimeter organised by *Maréchal* Villars, but this time they were serving together and were clearly referred to as the Brigade Irlandoise. An anonymous account of the battle showed them holding a centre-left position on the battlefield in front of Marlborough's forces. The French were badly mauled when the English stormed the defensive positions established along their line, and Louis XIV's regiments suffered accordingly. Another French source, the correspondence of the Duc du Maine, showed that the Irish were sent to plug the gap created by those casualties:

> At that moment, I joined *M. le Maréchal* and reported to him what I had seen of the emptying of the centre and the danger which could occur thereof. He answered that it was necessary to bring in infantry from the right. At that point, the enemies fired 50 or 60 musket shots at us, from which he was dangerously wounded in the knee and he left. I quickly sent for 15 pieces of artillery to beat the enemy's infantry there, but before they arrived the enemy made such a fierce charge on our left that our infantry gave way and abandoned their ground, and I saw only the Irish brigade standing firm in front of the enemy holding their ground.[110]

The Chevalier de Quincy mentioned that the Irish had asked *Maréchal* Villars to attack the English on sight:

> At 3 o'clock after midday our cannon began to fire on the enemies who had advanced into the gap to take positions. The Irish brigade, which recognised the English standards, came to ask *M. le Maréchal* for permission to go and charge them, as they desired to fight with them, which *M. le Maréchal* did not find appropriate to grant them.[111]

The Irish were praised, alongside most French units, for having resisted the onslaught in spite of the gruelling musketry and artillery fire. But their red uniforms led to deadly mistakes:

> The Irish brigade which had the Comte de Villars and the Marquis de Nangis for generals, returned to the wood which it pierced to the extreme left, overthrowing all that it found standing in front of it, but not without losing a considerable number of officers and soldiers: It was there that *Brigadier* Rooth who had remained dangerously ill at Douay joined it. He put the brigade in order, and marched with Messieurs de Villars and de Nangis against a body of enemy infantry which was posted in the vicinity of some houses, and received them with a prodigious fire, after which several of them threw down their arms; but the Irish, heated by the fight, paid little attention to this ceremony, and killed nearly

---

110   Monsieur de Saint Hilaire au duc du Maine, Quesnoy, 12 September 1709. Quoted in Maurice Sautay, *La bataille de Malplaquet: d'après les correspondants du duc du Maine à l'armée de Flandre* (Paris: Service Historique des Armées, 1904), p.129.

111   Léon Lecestre (ed.), J. Sevin de Quincy, *Mémoires du chevalier de Quincy* (Paris: Librairie Renouard, 1898), vol.2, p.365, footnote 11.

1,500 of them right here and there, and took two of their flags. It was at this time that the Brigade du Roy made a discharge on the Irish which killed nearly 100 men, both officers and soldiers, and without Messieurs de Villars and Nangis who were aware of this mistake, there would have been carnage between them. The Irish officers assure us that if their soldiers had wanted to take on flags they would have brought back more than twenty, but as their flagbearers had been killed, they had great difficulty in saving their own colours through the brush and thickets where they had been obliged to pass.[112]

Incidentally, the Duc du Maine's correspondence shows the exact same episode, but with the Irish confusing the Régiment du Roy with the enemy and firing upon them 'killing quite a lot of them',[113] proving that memories of a battle can be misleading in subsequent accounts.

A particular engagement that took place during that battle offers a precise description of a firefight between two infantry battalions in the early eighteenth century. Ironically, it involved two Irish units, Dorrington's on the French side versus the Royal Irish Regiment (later the 18th Foot) serving in Queen Anne's forces, from the ranks of which the following account comes:

We continued marching slowly on, till we came to an opening in the wood. It was a small plain, on the opposite side of which we perceived a battalion of the enemy drawn up, a skirt of the wood being in the rear of them. Upon this Colonel Kane, who was then at the head of the Regiment, having drawn us up, and formed our platoons, advanced gently toward them, with the six platoons or our first firing made ready. When we had advanced within a hundred paces of them, they gave us a fire of one of their ranks; whereupon we halted, and returned them the fire of our six platoons at once; and immediately made ready the six platoons of our second fire, and advanced upon them again. Then they gave us the fire of another rank, and we returned them a second fire, which made them shrink; however, they gave us the fire of a third rank after a scattering manner, and then retired into the wood in great disorder; on which we sent our third fire after them, and saw them no more.[114]

As explained by Parker himself, the superior weight of the musket ball fired by the British infantry and its use of platoon firing, which ensured a continuous rate of fire along the line of a regiment, probably explain the end result of this particular encounter. Incidentally, the majority of the wounds reported on the files of Irish soldiers involved in that battle and later admitted to the Invalides had been inflicted by either musket volleys or cannon shots. According to Vault's memoirs, the regiments of Lee, O'Brien, Dorrington, O'Donnell

---

112 Archives Municipales de Reims (AMR), Fonds Tarbé, carton xv, n° 293, *Relation anonyme de la bataille de Malplaquet, rédigée au camp de Ruesne le 13 septembre 1709 par un militaire qui servit à l'aile gauche de l'armée française.*

113 See André Corvisier, *La Bataille de Malplaquet, l'effondrement de la France évitée* (Paris: Economica, 1997), p.112.

114 Richard Parker, quoted in John A. Lynn, *Giant of the Grand Siècle* (Cambridge: Cambridge University Press, 2008), pp.486–487.

and Galmoy had more than 20 junior officers killed during the battle while sixty where wounded.[115]

The Irish were not just used as regular units in pitched battles. They also served as shock troops in mountainous regions to counter the actions of barbets and Vaudois in the Alps, miquelets in the Pyrenees and Camisards in the Cévennes, a mountain range south of the Massif Central. These operations, which today would be designated as counter-insurgency actions, also had an impact on the Irish headcount. There are traces of their presence in the Languedoc province where local authorities had a firm grip on their behaviour:

> The company of Irish fuziliers of Cotte which is in Vauvert is ordered to leave with their weapons and equipment as soon as they are relieved by a detachment of eighty men of the navy to go to Lunel and the following day in this city where they will remain until further notice, living everywhere with their pay in such good discipline that no complaint will be made to me, and to the mayor and consuls of Lunel and Montpellier to receive them and lodge them there in Montpellier on 4 February 1704.[116]

The French press often reported about Irish casualties during those operations against Protestant people generally described as religious 'fanatics'.[117] The type of guerrilla warfare adopted by these groups could cost the lives of officers as this extract from a diary written at the time but published in the 1870s clearly shows:

> Yesterday, at 12 o'clock, a poor Irish officer, who had just accompanied M. de Baville [the provincial intendant] to Lunel's bridge was attacked on his way back between Bernis and Uchaud [both situated near Nîmes] by eight ruffians who, after robbing him, hacked him to pieces.

The same diary also documented how the Irish fought against the Camisards. Cavalier, the famous leader of this Protestant insurgency, was ambushed by a French officer, M. de Vergetot, who had led merely 300 men to face 300 Camisards on horseback accompanied by up to 800 foot soldiers. The Irish were outnumbered:

> This affair happened at Lussan in the plain of Fan which is a castle belonging to Monsieur de Lussan. There is a small bridge there that the Irish defended with awe-inspiring intrepidity. They noticed after the first encounter that the Camisards who were so numerous were starting to open up their formation to assault them from behind. [The Irish] using both their heads and their fists faced a large number [of enemies], seized the bridge and repulsed all those who dared to approach it, thus

---

115 De Vault, Peret, *Collection de documents inédits sur l'histoire de France*, vol.9, pp.378–380.
116 Archives Départementales de l'Hérault (ADH), *Ordonnance de Nicolas Delabaume Montrevel, Maréchal de France, Général des armées du Roy, Lieutenant Général pour Sa Majesté en Bourgogne, & Commandant Général dans le Haut & Bas Languedoc*, 1704.
117 *Recueil des Gazettes, Nouvelles ordinaires et extraordinaires de l'année 1703* (Lyon: François Barbier, 19 May 1703), vol.76, p.84.

supporting their comrades' efforts and the other [French] troops. ... we lost in this action 5 or 6 officers, of whom 2 or 3 are Irish, 14 soldiers and 15 wounded, many of whom are already healed and we killed a hundred camisards ...[118]

As late as 1714, Irish officers were still billeted in the Cévennes and the Vivarès, north of Montpellier. Every month, captains and lieutenants were paid respectively 30 and 15 *livres* each to live there and keep the king's peace.[119]

Alongside these battles and operations on the European continent, two Jacobite expeditions were organised in 1708 and 1715, this time with Scotland as the main objective. Both attempts had Irish officers involved, as Louis XIV was still willing to help a very young James Francis Edward Stuart – recognised by the Jacobites as James III after his father's death in 1701 and also known as the Chevalier de Saint George in French circles. According to a report written by a Scottish officer designed to convince Versailles to intervene directly in the British Isles in 1707, Scotland was supposed to raise 25,000 infantrymen and 5,000 horsemen to fight for the Stuart pretender. The same author also wrote that more than half of the British army consisted of Irish and Scottish soldiers who would join the Jacobites upon the Chevalier's arrival should Queen Anne send back her troops across the Channel to counter the threat.[120] Doing so would have forced the British Army to abandon the battlefields of Flanders, a prospect that was supposed to persuade the French authorities to send help in the first place. The Scottish noblemen loyal to James III and quoted by the officer clearly wished to see the Irish Brigade involved:

> They ask it might please his Majesty to have their king (The Chevalier de Saint George) accompanied by five thousand men; they prefer their Irish troops serving in France as they are more accustomed to their way of life and speak the two languages used in the country. There are two Irish battalions in the King's army in Flanders, to which could be added six other German, Walloon, or French battalions and a regiment of foot dragoons that the Scots could provide with horses.[121]

However, by that time these Irish units were technically no longer under the Stuart monarch's command and Irish officers willing to fight for the Stuarts had to surreptitiously leave France to land in Scotland. The Comte de Forbin, a French naval officer involved in the attempt, wrote in his memoirs that many Jacobites, mainly Irish and Englishmen, were

---

118 Louis Lacour de La Pijardière (ed.), *Mémoire et journal très fidèle d'une partie de ce qui s'est passé depuis le 11e de may 1703 jusqu'au 1er juin 1705 à Nismes et aux environs touchant les phanatiques* [sic] *ou autrement dits Camisars...* (Montpellier, c.1870), p.17 and 40–41. Incidentally, the Lussan family was to become linked with Jacobite interests since Marie Gabrielle de Lussan married Henry Fitzjames, Duke of Albermale, the second natural-born son of James II in 1700. After Albermale's death in 1702, she was remarried to Jean (John) Drummond, Duke of Melfort.

119 *Recueil des édits, déclarations, arrêts et ordonnances de l'année 1715 pour la Province de Languedoc, Ordonnance qui règle ce qui doit être fourni aux troupes qui sont en quartier dans la province, 27 December 1714* (Montpellier: Jean Martel, 1715), p.5.

120 Anon., *Révolutions d'Ecosse et d'Irlande en 1707,1708 et 1709* (The Hague: Pierre Aillaud, 1767), p.5. 'Mémoire du colonel Hoocke', 1707.

121 Anon., *Révolutions d'Ecosse et d'Irlande*, pp.7–8.

gathered in Dunkirk to be sent to Scotland in 1707 and 1708, but that their boisterous arrival, bad weather conditions and James III's ill health had all conspired to delay the operation.

About 6,000 Irish and French troops were kept ready to embark in northern France under the military leadership of the Comte de Gacé, who had been promised a *maréchal's* baton in case of a successful expedition. He urged the young Stuart to act regardless of the navy's misgivings, but old tensions between French army and naval officers were revived. Lack of resources and men meant that the Jacobite attempt on the English throne could not build upon Scottish nationalistic feelings that had been reignited after the Act of Union of 1707. The expedition also failed because the British sailed a fleet to counter the Jacobites once the Forth estuary was in sight and the French navy was not willing to risk everything on what was, ultimately, a gambit.[122]

Several hundred members of Irish regiments including officers on half-pay from Galmoy, Berwick, Lee and Fitzgerald were stationed in Arras. Some officers came back from Languedoc where they were fighting against Protestant partisans. They stayed in Dunkirk ready to embark. Some senior Irish officers such as Dorrington, Galmoy or Gaydon were also gathered to accompany the young Stuart pretender on his journey. One document from the French military archives gives a list of officers ready to leave for Scotland in 1708 who specifically asked not to lose their positions within the Brigade once they had left French soil:

> Request from the officers about to embark:
> Leave of absence requested by the officers to go into Scotland so that they can keep
>   their commissions.
> My Lord Galmoy, first Gentleman of the Chamber
> Le *Sieur* Sheldon, lieutenant général
> My Lord Clermont, reduced colonel in Lee's
> Le *Sieur* Middleton, reduced captain in Nugent's
> Le *Sieur* Booth, captain in Berwick's
> Le *Sieur* Nugent reduced captain in Nugent's
> Le *Sieur* Jacques Murray reduced captain in Nugent's
> Le *Sieur* Jean Murray reduced lieutenant colonel who has visited Scotland several
>   times.[123]

Yet the majority of the soldiers that Versailles had mustered to try and invade Scotland were French and belonged to, for example, the Régiment du Boulonnois or the Régiment d'Agenois.[124] Once it became obvious the operation had failed, the Irish officers detached from units fighting in Languedoc asked to have their long journey from southern France and their prolonged stay in the Northern provinces refunded.[125]

---

122 Comte Claude de Forbin, *Mémoires du comte de Forbin, chef d'escadre, chevalier de l'ordre militaire de Saint Louis* (Amsterdam: François Girardi, 1729), vol.2, pp.296–315.
123 MKWP, Copy of SHD, Section Correspondance, A1, vol.2089, microfilm n°352, p.993. 26 February 1708.
124 Anon., *Révolutions d'Ecosse et d'Irlande*, pp.200–201.
125 Anon., *Révolutions d'Ecosse et d'Irlande*, p.264.

Another project took shape in 1709 and counted on the reputation of the Irish troops serving Louis XIV. As the war was entering its eighth year, a strong offensive directed at the heart of Britain was offered as a solution to relieve the pressure put on the northern frontiers of France. The courage displayed by the Irish earlier during the century was noted as a form of guarantee that Catholic Ireland would join in the fight to restore the Stuarts:

> It is however known that there are surely at least six Catholics for every Protestant and that one can easily judge by the unblemished valour and comportment of the Irish regiments serving in France of what their countrymen would be capable of in that island if they had weapons.[126]

However, the project foundered and the following one of 1715, though resting on Scottish support, also ended in failure. Once again Irish officers tried to join the expedition, but, as they were by then fully integrated into the French army, and since peace was officially signed between France and Great Britain, Versailles officially forbade them from answering the call on pain of having their commissions revoked. A colonel could even lose his regiment,[127] a situation that was compensated by promotion within the ranks of the French army as the betrayal actually illustrated loyalty on the part of the culprits. Nevertheless, the Irish officers involved in the attempt had to leave Scotland, dodging Royal Navy patrols in the area since being captured inevitably meant their hangings as traitors to the British crown.

The last war of the Sun King helped the careers of some Irish senior officers, as proved by Dominick Sheldon's case. After reorganising the regiments in Brest in the early 1690s, he became a *maréchal de camp* in 1694 and ended up being the aide de camp to *Maréchal* Vendôme in the early eighteenth century. But in early 1715, as the war had officially ended, many battalions in the French army were once again dismantled. The military strength of the Irish Brigade also had to be reduced, spelling disaster for thousands of privates and lowly officers. An entire unit, Bourke's, then passed over to the Spanish service and became known as the Regimiento de Irlanda, where it joined other Irish units that had been raised there since 1709. In February of 1715, two Irish regiments, Galmoy's and O'Donnell's, were merged with Lee's and O'Brien's, while one of Berwick's battalions was *réformé*, in other words broken up, its officers dispatched to other Irish units. On 30 November 1715, the French authorities allowed all Irishmen who had served for more than 10 years to be naturalised as royal subjects of the French crown, putting a relative end to the difficulties encountered by the Jacobite exiles whose inheritance, up until then, could not be bequeathed to their families after their deaths. Finally, in January 1716, the number of companies in each Irish regiment was also reduced.

From 1691 to 1715, the Irish serving France proved their mettle in battles across the European continent. Their reputation improved immensely but documents from French archives tend to focus primarily on the fates of major noble Irish families rather than that of the average foot soldier. Though the Irish represented the bulk of the Jacobite forces available

---

126 Anon., *Révolutions d'Ecosse et d'Irlande*, p.377.
127 *Ordonnance du roi, pour défendre aux officiers des régimens Irlandois, qui à son service, de quitter leurs régimens pour passer en Ecosse, sur peine d'être cassés & privés de leurs charges* (Paris: Imprimerie royale, 6 December 1715).

for a possible invasion of the British Isles, their real influence at the Stuart court in Saint-Germain-en-Laye was actually restricted as English and Scottish nobles held the real seats of power, especially after the deaths of Tyrconnell and Sarsfield, the two major Irish figures surrounding the Stuart monarch. After the war, some Irishmen once again chose exile, either to Spain, Austria or even Russia, in order to make a living. But most importantly, the fact that some Irish became high-ranking officers in the Bourbon military hierarchy meant that the history of the Irish regiments was somewhat transformed. Its darker aspects slowly faded into the background. A few years after Louis XIV's death, the Abbé de Choisy wrote an extensive history of the Catholic Church in which political and historical aspects of the Sun King's reign were also addressed. His vision of the Irish campaign of 1689-1691, and of the Jacobite forces fighting in it, was quite different from what transpired in the documents evoked earlier in this chapter:

> A ferocious and rebellious people was then seen lining up under the banners of a standing militia, learning with inconceivable application military drills, old men exercising new soldiers, children handling weapons they could barely wield, women, in spite of their gender's weakness, wanting to take part in the arts of war, and the pleasures of victory, all of them contributing to the common defence... They would fashion weapons from anything and cut shafts in the woods, and believed themselves invincible when these sticks were tipped with some iron. They were accustomed to suffer the insults of the air, their bodies, which are large and well built, seemed to demand a great deal of food but received little, verifying by daily experience what has always been said: that the Irish are natural born warriors and good soldiers when they are battle-hardened.[128]

---

128 Abbé de Choisy, *Histoire de l'Eglise* (Paris: Coignard, 1723), vol.11, book 35, Chapter 1, pp.273–74.

2

'Most of the recruits coming to us are vagrants'[1] – Maintaining the Irish regiments in France (1700–1740)

From Irish officers wherever they be,
Who fight against England by land or by sea,
And treat bold Britons with Damn'd cruelty,
Good Lord deliver us.[2]

The lore surrounding the Irish Brigade in the service of Ancien Régime France, first made popular in the nineteenth century, generally commemorates regimental feats of arms, personal exploits, and exceptional military careers in which the Irish regiments inevitably showed physical and moral fortitude. These writings, though based on genuine historical facts, usually leave aside more ordinary aspects of daily life within the Irish Brigade. Peacetime offered its own brand of conflicts and difficulties for the 'Wild Geese', for even if the Irish managed to change their reputation by proving their valour several times over during the last two wars of Louis XIV's reign, their existence in France remained quite arduous.

To begin with, recruiting men was essential to the Brigade's survival. Sustaining a regiment or company at full strength could make or break an officer's career and intensified competition among recruiters. Frauds committed at the expense of the regiments, debts incurred for professional or personal reasons, and jealousies caused by promotions plagued the Brigade and were routinely reported back to the French military authorities, leaving countless documents allowing historians to paint a more accurate portrait of these units. Irish soldiers and their families also had to find ways to settle in a host country that was not as welcoming as subsequent historical accounts would have modern readers believe.

---

1 NLI, positive microfilm n°184, folio 201. Extract from a letter written by Piers Butler, Lord Galmoy, to Versailles, October 1703.
2 *The Irish Absentees New Litany; and the Character of an Irish Absentee*, in *The Pall–Mall Miscellany* (London: W. James, 1733), p.10.

On the other side of the Channel, accounts of the war in Ireland between 1689 and 1691 published in the press obviously depicted the Irish soldiers fighting for James II in an unfavourable light. The Irish Catholics embodied the perennial counterpoint to Protestant bravery, as they were systematically depicted in English newspapers and street ballads as running away from any fight to take refuge in bogs and forests even when outnumbering their foes 10 to one. Conversely, the Protestants of Ireland like the Enniskilleners of Newtownbutler or the defenders of Londonderry were praised as heroes and incorporated into official regiments in the British Army. Yet at the same time, Britain in the eighteenth century soon realised the military potential that the male Irish Catholic population represented at a time when numbers as well as experience offered a better chance of success on the battlefield. From the 1690s, the Penal Laws had rendered Catholics unable to join the British Army, but evidence from this time period prove that Irish 'papists' were indeed recruited in regiments fighting for the Hanoverian monarchs, even among the Guards regiments.[3] Ironically, the Irish Brigade in the service of the Bourbon monarchy happened to be at the centre of the ambiguous diplomatic and military relationship between France and Britain during the 1720s and 1730s, when its recruitment allowed London to get rid of unwanted rebels while Versailles sought to maintain a viable Jacobite threat against its enemy.

The Lives of Officers in the Brigade

Due to the Treaty of Ryswick, France could no longer interfere in English affairs and Louis XIV had to put an official end to his support for the Stuarts, which immediately caused turmoil among Irish regiments serving both his cousin and himself:

> [The King of France gave] his royal word not to assist directly or indirectly any of the king of England's enemies, that he [would] not favour in any way rumours, secret plots or rebellions that could occur in England. And consequently, he absolutely and unreservedly [vowed] not to help any person with weapons, ammunition, food, ships, money or other things by sea and by land who would pretend to trouble the said king of England in the peaceful possession of the said kingdoms.[4]

Many Irish military men and their families were left in very perilous personal situations once their regiments were disbanded in 1697 and 1715. In 1699, the Assemblée Générale du Clergé de France, a representative body of the French Catholic clergy, gathered in Saint-Germain-en-Laye and, following the orders of 'their Britannic Majesties', gave seven thousand livres to both Irish and English Catholic veterans and their families. The clergymen also offered to give the same amount to the exiled Queen of England's first chaplain for the

---

3   Jean–François Dutems, *Histoire de John Churchill duc de Marlborough* (Paris: Imprimerie impériale, 1808), vol.3, p. 503.
4   Archives du Ministère des Affaires Etrangères (AMAE), pp.172–173, Correspondance politique. *Traité de paix entre la France et l'Angleterre conclu à Ryswick le 20 septembre 1697*, (Paris, 1697), article IV.

Officers on a break. The lives of military officers in the French army during the eighteenth century were rarely this peaceful. Loo, Carle van, 'Halte d'Officiers' (1745). (Anne S.K. Brown Military Collection)

same purpose.[5] Saint-Germain-en-Laye gained thousands of new residents who struggled to find accommodation in such a small town. When James II fell ill and had to lay in bed, he 'left the Irish regiments in his service to Louis XIV's care'.[6] After his death in 1701, his widow endeavoured to maintain the aid given to Irish veterans but had to drastically reduce the number of pensions allocated to keep the scheme sustainable, until her own death in 1718 marked the end of that system altogether.

The harsh living conditions of the Irish in France did have an effect on some French people. The *Sieur* de Pointis, a French admiral who had served as the senior officer for the artillery in Ireland in 1689, wrote a report in the late seventeenth century pleading to keep the Jacobite regiments regardless of any treaty, arguing that they represented the only force capable of helping a return of the Stuart monarch on the English throne. He added that he believed that the regiments offered shelter to Irishmen willing to escape from oppression in Ireland and acted as a guarantee that few of them would convert to Protestantism in order to join William III's forces. For Pointis, a unit composed of 'capable and loyal men', unable to return home, could form the nucleus of a 'considerable body of troops' in case of an invasion of the British Isles. They constituted an elite that James II could actually count on since many gentlemen 'had accepted to carry a musket' for several years in the hope of better prospects.[7] Yet even with a growing respect shown towards the military valour of the Irish regiments, the reforms of the late seventeenth century left many of their officers and soldiers destitute and bitter. One officer from Clare's regiment named Callaghan wrote to his cousin in 1698 about the 'sad changes … of late touching [the] … reformation and breaking of officers and souldiers [sic]'. Half of the 36 second lieutenants and ensigns 'together with about 400 souldiers' in his regiment were dismissed and Callaghan advised his cousin not to 'depend [on] any honour or promise of honour' made to him.[8] As we saw earlier, only the return of hostilities in the early eighteenth century allowed the Irish to find regular pay once again as their units were reassembled.

French archives provide researchers with the means necessary to study these Irish units. In the late seventeenth and early eighteenth centuries, the French army had grown to a gigantic size not only in terms of the number of men who fought under its flags, but also when it came to the administrative apparatus accompanying each and every unit. Decrees and regulations were regularly published specifying how regiments were to be organised and paid, down to the minute details of their uniforms and drills. According to the rules in practice during the War of the Spanish Succession, most Irish foot regiments had 14 companies of fusiliers and one of grenadiers[9] while Fitzjames', the only regiment of Irish cavalry left, had 12 companies of horsemen.[10] The *Ordonnances* detailed the workings of each Irish company:

---

5   Abbé Desmarets, *Procez [sic] verbal de l'assemblée generale du clergé de France, tenue à Saint Germain en Laye au Chateau–Neuf* (Paris: François Hubert Muguet, 1703), p.220.

6   *Mercure Galant*, September 1701, vol.11, pp.369–385.

7   Service Historique de la Défense (SHD), *Mémoire sur les catholiques irlandais*, série 75, n°173.

8   Micheline Kerney Walsh Papers (MKWP) at Cardinal O'Fiaich's Library in Armagh (COFLA), Copy of SHD, Section Administrative, Dossiers personnels, O'Callaghan.

9   *Ordonnance du Roy portant réduction des compagnies d'infanterie françoise et irlandoise* (Lyon: Imprimerie de P. Valfray, 25 April 1736), pp.2–3.

10   *Ordonnance du Roy portant augmentation de troupes* (Lyon: Imprimerie de P. Valfray, 1 November 1733), p.2.

Each company of the regiments of [Irish infantry], with the exception of that of grenadiers, must have a Captain, a Lieutenant, one Ensign in each of the Colonel and Lieutenant-colonel companies, a Second lieutenant or reduced Lieutenant in the other companies, two Sergeants, three Corporals, five Lance Corporals & forty Fusiliers including a Drummer. [11]

Service records were regularly kept in order to manage senior and junior officers, both *en pied* (full service) and *réformé* (reduced or on half-pay and attached to a particular unit). These papers, now held in the archives of the *Service Historique de la Défense* in Vincennes, detailed as precisely as possible the careers of captains and lieutenants at regular intervals and served to establish seniority among peers as well as promotion for the most deserving. In the case of the Irish, these records were all the more important as they listed their complicated career paths. Many officers had reached a certain rank when fighting in Ireland only to be relegated to a lower status in the newly created Irish regiments of the early 1690s. The distinction between officers on full or half-pay was entirely left in the hands of the Irish colonels whose decisions were then sanctioned by the French administrative machine.[12] For instance, the service records of Fitzgerald's Regiment, stationed in Italy in 1705, gave for one of its captains the following pieces of information:

Mulchail [Mulcahey?] lieutenant [in the colonel's company] has served as ensign in 1688, lieutenant in 1689, captain in 1691, second lieutenant in Dublin's regiment on 5 February in 1692, put on half-pay attached to this regiment on 17 March 1698 and promoted to full lieutenant in 1705.[13]

Mulcahey's irregular career path was quite common among junior Irish officers of the time. Even senior ones wrote to Versailles to obtain a higher rank within the French military hierarchy. Mulcahey's own superior, Colonel Nicholas Fitzgerald, wrote to Versailles about having been 'forgotten' in the list of senior officers rewarded by Louis XIV in 1704. In his 'just and very respectful complaint', he underlined not just his faithfulness first to James II and then to the King of France and his diligence in commanding and maintaining his regiment, but also his frustration at seeing younger men advancing in their careers when his own seemed to have stalled.[14] Fitzgerald died in 1708 at Oudenarde a *brigadier* after having been captured on the day of the battle.[15]

Irish officers on half-pay were always on the lookout for commissions. When Nugent's cavalry regiment came through the city of Abbeville in northern France in 1723, it was

---

11   *Réglemens [sic] et Ordonnances du Roy, pour les gens de Guerre* (Paris: Léonard, 1706), vol.14, p.109.
12   SHD, Administrative Archives, Older Section, infantry, reformed or incorporated regiments before 1715, série XB 1 (p.249), régiment de Fitzgerald.
13   SHD, document copied by Mrs Kerney Walsh, O'Fiaich Library. *Estat des noms et service des officiers tant en pied que réformé du régiment irlandois de Fitzgerald au camp de Moscolino [sic] ce 6 juin 1705.* The colonel's company was the most prestigious one in an infantry regiment in Ancien Régime France alongside the grenadiers' company.
14   NLI, negative microfilm n°1094, positive microfilm n°184.
15   Abel Boyer, *The History of the Reign of Queen Anne, Digested into Annals* (London: M. Coggan, 1709), vol.8, appendix, p.37.

accompanied by a *brigade à la suitte* [sic], meaning a group of reduced officers waiting for a full commission either in that unit or elsewhere. A regiment could be escorted by several of these groups, but priority was given to those belonging to the first brigade whenever a position opened up. Networking and kinship affiliations were the basic elements of all Irish troops and several members of the same family often served together. This situation provided a justification when a more advantageous position appeared, as in the case of '*Sieur* MacMahon ... a lieutenant on half-pay of the third brigade' who asked to be transferred to the first 'where *Sieur* Bernard MacMahon his father also [served] as a lieutenant on half-pay'. The father had 'thirty-one years of service', while his son only had 10. But allegiance to one's family did not necessarily imply loyalty to a single regiment, and reduced officers from one unit could and did ask to serve in another brigade attached to another Irish unit to increase their chances of getting a permanent commission. Another advantage was that while Edmond MacMahon retained the same rank, his move to Lee's Regiment gave him an extra 140 *livres*, bringing his pay to 540 *livres*. A son could easily succeed his father, as was the case in Clare's Regiment, whose colonel chose 'in place of *Sieur* Macarty *Sieur* Stapleton son of an officer of the same name who has served in the regiment. He is 19 years old'.[16]

These brigades of officers on half-pay provided candidates ready to fill any empty position in the Irish regiments, which in turn made spots available in the brigades themselves. Though there was a strict official order regarding seniority, colonels could promote any captain or lieutenant of their choice, which could lead to a complicated game of musical chairs to satisfy both the service obligations and the networking needs of an Irish regiment:

> Sir,
> I have the honour of proposing you to fill in the place of Captain *reformé* attached to the company of Mac-Elligot made available by *Sieur* Fitz-Maurice's retirement. *Sieur* Kenedy [sic], full Lieutenant in the Lieutenant Colonel's company, is the most senior full Lieutenant, except for *Sieur* Maguire, full lieutenant in the Colonel's company who wishes to remain where he is. In place of *Sieur* Kenedy, I propose to transfer *Sieur* Butler from the full lieutenancy in Jacques Lee's Company, to that of Lieutenant Colonel Oshagnussy's Company because *Sieur* Butler is Mr O Shagnussy's [sic] nephew. In the place of *Sieur* Butler, *Sieur* Grace is a reduced lieutenant attached to Denis O Brien's company and the senior reduced lieutenant. In place of *Sieur* Grace is *Sieur* Pierce Mac-Elligot, a cadet in Mac-Elligot's Company. This cadet has served with the Regiment for four years and led a recruiting party of seventeen men last summer. [17]

Getting a promotion could arouse jealousy among officers, especially during peacetime since commissions were then few and far between. In February of 1730, two officers stationed in Lille, named Barrett and Fitzgerald, got into a fight that led to a deadly duel in which 'Sieur Fitzgerald' killed his comrade Barrett after a very drunken all-nighter. They

---

16   MKWP COFLA, copy of SHD Administrative Archives, Older Section, Personal files, Travail du Roi, carton 2 1740 1 April 1740, Clare's Regiment.

17   MKWP COFLA, copy of SHD, Administrative Archives, Older Section, Personal files, Travail du Roi, Carton 7, Paris, 28 June 1742.

had been celebrating the recent promotion of the former to the rank of *capitaine réformé*. All the witnesses gave the same information about how the two men had been close friends and had been seen chatting amicably together shortly before the duel. The investigation confirmed jealousy as the motive for the murder. The inventory of the belongings left behind by Fitzgerald after his escape gives an insight into the life of Irish officers at the time: he only had 'half a dozen shirts both good and bad and several other rags not worth inventorying. One pair of new shoes …'[18] and above all the official commissions of his career from his first post as ensign in 1717 to that of 2 February 1730. He fled and was never seen again.

The French military hierarchy found promoting or rewarding the most deserving Irish officers in the 1730s and 1740s quite difficult since it required them to discriminate among men who very often had similar careers. Those who sought to showcase their exploits frequently had to wait for their turn. After the Battle of Fontenoy, Captain Patrice MacMahon needed the help of his superiors who appealed to the Comte d'Argenson, the French Minister for War, in order to be awarded the coveted *Croix de Saint Louis*:

> The *Sieur* de MacMahon, a reformed captain, is asking to be accepted as a knight in the order of Saint Louis as well as a gratuity. He says that for the past seventeen years he has been … present on all the occasions in which this regiment has been employed, and among others at the Battle of Fontenoy, where he took two cannons from the enemies, that this action earned him the applause of his superiors, and that they quite willingly promised to grant him the cross of Saint Louis. He adds that he has just arrived from Scotland, where he was sent, that he dares to flatter himself that he has fulfilled the court's wishes and that this journey has caused him considerable expense.
>
> Note: There are fourteen reformed captains before him who do not have the cross, three of whom have had companies [in the past] and four of whom are attached to the regiment.

In response to this request, Versailles sought to know whether 'the action he had done at Fontenoy was brilliant enough to deserve him such a distinction over his comrades who were older than him'. On 17 September 1746, Major MacDonogh of Bulkeley's had to testify of the support provided to MacMahon by his comrades in arms. Milord Clare in turn wrote in the officer's favour on 12 October 1746, and finally Captain MacMahon was awarded the precious medal which opened so many doors in Ancien Régime France.

When moving up in France's military hierarchy proved almost impossible due to disbandment or reductions of the number of officers per unit, some Irish captains or lieutenants left France or even joined the enemy. In the early eighteenth century, the British government had a list of officers serving in the Irish regiments of Louis XIV who had decided to be incorporated in Italian, Austrian or even Russian regiments, sometimes managing to return to the British Isles as can be seen for those in Clare's Regiment:[19]

---

18   ADN, Parlement de Flandres, series 8 B, Barrett case, 1730.
19   TNA, PC 1/2/238, *Extract from Minutes of the examination of Irish officers who quitted the French service*, dated 11 December 1713.

A generall (sic) list of all the officers that quitted the Eight Irish battalions and the regiment of Horse that serves in the French Kings service from the year 1700 to the year 1709 with the names of all the regiment that they were employed in the Allys (sic).

My Lord Clare's regiment	The Allys [sic]	The French	The Allys [sic]
Walter butler capt. Comodant [sic] was broake [sic] in the year 1700	Gott a troop of horse in Count Tafes regiment [Austria] and sold it and had lived this [sic] eight years in Ireland.	Lieutenant generall [sic] Darintons regiment	
Capt.n Thomas Mac Carthey was major of horse to King Philip in Naples and	Came to general Taun when Naples surrendered and is at present in London.	Leiutenant [sic] Goven	Capt in generall Ravenclows Regiment killed
		Lt Condon	Captain in genrall Arragh regiment killed
Captain Fernandino Callahan	Capt of granadeers in gen[era]ll Ravenclous regiment at present in London	Lt Nolan	Captain in count Tafel regiment
Leuiten.t Denish Mac Carthey	Capt. In general Effens [Russian]	Lt Bulger	Capt in the same
Lt Moor	Capt. In the same and killed	Ensign Marcy	Leuit in Gen. Revenclow's regiment killed
Lt Cronen	Captn in colonel Horn's regiment and killed	Lt O Daw	Capt in his royall highness the Duke of Savoy's service in Monseras regiment
Lt Clohosy	Captn in Hidlessin, was broke for killing a soldier	Lt Buttler	Captain in Prince Barith regiment
Lt. Oneale	Captn in the same and killed	Lt. Plunckett	Capt of horse in a Lorrain's regiment
Mr Obrian Cadiet	Lieutenant of granadeers [sic] in Prince Auzeneburg	Captn. John Mac Carthey	Capt in Marshall staremberg regiment [Austria]
Mr Mac nemara	Made lieutenant in the same	Mr Charles Mac Carthey his brother	Lieutenant in the same taken and wounded in the Battle of Birwaga now in London.

Source: The National Archives, Kew, PC1/2/238. The capitalisation and spellings are as per the original.

Even soldiers deserted when promotion within the ranks seemed impossible, with many Irish privates returning to the British Isles.[20] Officers who had left the service of France to go

---

20   Barbara White, 'The Criminal Confessions of Newgate's Irishmen', *Irish Studies Review*, vol.14, n°3, 2011, p. 315.

abroad sometimes tried to return and insisted on their allegiance not just to the Stuarts, but also to the French crown. An Irish captain named O'Berne wrote directly to 'Monseigneur d'Angervilliers' in the late 1720s to justify his subsequent career moves after the War of the Spanish Succession which involved service in Spain and Russia. Promises of promotion and financial rewards were binding only to those who received them:

> My Lord,
> O'Berne, full captain in Berwick's regiment, very humbly represents to his highness that he has served the king ever since the Irish troops landed in France in 1691, that he has been a captain in the said regiment for the past twenty-years and that since the beginning of the 1704 campaign in Spain up until the withdrawal of the troops from that country in 1709 he was employed under the marshals of Berwick and Tessé and finally under His Royal Highness the Duke of Orleans in building bridges for the passage of troops on the main rivers of Spain and that he was happy enough to have the approval of the senior officers who were successively in command and who commended his attention, his ability and exactness in bridge making on the days appointed on very hostile and precipitous rivers as an extraordinary and very useful service to the two crowns. On this consideration, his Royal Highness the Duke regent gave him a 600 *livres* pension and promised him some advancement. He also represents that Mr de Castillar, currently the Minister for War in Spain, as French troops left that country, would have promised him a position as lieutenant-colonel in his own son's regiment with a colonel's commission, but that [O'Berne] had refused to leave the service of France in time of war, and that ever since peace was signed he travelled in Europe and his Majesty the Czar forced him to serve in his country as an infantry colonel where he stayed for two years but as soon as he learned at the end of 1718 that war was brewing in France he got, with great difficulty, his full leave to return and serve in France. He hopes that in consideration for his services, both ordinary and extraordinary and because of the offers he refused in Spain and of the regiment he abandoned in Moscow, and because of his advanced age and his disease having consumed the best years of his life in the service of France during 38 years, your Highness will accept to grant him his full pay as a full captain and will maintain the said pension attached to the city of Paris.[21]

In order to stay within the military system which allowed them a meagre income for as long as possible, officers on half-pay systematically lied about their age to appear younger than they really were for fear of being dismissed. As seen above, family bonds could count more than years of faithful service. When Colonel Bulkeley wrote a letter in June 1742 announcing the 'death of *Monsieur* Everard and *Monsieur* MacMahon, both captains', he automatically freed two spots in the same regiment as well as two positions in the ranks of his brigade of

---

21   MKWP COFLA, copy of SHD, document from O'Berne personal dossier. The underlined segments appeared in the original document.

officers on half-pay. As a colonel, Bulkeley could disregard the rules and offered the posts to his protégés:

> Mr de Butler, whom I propose to be a reformed captain, is only the second lieu-tenant, but has some merit, moreover truly related to the Duke of Ormond, even of the oldest branch of this house, I believe, Sir, that you will grant him this distinc-tion. The Sieur Cantillon has not been in the regiment for long, but he is nephew to Madame de Bulkeley who is very interested in him, so I flatter myself that you will be willing to grant us this little favour, he is the only relative she or I have in this regiment.[22]

Officers who were passed over wrote directly to their superiors or even to the War Ministry in Paris to rectify what they felt was a slight to their honour. This is what the brothers Florence and Calahan Macarty did in 1742 when, after 25 years of service in Berwick's they complained to the Ministry about Thomas Barnewall, 'one of the last captains on half-pay of the said regiment and [who has been] in the service for only seven years', who had been promoted by Versailles on a position they had been eyeing for a long time. In compensa-tion for this preferment and to prove 'that they are only sensitive to the loss of rank, and not to the desire to have companies', they begged the Minister for War François-Victor Le Tonnelier de Breteuil to grant them commissions as full captains. They eventually got their wishes fulfilled in July 1742 with the support of Colonel Fitzjames who, according to his correspondence, was a close friend of theirs. Eventually, the situation was solved by Versailles as Barnewall became the captain of the grenadiers' company, one of the most prestigious positions in an Ancien Régime regiment.

Recruiting the Brigade

Junior and senior officers in the French army of the eighteenth century were constantly preoccupied by the idea of maintaining their companies at full strength since they received the equivalent of one to four extra soldier's pay depending on the number of soldiers regis-tered as their own.[23] This state of affairs posed an even greater challenge to Irish officers as their connections to their island home and potential enlistees had been mostly severed after the Jacobite defeat of 1691. For the officers of the Irish Brigade, recruiting soldiers meant almost as much as showing bravery on the battlefield when it came to prestige and promo-tion. They had few options to find Irishmen eager to join their regiments: they could scour France looking for volunteers, persuade deserters or prisoners to sign up, press into service British subjects or even recruit men who did not hail from the British Isles. Returning to Ireland to recruit young men there was also a possibility, although a dangerous one since British authorities had reinforced their legislation regarding any attempt to 'seduce men

---

22   MKWP COFLA, copy of SHD, Administrative Archives, Older section, Ancien Régime, Travail du Roy, carton 6 (1742) p.30.

23   *Réglemens* [sic] *et Ordonnances du Roy, pour les gens de Guerre* (Paris: Frédéric Léonard, 1706), vol.14, passim.

into foreign service'. Any offender caught in the act risked the death penalty as a traitor to the crown.

Between 1698 and the 1720s, finding Irishmen in France was the most obvious choice. The departmental archives held in Lille possess, for example, a unique document about an Irish soldier living in northern France after the 1697 reforms. He was interrogated in the autumn of 1700 as a key witness in a murder case involving two Irish officers. The circumstances of the homicide itself illustrate the daily life of an Irish regiment at the time. Jacques [James] Nolan and Denys O'Brien squabbled in Douai over a game of dice, which lead to the latter murdering the former. Several Irishmen were questioned, one of whom, a 22-year old soldier named Germain O'Brien, was a cousin of the suspected murderer who saw 'his kinsman' looking agitated. When he asked him if he had 'any quarrel with some officer from the regiment, [Denys O'Brien] did not answer and having taken wine did not really heed what was said to him'. Germain, who happened to be close to the inn *le logis de la teste d'or* where the murder took place, then heard the pistol shot that fatally wounded Nolan. Another *officier réformé* witnessed Nolan getting shot in the shoulder trying to grasp his sword before passing out. One of the victim's relative, François Nolan, testified that the murdered officer and himself had come to settle an argument with O'Brien about a game of trictrac, a form of backgammon. According to François, Nolan said that he preferred to 'send the game to hell rather than have a dispute', to which Denys O'Brien replied that he 'would send both Nolan and the game to hell'.

Most of the interviews related directly to the crime, but interestingly one Irish soldier, named Maurice Conil [sic] in the French official report, worked on the side as a servant to O'Brien and was interrogated as a possible accomplice. He declared himself as being 18 years of age and answered questions about his own life prior to joining the regiment. This constitutes a unique example of an interview with a private of an Irish regiment in the service of France in the early eighteenth century:

> Says he has served two to three months but that during the latest reform *Monsieur de Labadie* [brigadier in the French army posted in Flanders] gave him his notice, a document still in his sergeant's possession.
>
> Asked if he is still possibly enlisted in the regiment
>
> Answered yes and said Milord Clare having found him in Paris has ever since said in Saint-Germain-en-Laye that he worked at monsieur Helly, a tailor [illegible] he told him to join the regiment and this is how the [illegible] *Sieur* Milord gave him permission to come back and that at the beginning he served in the grenadier company for a month before being transferred into Berinoir's [sic] company.
>
> Interrogated on whether or not he wore the regiment's uniform,
>
> Said that while he was in the grenadier company he wore his own except on parade days
>
> When he was given the regimental livery and that ever since the last two months he has been in Barinoir's [sic] company he has always been wearing the regimental uniform.
>
> Interrogated in whether or not he knew sieur Denis O'Brien, the Irish gentleman who has fled the regiment and if he was his valet or not,

Said he knew him well for having served as a dragoon in the company where O'Brien was a lieutenant and that ever since he was attached to the regiment of Clare, any day when the respondant was not working as a tailor he would run errands for the said *Sieur* O'Brien wherever he needed to go.

Asked whether or not he used to make *Sieur* O'Brien's bed …

Said that ever since he was at Douai he only did his bed twice and since the said *Sieur* O'Brien could not afford to maintain a valet, the one serving sieur Filsgerald [sic] who stays in the same room hosted him…[24]

This interview warrants several remarks. As usual, several members of the O'Brien and Nolan families were serving in the same unit as patronage and networking were very common among Irish regiments. The fact that senior officers like Colonel Clare did not find it beneath them to request former privates to join their regiments is noteworthy as it proves that Irishmen with experience were hard to come by and were worth the trouble. Conil tried to avoid stating he was actually serving O'Brien not necessarily because he was linked to the officer's crime but rather in accordance to the strict rule in the French army regarding the use of domestics in the ranks. Such practices were officially prohibited as it could distort the actual number of men available to fight in a company during a troop review. Labadie, the French Inspector General for the King's infantry mentioned in the interview, had signed many documents in the late seventeenth century allowing Irishmen to go wherever they wanted without being considered as deserters, which confirms Conil's statement. Here is an example of such a document:

Leave of absence for a soldier of the regiment of Clare Irlandois
We, Inspector General of the Infantry, testify to all it may concern having given a full leave of absence to Thomas Nisby serving as a soldier in the company of Captain White so he can retire to any place he wishes, pray and request the king's officers and all others to let him pass without causing him any trouble or hindrance, done in Douay [sic] 25 December 1699[25]

Most importantly, Maurice Conil had already had a military career at a young age, since he had followed O'Brien to a new regiment and in the meantime had been able to find a job in the civilian world once the reforms reduced the number of positions available. In the end, O'Brien was sentenced *in absentia* by the French justice system to have 'his arms, legs and back broken alive on a scaffold' while Conil was sent to prison under the surveillance of his former comrades.

Other Irish veterans managed to join French units and, at the beginning of the eighteenth century, it was possible to find Irishmen in the regiments of Saintonge or Berry or even in the Royal Artillerie, though that last formation was officially a French preserve.[26] Documents from the period demonstrate that French officers had grown to respect the Irish and were

---

24   Archives Départementales du Nord (ADN), Série 9 B 276 175, O'Brien's case.
25   British Library (BL) Add MSS 21376 to 21381. 28 January 1700. The underlined parts were filled out in the original form.
26   BL, Add MSS 21376 to 21381. 1 May 1727.

eager to keep them in their own units at the expense of French soldiers when regiments were dissolved between wars.[27] With this in mind, Louis XIV had a royal decree published in 1702 sent to all French provinces enjoining all Irishmen living in his kingdom or serving in his other regiments to reenlist in Irish units as the War of the Spanish Succession was entering its second year:

> Irishmen:
> By decree from the twelfth of February 1702, all Irish, English and Scottish men from the ages of eighteen to fifty who live in the kingdom without any proper military discharge or employment are ordered to immediately join the Irish regiments on risk of being treated as deserters for those having already served or as vagrants for the others.[28]

The responses from local governors and mayors kept in French depositories offer a glimpse into some successful Irish integrations in French communities at the onset of the eighteenth century, redefining our understanding of their assimilation into Ancien Régime France. The Jacobite diaspora counted a large proportion of members of the nobility whose fruitful careers have already been the subject of extensive studies, but the provincial surveys offer examples of Irishmen of more modest backgrounds who also managed to assimilate into French society. Yet, as the investigation found few Irish or even British vagrants, any man who did not fit properly into provincial society could potentially find himself enlisted overnight. This meant that the local authorities got in touch with anyone who had ties to the British Isles, but were sometimes at a loss about how to deal with either English or Irish subjects living in France at the time. This turned out to be still true several decades later as shown in the correspondence between *Monsieur* de Marville, the head of the Parisian police in the 1740s, and the Comte de Maurepas, the then Minister for War:

> I find myself in great difficulty in the execution of the King's order of April the 25th last, which states that all English, Scottish and Irish who find themselves without a vocation or job will be obliged to join the Irish regiments which are in the service of His Majesty, under penalty, with regard to those who have already served there, of being treated as deserters, and with regard to the others, of being punished as vagrants. This order is all the more difficult to execute as there are no officers in Paris to engage these Englishmen, several of whom came to see me saying that they were ready to obey it, but that they had to be given money to go to the various regiments which they would join. Not having any orders in this respect, I am all the more embarrassed as to the course I should take, since it seems to me that, since these individuals have not entered into any commitment, and have no one to lead them to the regiments, the money which they would be given could be left to chance. Moreover, does this law, which applies to vagrants and people without

---

27 National Library of Ireland (NLI) positive microfilm n°183. Letter from Sieur de Thoy, 5 December 1701, folio n°524.
28 Michel Chamillart, *Les ordonnances militaires du roy, réduites en pratique, et appliquées au détail du service* (Paris: Frédéric Léonard, 1710), pp.271–272.

profession, apply indiscriminately to all Englishmen, and are those who profess the Catholic religion not exempt?[29]

These Irishmen living in France, referred to as *habitués* (as in accustomed or accepted), were willing to obey the royal decree and join the Brigade but usually imposed their own conditions before doing so. In 1702, two Irish veterans who lived in Valenciennes and worked as *commis des traites* (customs employees responsible for controlling grain trades) enjoyed a good reputation in their new home and refused to join the Brigade, backed in their decision by local bourgeois. Others accepted but only if they were reintegrated as officers, as was the case for 'MacMahon' and 'Macuene' [sic] who claimed to be both 'gentlemen and familiar with Milord Clare'. They had been incorporated in an Irish regiment as mere privates when they had first landed in Brittany. In 1702, at Béthune, near Calais, five former soldiers – all veterans from Lee's Regiment – were claimed by an Irish officer. Described as 'quite honest people who all work without any blame', they asked to stay in northern France or, should they be forced to join the ranks once again, wanted to be allowed to do so in Lee's Regiment since they had once belonged to that unit. Another document, this time from Limoges in west-central France, describes Irishmen living there who were fully adjusted to French society. One of them, 'Patrice Jean de Beaumont, born in the city of Cassel in Ireland', taught law and philosophy and, as a former officer in a German regiment, was chosen to lead the new recruits. He probably brought with him two of his students, a young man called 'Daniel Conel born in Trally [sic]', who was 'tall, aged 24 and fit to serve' and Daniel Mahony, who also worked as 'a private tutor for the children of a bourgeois'. Another former officer, Jean Heli from Cork, asked to be given a commission as well as a stipend for his 10-year-old son. His wish was not granted, though the practice of enlisting young boys whose physical appearance and family connections suggested they would make good soldiers in the following years was fairly common in Ancien Régime France. Other Irishmen who lived in Limoges did not join as they were either married, crippled or had turned to the priesthood.[30]

The majority of Irish people established in France after 1691 settled in and around Nantes in the west, or in the north, around Lille and Saint Omer. Saint-Germain-en-Laye, west of Paris, was also favoured as it brought them closer to the exiled court of the Stuarts. Local archives attached to these places have kept the names of Jacobite soldiers and officers, most often misspelled or transformed to sound more French. This was the case in the Nantes parish registers from 1692 to 1701. Irishmen could be found living in the area of the Quai de la Fosse which, at the time, was on the outskirts of the city. Weddings and christenings involving those who had settled in Brittany decades before the Treaty of Limerick and the Jacobite refugees of the 1690s allowed the Irish community to flourish for a time. Three examples from these records show the type of connections that were then established:

29   A. de Boislisle, *Lettres de M. de Marville, lieutenant général de police au ministre Maurepas (1742–1747)* (Paris: Champion, 1896), vol.1, p.180. Letter from Marville to Maurepas, 29 May 1744.

30   NLI, positive microfilm n°155, Letter from 5 April 1702. *Estat des Irlandois qui se sont trouvés à Limoges et qui sont en estat de servir.*

Guillaume Butler and Honorée Figerard [sic], Wedding,
On the fifth day of November 1696 were received in the nuptial benediction in the chapel of the Irish priests situated in the house of the *Touche* in the *Saint Nicolas* parish... Guillaume Buteler [sic] infantry officer son of the late Walter Butler and Helene Butler on the one hand and Honorée Figerard daughter of Jaque [sic] Figerard and Isabelle Figerard Irish 'habitués' for a long time in La Fosse, were present Guillaume Hogan, infantry lieutenant, Thomas Burke officer and Richard Carney and Thomas Routeler (Butler?) all of them Irish... signed: David Woudlokh [sic], priest, M J Cohan, Thomas Burk and Richard Carney.[31]

Anne Hogan, Baptism,
On the ninth of January 1697 was baptised in the church of *Saint Nicolas* in Nantes by me priest of the said church undersigned, Anne born this day, daughter of Guillaume Hogan Irish officer [currently] absent and Jeanne, the mother, his wife. Sir Thomas Dillon Irish captain, was her Godfather, Françoise Canelle her Godmother, [she] is unmarried residing near the Jacobin convent and the others at La Fosse district. So signed on the original Lea Connell, Tho. Dillon Cassard, priest.[32]

Anne Gorman, Burial,
On the eighteenth of May 1701 was buried in this church the body of the defunct Anne, aged one, who died yesterday, daughter of Sir Arnold Gorman, lieutenant in the regiment of Berwick and of Marie Aloran [sic] his wife. Were present the said sir Gorman and Jan Allorand [sic] her grandfather, all of them Irish and all signing. Jean Halloran [sic] Arnold Gorman, Bousseau rector.[33]

Irish endogamy turned out to be a double-edged sword: it did reinforce the links within their diasporic network, since officers and soldiers' widows tended to remarry other Irishmen, but it also weakened the ability of the Irish community to integrate French society right after their arrival in the Bourbon kingdom. After 1701, fewer soldiers and officers appeared in the records at Nantes as they were needed on the frontiers for the war. Around the same time period, Saint-Germain-en-Laye also attracted Irishmen who lived in cramped hovels, mostly begging or waiting for some alms coming from the exiled royal family. Paris and its hospitals, particularly the Pitié Salpêtrière, also received Irish people while the Quartier Latin and the Collège des Irlandais soon became an old haunt for these refugees. As the War of the Spanish Succession continued, Lille and the northern provinces of France welcomed the Irish regiments which served as garrisons in these border cities. As food and lodgings were scarce in those parts, the local authorities often had to deal with problems generated by Irish officers accompanied by their families. Letters exchanged in 1710 between Louis XIV and Michel Chamillart, his Minister for War, about the situation of the Irish reveal

---

31   Archives Départementales de Loire–Atlantique (ADLA), Saint Nicolas' Parish, 1696, Grosse 27, folio n°52.
32   ADLA, Saint Nicolas' Parish, 1697, Grosse 28, folio n°3.
33   ADLA, Saint Nicolas' Parish, 1701, Grosse 32, folio n°17.

how they were by then regarded as belonging to a 'brave regiment' but also emphasised the never-ending problems they provoked in the neighbourhood they inhabited.[34]

In the early eighteenth century, desertion towards the ranks of the Brigade constituted the second source of recruits for its regiments, to the point that Louis XIV and Chamillart sent 15 Irish officers to Flanders to enlist men leaving Marlborough's army. But these Irish captains immediately complained that they had to reach into their own pockets to increase the recruiting bonuses offered to each man. This was the only way these potential soldiers did not leave to join other, better funded units. The price of recruiting one man for an Irish regiment at the beginning of the eighteenth century was 27 *livres* and 10 *sous*. The enlistment itself amounted to 14 *livres*, the uniform seven, the combined cost of a pair of stockings and a shirt was two *livres* and 30 *sous* while a pair of leather shoes was valued at three *livres*.[35] Because they were facing English troops on the northern frontiers of the realm, Irish regiments stationed there were clearly advantaged compared to their counterparts serving in northern Italy, as deserters only had to cross a field or a ford to join them. The Italian front was also plagued by the fact that the Duke of Savoy himself had Irish troops initially recruited from Irishmen serving in the French army and which were better paid than France's.

The fact that Irish Catholics could be found in the English – soon to become British – army during the last two wars of the Sun King's reign should not come as a surprise as there is ample evidence of their presence.[36] The London government as well as Dublin Castle were eager to avoid such soldiers in their regiments but could hardly maintain their forces at full strength without such an expedient. The French authorities were aware of Jacobite feelings being still present within both the English army and navy in the 1690s and the 1700s and were keen to offer rewards, especially to any navy captain who was willing to join the Stuart cause:

> As we are persuaded that there are many good subjects of his Britannic Majesty in the English fleet who would be quite pleased to leave the service of the Prince of Orange if they were assured of having enough to sustain themselves, a promise is made to all who will sail into any French port or join his Most Christian fleet not only to maintain them in the same employs they currently enjoy but to reward them with two thousand *écus* given to any man bringing a warship counting more than 40 cannons.[37]

Irish soldiers regularly left the ranks of the English army to join those of the French. They would evoke Jacobite feelings to persuade French authorities and convince them of their

---

34   MKWP COFLA, copy of SHD, section correspondance, A1, vol.2232, microfilm n°353, pp.421–427. Letter from Leblanc, 19 October 1710.

35   NLI, positive microfilm n°184, *Mémoire pour la levée d'un soldat irlandois*, circa 1702. There were twenty *sous* to a *livre*.

36   BL, Anon., *A letter from a soldier, being some remarks upon a late scandalous pamphlet; entituled, An address of some Irish–folks to the House of Commons* (Publisher unknown, 1702), 16 pages.

37   AMAE, *Correspondance politique*, pamphlet inciting desertion dating from 1693 (article 271 in volume 272).

good intentions as illustrated by this petition signed by 19 Irishmen held captive in Dinan, northern Brittany, in the early eighteenth century:

> Your supplicants [sic] very humbly show to your highness that they are Irishmen of the Roman Catholic religion taken by force in Ireland to go to the service of the so-called Queen Anne of England and, being embarked at Corke [sic] to be taken to France which has given infinite joy to your supplicants for having been brought to a Christian country not only because of the freedom of religion but to show their zeal and fidelity to their legitimate Prince the King of England presently in Saint Germain and to show how naturally they are inclined to the service of his most Christian majesty. They have openly joined Sieur O'Maddin Lieutenant in Dorington's [sic] Regiment who, at his own expense, provided your supplicants with all sorts of necessary things which they needed. Your supplicants most humbly beg your highness to give his orders to send us to the service of the King and not to allow us to be brought back to England to be sacrificed there. Your supplicants pray to God for the Salvation and happiness of your Highness.

> Names:
> Michael Forlong, Richard Forlong, George Bryen, David Curling, William Boolen, John Smith, Will Veale, Darby Regan, Walter Louis, Jeremy Murphy, Francis Spencer, John Browne, John Marnane, John Lillée, Thomas Edmiston, John Linahane, John Mallon, John Crowly, Edmond McCarty.[38]

As the English arrived in the Iberian Peninsula during the War of the Spanish Succession, Philip V used religious arguments to convince more Irishmen illegally enlisted in British regiments to join the cause of a Catholic king battling Protestant troops. The Spanish Inquisition re-converted many Irishmen who had had to abandon their faith in order to become soldiers in Queen Anne's army.[39]

Competition for Irish recruits also created tensions among allies. In the opening stages of the War of the Spanish Succession, the French *Maréchal* de Boufflers was convinced that half of the English army present in Holland would desert and join the Jacobite side, which guaranteed enough recruits for the Irish.[40] But his assessment did not consider the attraction Spanish units had for Irishmen. Philip V, impressed by their military performance, wanted to enlist more Irish veterans for his own forces lacking in experience, and O'Mahony, of Cremona fame, offered to organise a royal Irish guard for him. French authorities saw this personal initiative as detrimental to the Irish regiments in the service of Louis XIV and flatly refused O'Mahony's proposal. Nevertheless, Irishmen, both soldiers and officers, started to flock into Spanish units serving in Flanders or directly into Spain, as they were looking for better living conditions under another Bourbon king. Andrew Lee, one the most famous senior Irish officers at the

---

38   SHD, A1 1896, n°255.
39   See Thomas O'Connor, *Irish Voices from the Spanish Inquisition, Migrants, Converts and Brokers in Early Modern Iberia* (London: Palgrave Macmillan, 2016).
40   NLI, positive microfilm n°183, letter from *Maréchal* Boufflers, circa 1702.

time, wrote directly to French authorities to complain about such an unfair competition which, according to him, was depriving the regiments of the 'only and unique means which can furnish the ability to maintain our Irish troops'.[41] Even though the governor of the Spanish Netherlands, the Marques de Bedmar, had officially prohibited his officers from recruiting English, Scottish and Irish deserters coming from Marlborough's regiments present at Roosendaal in North Brabant, the Irish still preferred serving in Iberian units or even be sent to Spain since they were guaranteed to find employment in units organised by Philip V. Most importantly, when Versailles demanded a plethora of genealogical documents and peer referees to accept foreign titles of nobility from would-be Irish officers, Spanish authorities were far more accommodating when examining Irish aristocratic claims because of the long-established historical links between the island and the Iberian kingdom. By 1709, the Spanish crown created its own Irish units, all named after direct references to the island rather than after their colonels – respectively Hibernia, Irlanda and Ultonia. They formed the other Irish Brigade which was to survive until the early years of the nineteenth century.

Getting Irishmen to join Irish regiments was still quite practicable at the onset of the eighteenth century, but actually incorporating them before they had had time to desert was entirely a different matter. One document from 1705 clearly states that officers struggled to keep the men they had recruited to complete their depleted companies. The list provided in 1705 by Monsieur de Rollivaud, a French *intendant* based in Lyon, gave details about six Irish 'companies', a term referring in this case to groups of enlisted men en route to join Irish regiments. They had been gathered in Douai and were destined to the Irish troops fighting in Italy. Each soldier had received 'from the king's magazine one musket, one cartridge and a uniform'. The groups, led by a captain, totalled 173 men and had left behind one soldier in a hospital while travelling to Lyon and had lost to desertion between six and 15 soldiers. The Irish officers in this recruiting party managed to arrive in Lyon with, on average, 25 soldiers.[42] In spite of this reality, reports were regularly written by Irish officers living in France to convince French political and military authorities of the feasibility of recruiting more Irishmen for the regiments, usually with the ulterior motive of obtaining permanent commissions for themselves in these newly created units. One example from 1702 written by an Irish officer on half-pay gives an optimistic view of the measures to be adopted:

> … the officer will begin his recruitments in La Rochelle, afterwards he will go to Rochefort where he will find several in the naval troops, he will pass to [the island of] Olleron [sic] where he will find all of those soldiers who, with those of Saint Martin de Ré, will be led to La Rochelle where they will be lodged and subsist under the care of some officers of the garrison… the Irish officer will [then] take the stagecoach to Brest where he will find a large number of Irish in marine troops, will return by way of Saint Malo where he will find some more, the officer will

41   NLI, positive microfilm n°184, Report written by colonel Andrew Lee about recruitment (24 October 1704).

42   MKWP, COFLA, copy of SHD, *Etat de la revue faite aux six compagnies irlandoises qui sont parties de lyon ce 4ème de May 1705, marchant en Italie.*

[then] pass into Nantes where he will take those who are there and he will come to La Rochelle from where he will leave with all these men, pass into Bourdeaux [sic] we will send to take those who are there then to Toullon [sic] and Marseilles [sic].[43]

Though probably unrealistic considering the difficulties seasoned Irish officers had to keep their recruits from decamping when moving from one city to the next, this plan at least provides confirmation of the locations in France then most likely to harbour Irishmen. In any case, money remained the most problematic aspect of these recruitment schemes which always rested on Versailles loosening its purse strings, a rare occurrence at the time.

Yet even the arrival of deserters from the enemy's ranks did not solve all the difficulties encountered by recruiters as shown by the case of six English deserters taken in 1705 in Toul in eastern France. Captain Butler from Dorrington's Regiment had spotted these men, who were initially promised to Irish regiments serving in Italy but ended up in one of Clare's companies, a regiment destined to the eastern frontier. Butler was all the more aggrieved about the situation as he had gathered no fewer than 26 men and had already lost 15 to desertion. As a compensation for his financial loss, he demanded 30 *livres* per man from the King's own funds.[44] Deserters from recruiting parties could be pardoned if they joined a regiment as most Irish units were in dire need of men, but they could also suffer the consequences of such an act, even during wartime. In 1706, Lee's Regiment had a war council to decide the fates of two soldiers who had absconded after being enlisted, and the two men were sent to serve on the King's galleys, a punishment which at the time was akin to imprisonment and hard labour.[45]

Captured enemy soldiers held in France did not guarantee an easier way to obtain men for the Irish regiments. British sailors were thus considered as unrecruitable since they were supposed to be exchanged with their French counterparts. Versailles feared London would exact reprisals by abducting French fishermen going to Newfoundland or would press the French sailors detained in Britain into serving in the Royal Navy. English and Irish sailors held in Dinan had to be left aside by a recruiting agent working for Dorrington's in 1705.[46] There were cases of forced enlistment of Englishmen, as this interview with a silk weaver captured by the French at the end of the War of the Spanish Succession shows:

> Testimony of John Lodge Skinner, resident of London: The Witness says he served most of the last war in the regiment commanded by Brigadier Hans Hamilton, that in the year 1712, when there was an attempt to set fire to the shops at Arras he had the misfortune to be taken prisoner by the French and taken to Arras, that the officers of the Irish Brigade came with a pretended authority from the king of France and forced him to serve, that he consequently served in Dorrington's regiment from which he deserted about a fortnight ago with the intention of making

---

43   SHD, correspondance générale de la guerre, volume A1, 1612, *Mémoire d'un officier irlandois pour le recrutement d'un grand nombre d'Irlandois.*

44   MKWP COFLA, copy of SHD, A1 vol.1857, microfilm n°351, pp.692–695, Captain Butler from the camp at Wissembourg, 16 July 1705.

45   SHD, correspondence section, A1, vol.1945, microfilm n°352, pp.176–178.

46   SHD, A1 vol.1896, folio n°255.

a report of all that he knows which might be useful to this nation, the witness says that during his stay in France he observed that several persons of the Irish Brigade in France were dispatched [illegible] into England and Ireland to bring men from thence to recruit the said Brigade & that accordingly several men have been brought over to France but, as he has been told & verily believes, they were deluded by hopes of employment & receiving other benefits from their friends but did not know they were to serve in the troops till their arrival at Calais, where they were usually thrown into prison and then forced to be soldiers. The witness... says that several men brought from England and Ireland to reinforce the said Brigade are dying of grief because they have been so trepanned.[47]

The suspicion that accompanied Catholics in the mainly Protestant units of the British Army had a mirror effect on the other side of the Channel as Protestant soldiers were officially barred from joining the Irish Brigade but could still be found in its ranks. Enlisting Protestants could bypass recruiting shortages but required a formal religious renunciation co-signed by either Irish or French clergymen. Some decided to convert to Catholicism for personal reasons, but most did it to be able to benefit from the *Invalides* institution where only Catholic soldiers could be admitted. Jan Ryan, an Anglican soldier in an Irish regiment, was thus presented to Catholic priests in Nantes in 1714:

Jan Ryan, Recantation,
On the nineteenth of February 1714, I, the undersigned high priest from the community of Hibernian ecclesiastics and by permission of his Lordship the Bishop of Nantes, have received the recantation from the Anglican Church of Jan Ryan, a soldier in the Regiment of Sir Lee, aged approximately 30, son of Thomas Ryan and Eleonore Pouurne, his father and mother coming from county Tiperarie [sic] in Ireland in the presence of the V[enerable] and D[evout] M. Daniel Nolan, priest, and Daniel Rian, cousin of said Jan,
    All signed John Rian Dan. Nolan, priest, Daniel Rian and H. de la Roche, priest.[48]

As mentioned above, obtaining a commission or benefitting from a promotion usually required patience and excellent social skills and relations, but an officer's ability to recruit men was highly valued in the Brigade and took precedence over the length of service, officially the only way to promotion. Although unwritten, this rule applied to all and tends to prove that maintaining an Irish character within the regiments was paramount. This is perfectly illustrated in a letter from the Comte de Fitzjames about Edward Nugent's appointment to the prestigious Colonel's Company. Nugent was appointed in spite of other, more senior officers, who belonged to the same unit and had been waiting for that very promotion for a long time:

---

47   British National Archives (TNA), State Papers Foreign, Marlborough, SP34/23/48, FF 93–94, Whitehall, 12 July 1714.
48   ADLA, 1J art. 266, Saint Nicolas' parish, B.M.S., 45 grosse, folio 9, Jan Ryan's abjuration, 19 February 1714.

It has always been the practice in the Irish regiments to promote, before their seniors, those who render great service in matters of recruitment; and this is what has sustained them, and still sustains them, in spite of the difficulties which are met with in getting [Irishmen]. As Mr Edward Nugent has been a great resource to the regiment for our recruits, I thought, according to established practice, that I should propose him for the post of reformed captain of the colonel's [own] company, even though others are veterans. I hope that these reasons will determine you to grant him this request. I have the honour to be with respectful attachment, sir, your very humble and very obedient servant.[49]

Competition did not only happen between officers. Irish regiments within the Brigade were rivals fighting over Irish recruits. Conflicts between Irish units were regularly reported back to French authorities and the unwritten rules governing such practices often trumped any official orders. This was the case in 1710 when an officer from Lee's Regiment complained to Tressemane, a French senior officer, about having lost potential soldiers to not one but two competing units:

Sir,
Monsieur de Lincoln, a captain in Lee's regiment writes to me that having discovered five Irish soldiers in the Régiment du Dauphiné he denounced them to Monsieur de Montviel as per the King's regulation ordering that those from that nation that will be found in French regiments will be sent to the Irish officer who will claim them first. As Monsieur de Montviel is reluctant to give them back on the pretext that he has promised them to Dillon's and O'Donnell's regiments, the king's will be that you made sure that they be returned to Mr Lincoln after you have justified that he did ask for them first. Please let me know what has been done about this, I am etc.[50]

Even when the War of the Spanish Succession was officially ended, relationships between Irish units were still strained because of recruiting rivalries. In July of 1714, Lee's and Berwick's were at loggerheads over the arrival of recruits illegally raised in Ireland by the former and enlisted in the latter. The French military authorities decided to side with Berwick since the financial burden of getting them to France by ship had been borne by Berwick's regiment:

[T]hese 14 soldiers have enlisted with the officer from Berwick's who paid for their passage and brought them here therefore they should remain with him, as it is customary among troops from your nation serving the king that the recruits belong to those who brought them over regardless of what happened in Ireland for their enlistment.[51]

---

49   MKWP COFLA, copy of SHD Administrative Archives – Older Section, personal files, Travail du Roi, Carton 3 (1740).
50   MKWP COFLA, copy of SHD, facsimile, 4 January 1710 at Versailles.
51   MKWP COFLA, copy of SHD, correspondence section, A1, volume 2479, film n°353 (p.1168). Letter dated 29 July 1714.

Even though until the 1740s a steady stream of men coming over from Ireland allowed most regiments to keep their Hibernian identity, Irish recruiters sometimes resorted to the impressment of Frenchmen. D'Argenson, the French Minister for War during the War of the Austrian Succession, received a 'petition from a man named Gilles Labé who complain[ed] that the horsemen from Captain Nugent's company first tried to force him to sign a contract then led him to the gaols at Lambale [actually Lamballe in Brittany]'.[52] Even after having joined an Irish regiment voluntarily, getting settled in such a unit could be dangerous for outsiders, especially since Gaelic remained the main language spoken among privates, at least when not on duty. In 1745, a Frenchman named Nicolas Gauthier, born in Picardie, joined the cavalry regiment of Fitzjames but 'could not understand the language of his comrades who, in return, could not stand him and often sought quarrel with him, bullying him and headbutting him like rams'.[53] When it comes to the question of language used in the Brigade, most records from Irish regiments indicate the presence in the ranks of an interpreter, though it is hard to know whether this man worked to facilitate communication between the Irishmen and the French population or between Gaelic–speaking privates and English–speaking officers. Foreign regiments were expected to use their own language in daily life as well as in battle. To this day there is no document explicitly stating which language was actually used in the Brigade though most officers came from an Anglo–Irish background, suggesting English as the most probable option for day-to-day interactions in the early decades of the eighteenth century.

The Ambiguous Franco-English Agreement of the 1730s

After Limerick, the Penal Laws formally prohibited the enlistment of Catholics in English regiments, a rule taken up by Queen Anne in 1714, quite clearly stating that her written consent had to be given for the raising of troops in Britain for an army other than her own. Nevertheless, the antipathy shown towards 'Papists' did not prevent them from being found in British units. The law provided for the dismissal of any English captain and the suspension of any colonel, in addition to a cut in his salary, whose troops harboured a Catholic, and a reward of five pounds was offered to denounce any Catholic soldier. Concerning Irishmen joining the Irish Brigade, recruiters from France were obviously the priority target of British authorities in Dublin as well as in London. Captain Kelly, accused of high treason for enlisting soldiers in the service of the Pretender in 1715, was imprisoned in the English capital and then released for lack of evidence.[54] Death sentences were commuted to exile in the West Indies for the same acts committed in Dublin. London also kept a watchful eye on Jacobite officers in Calais as they left for England in 1716. This did not prevent Irish recruiters from arriving on British soil in the early 1720s, provided they had a passport when they went 'for the good of their particular business' in Ireland:

---

52 Archives Départementales Ille–et–Vilaine (ADIV), 1F 1204, Military matters. Letter dated 14 February 1744.
53 ADIV, 8B550, 23 January 1745.
54 *Gazette* (Paris: bureau d'adresse, 18 March 1715), p.153.

A map of Ireland in the eighteenth century. (*The New York Public Library Digital Collections*)

From the King to all our governors, to our lieutenants general in our provinces, to our particular governors of our cities, places, mayors and aldermen of the said cities and all other of our officers and subjects… greetings having kindly agreed to heed the opinion of our very dear and much loved uncle the duke of Orleans regent, by allowing Bourck reformed captain in the regiment of infantry of Berwick to go to Ireland for the good of his particular affairs we want and mandate you to let him pass safely and freely both on his way in as on his way out without stopping him, to allow that no disruption or hindrance may come his way, the present passport valid for eight months for such is our pleasure given in Paris on August 8, 1720 signed Louis and lower by the King the Duke of Orleans Regent.[55]

The Irish Parliament in Dublin passed an Act in 1722 prohibiting illegal recruitment for a foreign army in Ireland on pain of death. In the Summer of 1726, one recruiter, Moyse Newland, paid the ultimate price for breaking the law:

IRELAND. August 1726, Dublin. Captain Moyse Newland, convinced that he had enlisted people for the service of a Foreign Prince, was executed on the ninth of last month in [St Stephen Green]. After he had been hanged, his body was quartered and his entrails burnt; but his limbs were given back to his Parents, to be buried. It is said that he had already taken 200 men on board; and that the night he was taken he had another 100 ready.[56]

Despite the draconian British laws, smuggling between Ireland and France continued. Allegedly, Irish merchants would hide volunteers in the hold of their ships and list them among other goods as wild geese feathers, which is thought to be one of the origins of the nickname 'Wild Geese' given to Irish Catholic soldiers in the eighteenth century. If there is no historical reference confirming this explanation, there is however a document published in Britain in the 1720s clearly using the expression 'Wild Geese' deriding Irishmen while referring to the Brigade. The joke consisted of a dialogue between an Irish dragoon sergeant and new recruits freshly arrived from Ireland being drilled on horseback.[57] The thick Irish accents of both the NCO and the men ('Fer vas yo Born' for 'Where were you born?') and the repetition of the same orders ('To de right, put in your toe, put out your heel, shit up straight') made light of the Irish Brigade itself as well as of the Jacobite threat. The sergeant's brogue rendered all his orders unintelligible and turned the exercise into a catastrophic failure. The exact date of this document is not known, though one source gives the tentative date of 1727,[58] which would correspond with the relative thawing of Franco-British rela-

---

55   MKWP COFLA, copy of Archives départementales de la Gironde, (ADG), amirauté de Guyenne, 6B 46. 3 October 1720, "Passport for *Sieur* Bourck, captain alongside Beau and Cake his servants".

56   *Lettres Historiques contenant ce qui se passe de plus important en Europe* (The Hague: Adrian Moetjens, August 1726), p.225.

57   William Finemore, *The Pretender's exercise to his Irish Dragoons and his Wild Geese* (London, 1720s) Trinity College Library, Ireland, Press A.7.4 n°120.

58   Raymond Hickey, *Corpus Presenter: Software for Language Analysis with a Manual and 'A Corpus of Irish English' as Sample Data* (Amsterdam: John Benjamins Publishing Company, 2003), p.261.

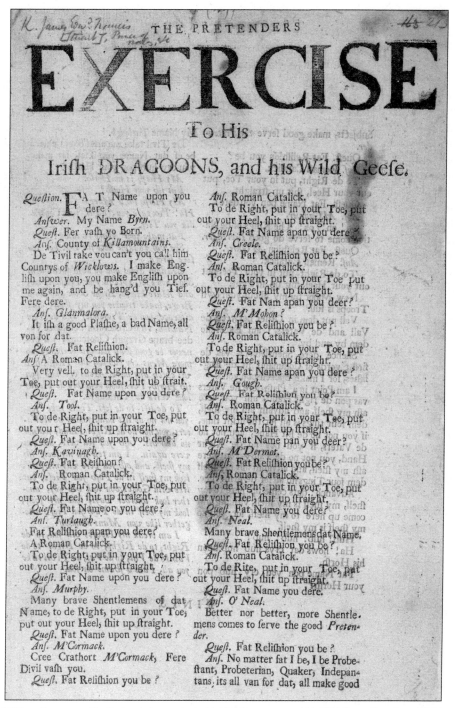

William Finemore, *The Pretender's exercise to his Irish Dragoons and his Wild Geese*. (London, 1720s) Trinity College Library, Ireland, Press A.7.4 n°120.

tions between that year and 1731. Versailles was by then attempting to negotiate an official permission to raise men in Ireland while London was trying to have the port of Dunkirk demilitarised as promised by the Treaty of Utrecht. Once peace had been signed, the main target of British suspicion over illegal enlistments was Spain. During the 1720s and early 1730s, recruitments in Ireland for the French Irish Brigade were tolerated when kept under wraps while Spanish enlistments were strictly banned.

After two failed Jacobite rebellions in Scotland in 1715 and 1719, tensions rose in Ireland and any man caught recruiting for the Pretender faced at least severe imprisonment if not death, and yet there was a form of toleration regarding the enlistments of Catholics in the 1720s as a way of removing as many potential agitators as possible. A contemporary Protestant observer explained that 'this country is better off being rid of them and their offspring, for not one in twenty survives to see his native island again.'[59] Thus, the first signs of a *détente* between Versailles and London appeared in Horatio Walpole's correspondence in the early 1720s, a period certainly marked by a relaxation of the rules governing how Irish Catholics could serve in a military capacity. The then Chief Secretary to the Lord Lieutenant of Ireland received and sent letters in the summer and autumn of 1720 about newly appointed officers or pensions needed by British war widows, but also about Irish recruitment directed to the continent. Walpole thus mentioned 20 to 30 men, 'either Protestants or Papists' that were to be selected on the grounds of their impressive physique so they could serve as grenadiers in the King of Prussia's personal guard. The Chief Secretary was confident such men could be found and did not seem worried about the prospect of Catholics becoming soldiers, even if in this case they were to serve a distant foreign power keen to get its hands on exceptionally tall soldiers.[60] A few days later, he was made aware of 'men listed and designed to be shipped off for foreign service', but once again there were no signs of any apprehension in his writings.[61] In early September 1720, the Lord Justices of Ireland informed the Lord Lieutenant of illegal recruiting practices, but received no specific orders in return. By mid-September, a copy of a letter written by the mayor of Cork was sent by the same Lord Justices to report what clearly appeared as unlawful actions occurring in the south of Ireland. The document, an examination of travellers about to embark for the continent, showed that several people who were 'bound for France on account as they pretended of their private affairs' were actually suspected of 'going on another errand', in this case, the men were 'suspected to be going into the Spanish service and pretend[ed] only to be bound... for France, a kingdom in amity with his majesty.'[62]

Though the enlistment of men for the Prussian army caused little to no complications and France at this point appeared as an ally of Britain, recruiting directly for the Irish Brigade in Ireland was quite another matter and the relaxed attitude mentioned above had its limits. A file held in the French military archives describes the career of Daniel O'Connor, an 'Irish gentleman bearing arms in Clare's regiment' who spent '8 months and 18 days' in 1727 with his neck, hands and feet bound in iron chains in a Cork dungeon. His life was only

59 Terence Denman, '"Hibernia officina militum": Irish recruitment to the British regular army. 1660–1815', *The Irish Sword*, vol.20, no.80, Winter 1996, pp.152–153.
60 PRONI, T2806 9840, Walpole, 6 August 1720.
61 PRONI, T2806 9840, Walpole, 20 August 1720.
62 PRONI, T2806 9840, Walpole, 15 August 1720.

saved by a letter sent from the French War ministry to the French ambassador in England. Ironically, while he did manage to return to France with 12 men, Versailles and London started to negotiate in earnest. On 31 January 1727, the Duke of Newcastle had reported to the Attorney General that the French were proposing a new method to enlist Irishmen. The correspondence proved quite affable, but soon suspicions and difficulties were accumulated grinding the scheme to a halt:

> From Harrington to Broglie[63] on the Brigade's recruitments in Ireland
> Monsieur,
> His Majesty having considered the letter your Excellency wrote recently to the Duke of Newcastle [secretary of State to Foreign Affairs] about the recruits desired from Ireland in the service of the [French] king... there is a very essential circumstance missing [in the papers] which is the number to which these recruits will amount to. As soon as we will be informed onto that subject, the King [of Great Britain] will issue orders that were promised so that only three months can be devoted to the task, still under the condition that the recruitment and the officers in charge of it will be so exempt from any blame or scandal that the government of Ireland will not find itself in the obligation of abandoning them to the rigours of law of the land. I am, etc.
> Harrington[64]

The recruiting officer, Lieutenant Colonel Hennessy from Lee's Regiment, was supposed to assemble 750 men and was helped in his task by several junior officers and sergeants. The period of three months granted by London was deemed too short by French authorities who thought that six months would barely be enough. Hennessy was told not to announce himself and his fellow Irishmen as a recruiting party once on the island and to work there as if he had not been granted any permission. Each officer was instructed to enlist men from the provinces they originally came from and to send 20 to 30 men at a time rather than wait until all 750 recruits had been gathered before shipping them to France. Specific orders were given not to enlist any deserters from the British forces. The French hoped that the three months allotted to them could be extended, but the British authorities estimated that it would coincide with the return of the Parliamentary season in England, which would provoke unwanted attention and resentment at the prospect of a foreign power openly recruiting in Ireland.

From the onset, these negotiations angered British pamphleteers. One of them, Charles Forman, who had served in Queen Anne and George I's war cabinets before moving to France under John Law as Comptroller General, wrote an article about the recruitment of Irishmen bound for France. While he showed some sympathy for James II, he was not a self-styled Jacobite and was at odds with the officers of the Brigade. In his writings, Forman directly addressed Robert Sutton, the former British ambassador to Versailles, urging him

---

63 As a French officer and diplomat, François–Marie de Broglie, 1st Duc de Broglie (1671–1745) was the French ambassador to England from 1724 to 1729.
64 Lord Stanhope, a former military man himself, was an English diplomat who had served a few years prior in Spain.

to be wary of the Irish military presence in France and of French endeavours to recruit for the Jacobite cause, although his remarks ended up focusing more on illegal importations of Irish wool into France rather than on the military issue itself. As France was rebuilding its forces after 1713, Forman expressed his fear that the Old Pretender would once again try to invade the British Isles and proposed to dismiss the Irish troops in the service of the Bourbons since they were made up of British subjects:

> I cannot comprehend by what honest Policy it is that the Irish Regiments are still permitted to remain in the Service of France. If that Nation is sincerely resolved to keep her Treaties with BRITAIN, she has no great Occasion for their service: But if she is only wheedling us to gain Time to re–establish her former Power, which we can still give a Check to, we shall be very much wanting to Ourselves, if we suffer those Regiments to continue any longer on Foot. As long as there is a Body of Irish Roman Catholick Troops Abroad, the CHEVALIER [James III] will always make some Figure in Europe by the credit they give him and be considered as a Prince that has a brave and well-disciplined Army of Veterans at his Service.[65]

The brigades of officers on half-pay, mentioned above, provided reserves of highly trained and motivated men ready to lead the Catholic male population once in Ireland. Forman frankly condemned the recruiters caught in Britain, but asked why there was a need to hang people whose regiments could easily be disbanded, their soldiers dispersed to French or Spanish units rather than in Jacobite ones to avoid so many 'brave men being reduced to misery' and because Spain and France would refuse to deprive themselves of their services:

> I only mean to abolish the name of the Irish forces abroad by incorporating them into French and Spanish regiments: by such means that military nursery of inveterate enemies to His Majesty's title and the British constitution will be entirely broken and dispersed... Their method of recruitment is certainly as base as it is savage, and void of all sentiments of humanity; and the gallows is too mild a punishment for the vile lies they spread among the poor ignorant creatures whom they spirit away.[66]

Talks between the two old enemies continued, but obstacles started to accumulate. By September 1730, the French authorities agreed to officially recall the officers in the face of the outcry. Harrington noted that 'spirits were... heated in Ireland judging by all that came back to him'.[67] In November 1730, London wanted the French court to 'cease insisting on the fulfilment of a promise which [could] be of little service to them and could only be treated with a great deal of inconvenience here' to calm the debates that had appeared by then in the

---

65   Charles Forman, *A letter to the Right Honourable Sir Robert Sutton, for disbanding the Irish regiments in the service of France and Spain* (London: George Faulkner and James Hoey in Christ–Church–Yard, 1728), p.19.

66   Forman, *A letter to the Right Honourable Sir Robert Sutton*, p.44.

67   SHED, A1 2770, recueil 1636-1734, Dépôt général de la guerre, n°78. Letter from Broglie to Harrington, 7/18 August 1730.

English press. The *Daily Courant* announced the arrival of Irish officers in Dublin, a piece of news that was picked up on 7 November 1730 by the *Craftsman*, a newspaper financed by an alliance of Whigs and Tories hostile to Robert Walpole, the then British Prime Minister. In the ensuing controversy, The *Craftsman* wrote the following text about the Irish Brigade:

> A very considerable body of men … They are generally esteemed to be the best forces in the French service. That they have always behaved themselves as such in the late wars, and are commanded by officers of approved courage as well as great skill and experience in military affairs. … they are generally looked upon abroad as a standing army kept on foot to serve the pretender upon any occasion … [they] speak our language, are acquainted with our manners and do not raise that aversion in the people which they naturally conceive against other foreign troops who understand neither. … Now, though it may not be safe to trust them into our armies, yet certainly we ought not to give the least encouragement to their entering into foreign service.[68]

A Whig newspaper, *The Free Briton*, responded to the *Craftsman* on 2 December 1730 by defending the government's position. In it, the warlike reputation of the Irish was deemed 'greatly exaggerated', and the author wrote about them that 'in truth these troops are like other troops, I am persuaded they are no better, and I will not say here that they are worse than the other armies of France are in general'.[69] The article even claimed that the men asked by Versailles were not a threat, as Cromwell had let thousands of Irishmen go into exile with Charles II. The Irish were after all in the author's eyes 'sadly known for their cowardice whenever they fought Englishmen', before pointing out several contradictions in the *Craftsman*'s logic. In a postscript, Francis Walsingham, one of Walpole's supporters, recalled that at the time of publication there was no official permission for the French to recruit in Ireland. For his part, Jonathan Swift responded to the *Craftsman*'s controversy on 12 December 1730 with the same kind of irony he had used in *A Modest Proposal* a year before. Swift attacked Nicholas Hamhurst, the *Craftsman*'s editor, and his article against the recruiting of Irishmen by comparing them to cattle and proposing to reduce the Irish population to just over 60,000 souls and turning them into shepherds guarded by 20,000 English soldiers.[70]

This was above all a journalistic controversy about Walpole rather than a genuine debate about the warlike value of the Irish in the service of France. Only Forman, in a second essay about the Irish, actually defended their merits. In contrast to the *Craftsman* and the *Free Briton*, he emphasised the fire discipline of the Irish, whom he regarded as his countrymen ('I defy even the vilest and most prejudiced of men to name the place where the Irish have misbehaved either at home or abroad since they have become disciplined'). He rehabilitated their participation in the Battle of Aughrim in 1691 and the usefulness of the Irish diversion

---

68   The *Craftsman*, 18 November 1730, pp.139–140 and 145.
69   The *Free Briton* n°50, 2 December 1730, "Reflections on the Irish troops in the service of France; with a defence of royal licences to raise recruits in Ireland", p.7.
70   John Nicholls, (ed.), *The Works of the Rev. Jonathan Swift* (New York, William Durell, 1812), Vol.13, pp.106–112.

for Louis XIV's France. On their recruitment, he referred, as mentioned above, to the presence of Irish in the English ranks:

> It was not only a common thing to recruit there [in Ireland] before, but even entire
> regiments were raised in that kingdom, of which I can name several, until the expe-
> rience we had of their frequent desertions to the French and Spaniards showed us
> that to list in Ireland was recruiting for the Irish troops in the service of France and
> Spain and, consequently, to raise forces at that time for the Chevalier. It demon-
> strated where their inclinations lay.[71]

Eventually, the whole operation was abandoned. Broglie suggested leaving only corporals
and sergeants to recruit more discreetly, but even though Harrington was disposed to help,
the local reactions in Ireland were that of outrage as the NCOs were 'too well known' in
their own island, hinting that loyalty towards Jacobite nobility in Irish counties was not
the only reason why men enlisted in the first place. Hennessy and his men were urged to
return to France with as many recruits as possible while Harrington admitted that once
these Irish officers were gone, clandestine recruitment could resume, assuring the French
that their regiments 'could get recruits using the same manner than during the reign of the
late King of England [George I] and even this one [George II]'. He promised Broglie that if
any member of the Irish Brigade was to be arrested in Ireland while recruiting, he would
help set him free. By the end of 1730, James Waldegrave, the British ambassador to France,
was able to announce that the French had agreed to destroy Dunkirk and give up their
recruits, much to the dismay of Cardinal Fleury, the *de facto* French Prime Minister, who
complained that Britain had ultimately won.

And so, by January 1731, clandestine enlistment resumed. The records of the Old Bailey in
London give some examples of sentences related to recruiters taken prisoners in the English
capital after that date. For instance, in 1737, Philip Dwyer and Bryan Macgrass were both
tried for 'seducing from [the King's] allegiance' an Irishman called Richard Murphy in the
name of 'Buckley's [sic] regiment'. Murphy had met them in a pub where he had enquired
about enlisting in the French service. He had missed an opportunity to leave on 1 February
1737 with a sergeant from the Irish Brigade working in Lincoln's-Inn-Fields. Murphy was
promised 'seven pence half-penny a day' and, though deemed slightly too short to serve in
time of peace, Dwyer had assured him that the Irish Brigade would not turn him down and
that he could 'follow [his] trade too'. The judge insisted to know whether Murphy had been
ready to sign to continue his trade in France and bring with him one or two volunteers or
if he had wanted to 'serve himself', questions to which Murphy did not answer straightfor-
wardly. At the very moment he had been apprehended, Dwyer had dropped a piece of paper
in the inn's hearth, which turned out to be his safe conduct:

> The Irish Regiment of Buckley. Soldier' Furloe [sic]. We who have undersigned, to
> all unto whom it may appertain, we have given Leave to Philip Dwyer, a Voluntier

---

71   Charles Forman, *A Defence of the courage, honour and loyalty of the Irish Nation, in answer to the
     scandalous reflections of the Free–Briton and others* (London: J. Watson, 1735), p.48.

in the Colonel's Company in Buckley's Regiment, to go to England for 6 Months, to recruit for the said Colonel's Company. The said Dwyer was born in Tipperary, aged 43 Years, five, Feet five Inches high, Chesnut colour'd Hair, Blue Eyes, short Nose, and good Legs. Signed. Macgray, Capt. Lieut. Dated at Avence, Counter-sign'd. Macheire, Major. Oct. 12, 1736. Approv'd and sign'd. Henezie [Hennessy], Lieut. Col. Enter'd. Dettez, Commissary of War.[72]

Dwyer had tried to burn the very paper that actually saved his and his friend's life. They were both acquitted.

In the absence of legal recruitment documents that usually led to their acquittal, defend-ants were systematically executed. Official commissions sent from France to serve as safe-conducts for Irish or English recruiters were often backdated to save the lives of potential Irish prisoners by making them officers of the French army rather than traitors to the British cause. The scheme did not always work, as illustrated by a man named Mooney held in Dublin for whom the *Maréchal* de Berwick personally wrote a commission making the Irishman's activity if not legal at least not punishable by death. However, the Protestants wanted to make an example and Mooney was eventually hanged.[73] In 1734, with the return of the Irish regiments to northern France, the Duke of Newcastle received a letter from a man named Ellys, postmaster at Dartford, reporting on the arrival of Irish deserters and farm labourers to Kent via Dover:

> I have often thought with horror that if the disaffected Papists, Jacobites, Tories, and Whigs who soon unite in a single resolution to destroy the present government, though they perish with it, if they should ever foment a rebellion, how easy it would be for them to assemble an army of Irish Papists in the very bowels of our kingdom, to cut our throats ... [74]

With the rise of tensions in Europe in the late 1730s, the English once again made it abso-lutely illegal to recruit for foreign Catholic powers to prevent both Spain and France from strengthening their respective regiments. The following decade saw a slight influx of volun-teers from Ireland, as the municipal archives of Angers show.[75] This increase was probably a result of the Irish famines of 1739–1741 which ultimately led to the creation of Lally's Regiment during the War of the Austrian Succession. The records of the city of Nantes reveal that in 1741 Irish recruiters had to be received periodically. Recruiting problems led the authorities to resort to a more enduring solution, and there is evidence of a permanent representative of the Irish Brigade posted in Nantes. A document signed by d'Argenson indicates that an Irish merchant, *Sieur* André Galloway, 'was in charge of recruiting for the regiment' of Rothe and that he was 'responsible for the correspondence of all the Irish regi-

72 February 1737, trial of Philip Dwyer Bryan Macgrass (t17370216–31), *Old Bailey Proceedings Online* <http://www.oldbaileyonline.org> (accessed 20 May 2022).
73 See PRONI, T3019/110 and T3019/108. Moony was a repeat offender.
74 TNA, SP 36 /33, 17 December 1734.
75 Municipal Archives of the city of Angers (AMA), EE 11, p. 112, 115 and 116 (14 May 1744, 14 January 1745).

ments and to whom they apply for their subsistence and the passage of all their recruits'.[76] This is, as far as can be ascertained, a unique example of this type of arrangement as Ancien Régime officers usually retained control over their recruiting schemes since their careers heavily depended on them.

Surviving After the Wars

For both officers and soldiers, life in the Irish Brigade when not in campaign proved complicated. The men did their best to remain as part of a company since obtaining a pension or being accepted in the *Hôtel Royal des Invalides*, France's first official military hospital, was far from guaranteed. Getting there meant that for a period of time the veteran was taken care of and could recuperate. If his health improved enough, he could be sent out to a provincial fortress or garrison as an invalid soldier. This solution offered him lodgings, food and put clothes on his back, a veritable form of retirement plan. Since obtaining men proved such a headache, many Irish soldiers were kept within the Brigade long after their infirmities and long years of service had eroded their martial abilities. But injuries sustained during battles, or simply long army careers, forced senior officers to sign papers finally letting veterans go. One example from Bulkeley's correspondence suffices to illustrate how Irish soldiers could be admitted in the venerable Parisian institution. The document, printed in advance with blanks to be filled in with the relevant pieces of information by the regiment's clerk, detailed the physical appearance of the candidate as well as his age and services and constitutes a precious source of information about the careers of Irish privates and NCOs:

> *Congé militaire* [military leave]
> We, the undersigned, testify to all it may concern having given his leave to join the Invalides, having faithfully served thirty-six years, to Philippe Nolan, corporal, from the company of Kearney in the Regiment of Bulkeley born in County Limerick in the province of Munster, in the jurisdiction of Ireland [sic] aged sixty-eight years, height: five feet three, grey hair and grey eyes, long and wrinkled face, good shoulders. Done at Ypres, on the fourth of the month of January one thousand seven hundred and forty-five.[77]

Getting accepted by the royal institution required both persistence and interpersonal skills. One soldier from Lee's Regiment was lucky enough to be directly helped by his colonel who personally wrote to the governor of the *Invalides*:

> At Saint-Germain this 9 September 1723,
> Sir,
> The man called Neal O'Byrne who has been serving for more than thirty-three years from the company of Sir Macmahon, captain in the regiment I have the honour of

---

76   ADIV, 4F folio n°9.
77   BL, Add MSS 21376 to 21381", Documents relating to the Irish Brigade chiefly consisting of soldiers' certificates and discharges, in 6 volumes. 21 January 1745.

commanding has been sent [out from] the regiment to see if at the Hotel Royal he could find a way to be cured from an infirmity that has already cost him an eye and could well make him lose the other. It is true that he has not been counted among those inspected to be sent to the Hotel but the long services and his disability make me hope that you will have some consideration for him... should you, sir, not find appropriate to have him accepted in your Hôtel Royal, please at least have him examined by the Hôtel's ablest surgeons and oculists to know if he can be cured or not and should his illness be incurable, please write me a word and send him back to me.[78]

The letter obviously opened the doors of the institution since one of the doctors from the *Invalides* came to see O'Byrne and recognised that his disease rendered him unable to serve as a soldier. But not all Irish soldiers were this fortunate, or this honest. Though supported by their superiors, some lied about their past to be admitted. One of them, Terence O'Bryen [sic], was diagnosed in 1700 as deaf and suffering from a fistula on his back rendering him incapable of performing his duties. His claims of having served in previous Irish regiments like Hamilton's in the 1670s before being transferred first to Furstemberg, then Greder and finally being incorporated in the Irish regiments of the 1690s were backed once again by Andrew Lee. The colonel's letter allowed O'Bryen to be admitted to the *Invalides*. But once there his file mentioned unequivocally that another Irish officer, Roth, found out that his certificate had been a fake. His application was eventually rejected with the word 'expelled' added underneath his name.[79]

Irish veterans sometimes refused to obey the strict regulations that still existed even after having left a regular regiment to enter a company of invalids. This was evidently not uncommon in Ancien Régime France, but the Irish seemed to have retained in the early years of the eighteenth century the lack of respect towards military discipline that had prevailed in previous eras, much to the despair of French authorities. One document from Antibes in southeast France provides a colourful portrait of Irish invalids taken from the minutes of a court martial responding to complaints against these veterans wreaking havoc in Provence:

The following men, Bernard Reilly, Irish, Daniel Rian [sic] Irish, Denis Hogan (Irish) Jean Michel, (Scottish), [are] all four addicted to wine and incorrigibly quarrelsome mutineers so furious when drunk, according to what was reported to us by the officers of the garrison, that they would know no one and, in this state, would be in the habit of shutting themselves up in their rooms where they would fight cruelly like beasts.[80]

---

78 BL, Add MSS 21376 to 21381, Documents relating to the Irish Brigade chiefly consisting of soldiers' certificates and discharges, in 6 volumes. 11 November 1723.
79 BL, Add MSS 21376 to 21381, Documents relating to the Irish Brigade chiefly consisting of soldiers' certificates and discharges, in 6 volumes, 18 November 1700.
80 BL, Add MSS 21380 0372, Iles Sainte Marguerite, 2 October 1717.

After having drawn lots to choose who would be punished, Reilly and another Irishman, Philippe Rhedan (probably Riordan) were both expelled from the invalids' company and left to fend for themselves. No wonder then that some Irishmen, with no other option or looking for better situations, ended on the wrong side of justice. Around the same time period, one of the accomplices of the notorious highwayman Louis Dominique Garthausen, better known in the Parisian underworld as Cartouche, was Nicolas Moure (probably Moore), a 24-year old Irish soldier convicted of theft and murder who was sentenced to death by the wheel in 1722.[81]

The bad reputation of Irish regiments was such that demonstrations of strict discipline and devotion were always welcomed. One letter from 1704 published in the *Mercure Galant* tried to mend the character of the Irish using the celebrations surrounding Saint Patrick's Day:

> As I know that you take a great deal of interest in what concerns us, I thought that you would not be displeased to learn the manner in which we celebrated the Feast of the glorious Saint Patrick. I will tell you first of all that all the companies of our Regiment spent this Feast with an extraordinary fervour and a very impressive devotion. All the Officers & all the Soldiers, were prepared to celebrate this Feast with much Religion. We had first of all a solemnly ordered Procession, then the great Mass sung in the Collegiate Church with much enthusiasm, all the Clergy of the Chapter, the Clergymen and all the Gentry of the City attended with piety, admiring the fervour and recollection of our Soldiers. After the first Mass the Benediction of the Blessed Sacrament was given; At three o'clock after midday everyone attended the Sermon in the large Church, preached by the Reverend Father Gaulaud, and after the Sermon, the Blessed Sacrament was consecrated. What contributed to making the Procession magnificent and solemn, was the order of our Officers & Soldiers, who being aligned in a row from the Church, made on both sides as it were an alley through which the Procession was to pass, the principal Officers saluting it with their Pikes & the Flags displayed in ceremony & in the most respectful manner they could. The Clergy had no sooner entered the Church than there was a general discharge of musketry. A similar discharge was made at the elevation and at the two Benedictions of the Blessed Sacrament, and during all this time the chimes of the bells together with the drums beating continuously, made a very agreeable concert which astonished and surprised the Religionists, who had never seen such a feast among them, and which was to the Catholics a great subject of consolation and edification, to see among the Soldiers such a rare, regulated, and exemplary piety. But if some were impatiently waiting to see the end of the day, persuading themselves that debauchery and excess of wine would disgrace the feast among the Officers and Soldiers, they were well deceived in their expectations, for after the whole of the Office was over, I retired with them to the Religious Cordeliers, where we remained until the hour of the supper, which I had

---

81   Parlement de Paris, *Arrêt de la cour de parlement portant condamnation de mort contre Nicolas Moure dit More, complice de Cartouche* (Paris: Delatour & Simon, 1722).

brought to their Refectory, and where, having only the Religious and the Officers, all were able to enjoy the meal, We completed the solemnisation of the feast by making wishes that the Lord would pour every kind of blessings on the sacred persons of our King, Queen, and all the Royal family, wishing also continual prosperity to the arms of France, to the Royal family, and above all, growth, triumph and victory to the Catholic, Apostolic and Roman Church. Then I sent everyone back to their quarters, without there being the slightest confusion; but everything was carried out with surprising devotion, and this devotion did not end with the Feast; for since that time both the Officers and the Soldiers, continue every day to attend Offices, Sermons and High Masses with great devotion.[82]

Officers could also join the *Invalides*, and the reports they sent to Versailles listed not only their campaigns but also their wounds, proving if need be that Irish junior officers led from the front and could sustain a great number of injuries while still remaining active within their regiment. Lieutenant O'Connor, who had joined the French army in 1690, suffered from an impressive series of war-related injuries:

A mutilated right arm, a left arm which received a musket shot and two sabre slashes, a musket shot across the neck causing him dizziness and another shot on the right shoulder, [he] has been a prisoner in Holland for six years without having received any pension or gratuity and begs his Highness to grant him a gratification so he can take to the spa waters.[83]

O'Connor was earning 1,200 *livres* per year but had to spend quite a lot of that money to maintain his unit as explained above, and so was granted a 300 *livres* bonus to ease his pains.

French military archives have kept thousands of muster rolls dating back from the eighteenth century, allowing researchers to study Irish regimental records. Samples taken from Lee's infantry regiment and Nugent's cavalry regiment reveal quite a lot about privates in the Brigade in the 1720s, though the information gathered requires a cautious analysis.[84] Firstly, muster rolls could be misleading about the men's personal information, for instance because of the ambiguity between the actual age on the date of enlistment and the age of the soldier at the time of the muster roll itself. Similarly, soldiers were recorded in the order in which they arrived in the regiment. If we follow this rule for Nugent's Regiment, whose muster rolls for the years 1723 and 1729 are available at Vincennes, the men do appear in the order of their enlistment date, but it becomes clear that the major responsible for recording the information in 1729 was more than happy to reuse the 1723 ages without adjusting

82   Mercure Galant, "Extrait d'une Lettre de Grenoble, écrite par un Officier Irlandois, touchant la manière que les troupes Irlandoises solemniserent à Montelimart, il y a quelque temps, la Feste de S. Patrice leur principal Patron & Apostre, qui se célèbre au 17 Mars" (Paris: Michel Brunet, avril 1704), vol.4, pp.128–134.
83   SHD, Administrative Archives, Older Section, Personal files, Ancien Régime, O'Connor. 5 May 1722.
84   MKWP COFLA, copy of SHD, 2151, 3Yc 198 "NUGENT", 1723. 2152, 3Yc 199 "NUGENT", 1729. GR 1 Yc 407 "LEE" 1690–1728.

them, even though his annotations for the origins and descriptions of the men had in the meantime become much more accurate:

	Names, proper names and nicknames	Birthplace	Description
1723 muster roll	Marcus Murphy	From Casselellie in Irland [sic] Wexford	Age 32 years old, height 5 feet 6 inches, black curly hair
1729 muster roll	Marc Murphy	From CastelEllis in Irel[an]d Lagenie province, jurisdiction and county Wexford	Aged 32 years. Height (sic) of 5 feet 6 inches, black curly hair and grey, broad of face and marked with the smallpox

Nevertheless, the muster rolls do paint a picture of Irish companies before the War of the Austrian Succession. This is for example a grenadier from Lee's Regiment as he appeared in 1729 who had completed his entire six-year enlistment. After 1716, enlistees in the French army had to have their description noted down to help authorities in case of desertion at a time when identity cards did not exist:

Names, proper names, and nicknames	Birthplace	Description	Date of enlistment	Date of death, notice and desertion
Denys Ryan	Native of the county of Tiperery [sic]	Twenty-five years old height of five feet six inches square [sic] good legs chestnut hair [sic] grey eyes, full face.	1 April 1726	Full leave in July of 1732

The descriptions tried to be as precise as possible, and there were many examples of soldiers with 'good legs' or 'beautiful eyes' or 'fresh complexions', while others had traces of smallpox, typical of the time, or wore wigs to conceal a receding hairline. While there were some inevitable exceptions noted down in 1722, it seems that the physique of Irish recruits who joined the Brigade between 1726 and 1729 was quite impressive, with most men having 'good legs', the phrase 'poor legs' disappearing almost entirely from the second troop review. In contrast, the dates of death for 17 men throughout the regiment indicate that the autumn of 1726 was a deadly one. Some of these casualties were relatively old when most of the men were still young and had been brought over from Ireland the previous summer.

The cavalrymen in Nugent's troops had an average height of around 170 centimetres (five feet seven inches), which corresponds to what a historian like Eoghan Ó Hannracháin found in his study of Fitzjames' Regiment (as Nugent's had then become) in 1737 when he noted the respectable appearance of the veterans, then in their fifties, who were described as 'well–built of body and legs'.[85] But even they were not free of problems related to illnesses, as in August 1729 and in January 1730 when five soldiers died within a few days of each

---

85   Eoghan Ó Hannracháin, 'An analysis of the Fitzjames Cavalry Regiment, 1737', The Irish Sword, vol.19, No.78 (Winter 1995), p.265.

other, probably due to an epidemic. In 1733, the soldiers of the colonel's company in Lee's Regiment, who were mostly young, were taller than their French comrades, who were on average 160 centimetres (five feet three inches), while the tallest Irishman was 180 centimetres (nearly six feet tall). The ages of the non-commissioned officers ranged from 50 to 65, although care must be taken with this type of information given the inconsistency of the information they usually provided.

As part of the regiment's elite, Lee's grenadiers were obviously taller and older than other soldiers. The records show that they were still predominantly Irish, with 46 of the 52 soldiers listed having direct Irish connections, and only three born in France to 'Irish' parents. The five remaining were either Scottish or English, accompanied by a lone Belgian. The geographical distribution of the 39 Irish people with full profiles shows that all of Ireland was involved in the recruitment of this company, with Leinster slightly in the lead. The longest registers, those of the *Maistre de Camp* and 'Swiny's' companies, with 99 and 125 names respectively, are also very valuable information–wise. The first company was largely Irish, with only one Scotsman and one Belgian answering the call. Three of the Irish had been born within the regiment. The province of birth for 43 of them is unfortunately not known, but, for the others, there was a clear domination of the Irish province of Leinster, particularly County Tipperary and the Queen's County in the centre of the island.

Numerous transfers between companies appear in the documents, which could have been internal exchanges between captains to bring together men who knew each other or hailed from the same family. In Coghlan's company, Leinster seemed to have been the most common province of origin and there was a significant number of soldiers' sons (12, over 16 percent of the total, four times more than in the other companies). When the son of a soldier or of an officer joined the ranks, his age was noted but, instead of the corresponding height, the chart only indicated that the boy was 'expected to grow'. Finally, there were at least nine soldiers from England, Scotland or Wales. For Swiny's company, this percentage of British people fell to fewer than six per cent. After the 1730s, enlistments were more likely to be in the Munster region, with Cork and Limerick in the lead, followed closely by Dublin and, to a lesser extent, by Connaught. The same percentages appear in parallel in the entries to the *Invalides*, with Munster accounting for just over 40 percent of the applicants, and the city and surrounding area of Cork amounting to a large proportion of the men enlisted. It seems that the men's birthplaces no longer necessarily corresponded to that of the officers', and that being from Ireland trumped being from any specific Irish county. Purely regional recruitments disappeared when the higher interests of a regiment or a company prevailed. Furthermore, the population of Ireland in the eighteenth century was much more mobile within its geographical boundaries than in previous eras, and by then names did not necessarily correspond exclusively to a particular region.

The Womenfolk of the Wild Geese

Earning a living was not only a major concern for the men; it also forced the women of the Wild Geese community to fight their own battles for survival. This was already true when the Irish settled in Brittany in the late 1690s and early 1700s as the husbands and sons left to fight Louis XIV's wars, but proved even more of a pressing matter when those conflicts ended and the relative regularity of an army pay suddenly ended, either because the men had died or because their regiment had been disbanded. For most Irish women, the army represented a better chance to feed their families, especially as the last years of Louis XIV's reign were marked by bad harvests and diseases. Many of them asked the French for certificates that would have allowed them to benefit from the army's provisions, a request resisted by the military authorities as they feared other Irish families would flock to the front, depriving French regiments of much needed food supplies. The quartermaster for the French army stationed in Italy, Etienne-Jean Bouchu, wrote in October 1701 that 'more than sixty wives of Irish officers' living in Grenoble wanted to join their husbands on the frontline.[86] They asked for documents allowing to be fed and lodged alongside their children while en route. Bouchu refused to give them any money for fear they might spread diseases in the camps or use it to settle in or around Grenoble for good, and only allowed them to stay in the town's hospital for a while.

Women were far from inactive members of the Irish community and French authorities noted in the early eighteenth century that their great number burdened the regiments when on campaign. They would threaten French commissaries in charge of supplies and urged their husbands to desert to the enemy if such a move promised better prospects. Some Irish women even turned to a life of crime. A French abbot called Séguier wrote to Pontchartrain about Irish bandits led by a man called O'Driscol (spelled Iriscol in his letter) who operated in Paris in the early eighteenth century. The priest explained to the minister that in case of a trial, he refused to see his name being mentioned for fear of reprisals and that 'sooner or later this would cost him his life as the women would have him killed by some soldier or friend of Iriscol's'.[87]

The arrival of the Irish in the early 1690s did not mean they were immediately fully accepted as equals by their French hosts. For instance, inheriting in Ancien Régime France required foreigners to be recognised as *régnicoles*, that is fully-fledged subjects of the Sun King, while the Irish were often treated as *aubains*, in other words foreigners whose possessions were normally offered to the king after they had died. As mentioned above, all Irish military men obtained the French nationality after Cremona, with a royal decree dating from 30 November 1715 confirming that all Irishmen who had served in the French army for more than 10 years did not have to provide any proof they had been naturalised as they were automatically considered as such. Nevertheless, French local and national archives do possess collections of documents produced in the eighteenth century in which Irish people requested 'letters of naturalisation' that guaranteed their possessions could be legally passed to their children after their deaths, rendering the *droit d'aubaine* null and void.

However, the death of a soldier or an officer serving in the Brigade usually meant dire consequences for the women depending on their wages, leading to poverty or even vagrancy. Reversionary benefits did exist for military families in Ancien Régime France, but rested entirely on the good will of French authorities. Having the support of high-ranking people at Saint-Germain-en-Laye or Versailles, or within the Catholic Church, was usually the only

---

86   NLI, positive microfilm n°183.
87   See David Bracken, 'Irish migrants in Paris hospitals, 1702–1730: Extracts from the registers of Bicêtre, La Charité, la Pitié and la Salpetrière', *Archivium Hibernicum*, vol.55, 2001, p.131, Séguier to Pontchartrain, 24 August 1701.

'Un Camp Volant' ('A light camp'). Watteau, Jean-Antoine, «Camp Volant» (1710). Armies in the eighteenth century were usually accompanied by camp followers. This type of scene with wives and children would have been quite common wherever the Irish Brigade was encamped. (Anne S.K. Brown Military Collection)

way to obtain such help. As a rule, those pensions were given to families whose head of the household was an officer and in which a son or sons were serving in the army as well. When a mother was left alone with no male offspring or with a daughter to take care of, charity was the only way to get by as shown in a letter written by the widow of an officer called Brennan to d'Angervilliers, the Minister for War in 1735:

My Lord,
Your Excellency having promised to take me into consideration in recognition of my husband's services who died as a Captain in Rothe's regiment after forty-five years of service as featured in the certificate attached to this letter, I cannot but renew to your Excellency in sadder times for me your generous promise, my daughter being dangerously ill from all the destitution we have both suffered for the past three years while I had the honour of requesting the favours of His Majesty and yours without obtaining more than six louis d'or that your Excellency was charitable enough to offer me, and which I will remember all my life with a strong appreciation, as I ceaselessly pray the heavens to shower you with graces, and begging Your Excellency to take me into your pity, as I am the saddest and most unfortunate widow that ever appeared in court, having no help after selling my belongings to subsist very cheaply, I am on the verge of seeing my child and myself perish from want, lacking all life necessities, from a violent disease. Please do open, your Lordship, I beg you in the name of Jesus Christ our saviour the bowels of your mercy on my woes, do not let me fall into despair for want of some help which will attract the blessings of Heaven upon you and will make me for the rest of my life, with a great respect and a perfect acknowledgment, your Lordship, your very humble and very obedient servant.
      Signed Widow Brennan[88]

On the side of the letter, in a different writing, was a quick summary of her husband's career which proved how difficult promotion could be for Irish officers who did not benefit from an effective family network or from Versailles's benevolence. Brennan had been a cadet in 1691 but waited until 1710 to get a lieutenant's commission, only to become a lieutenant on half-pay the following year. He waited another 11 years to be commissioned as a captain of a grenadier company in 1722, and his career ended when he was made a captain on half-pay in 1730. Her request was transmitted to Louis Achille Auguste de Harlay, a civil servant in charge of the finances for the city and jurisdiction of Paris, and his answer to her claim is worth quoting as it shows how widows could hope to be assisted:

I acquainted myself as best as I could about Captain Brennan's widow, who asks for a pension to help her survive. This widow, to prove her nobility, has submitted a *bona fide* certificate from the archbishop of Waterford and from several of the principal officers of the late king James, by which it is justified that she bears the name of O'Brennan, which is close to and from the same family as her late

88   SHD, Administrative Archives, Older Section, Personal files, Brennan.

husband's. According to the same certificate, this Irish family is indeed noble, did serve well and was never rich. This widow is nearly sixty-years old and was married for twenty-seven years to Mr. Brennan. It does not seem that she received anything from her father and mother as they were both already dead when she married. She has no other children than a daughter about twenty years of age who lives with her and who has been taken ill for almost two months. As for any succession from her side of the family or her husband's, she has none to hope for, one cannot define the extreme poverty in which she and her daughter live. They do not have forty francs of furniture in their room and without relief, often coming late, from charitable persons, they would starve to death. The Saint Benoist priest who gives them alms from the parish and to whom we asked about the conduct of the widow and her daughter has testified that they lead an exemplary life and they behave in the midst of the greatest poverty in a manner to be respected in their neighbourhood. His Excellency the Cardinal de Fleury [the equivalent of France's Prime Minister at the time] who learned about their situation has already been kind enough to get them some help at the beginning of the year.

I am respectfully,

Your very humble and very obedient servant,

(signed) Harlay[89]

The case of Brennan's widow is quite revealing. First, the connection with the Catholic Church of Ireland was not entirely severed as the Archbishop of Waterford, Richard Piers, who lived in France (he died in Sens in 1739) confirmed her status as a noblewoman. The Catholic Irish clergymen exiled on the continent usually served as priests in local parishes or as teachers in the Irish colleges established in the kingdom. They served as genealogists for members of the Irish regiments who needed proofs of nobility to request advantages and bonuses from the French aristocratic system. She then received help from her local French priest as well as from her husband's peers in the Irish Brigade. The importance of a good Christian reputation should also be noted as this argument was often put forward in official requests for gratifications. Having left Ireland because of religious intolerance, Irish Catholics could resort to recommendations from the clergy to be relieved as Lieutenant Colonel Skiddy's daughter did in 1725 after her father's death. Complaining of living 'in the unhappiest of situations' she asked that part of her father's pension, amounting to 1,200 *livres* per year be passed on to her. Being already 55 years of age, she could not count on her parents' assets which, having been invested in Paris, only yielded 80 *livres* of annuity, and then again in paper money. She eventually received 300 *livres* with the help of the Archbishop of Sens in north-central France who reminded the French authorities that she had 'left her country because of her religion'.[90]

Obviously, solidarity between exiles could not replace the support of a family and some documents offer a dark glimpse into the lives of Irish refugees. The loss of a father meant financial instability, but the loss of a mother left orphans without any prospects. A lieutenant

---

89 SHD, Administrative Archives, Older Section, Personal files, Brennan.
90 SHD, Administrative Archives, Older Section, Personal files, Skiddy, 8 October 1725.

in Clare's died in 1723 leaving behind two young sons who had previously also lost their mother. Two certificates were drawn up for them:

> We, brigadiers of the King's armies, testify that sieur Jean Odonelle [sic] formelly a lieutenant in the regiment I was in charge of and then in the second brigade of Clare's regiment served in the said quality as a brave man and good officer, diligent in his tasks and quite zealous in the service of the king. And as his two sons, the eldest being only six years of age have been left after his death in August last orphans of both father and mother we gave them this very certificate to which we added the seal of our coat of arms to serve them well, done in Saint-Germain-en-Laye, this 22 December 1723.
>
> We, the commanding officer of the second brigade of officers attached to Clare's regiment testify that Sieur O'Donnel formerly a lieutenant in the said brigade died in this place at the end of the August last leaving his two sons as orphans, one aged six the other eighteen months, without any belongings or support, their mother having died three months prior. We moreover testify that the said sieur O'Donnel served in the said brigade as well as O'Donnell regiment with great zeal, being assiduous and paying attention to his duties in witness whereof we have given this certificate to his eldest son to his benefit, done in Béthune, 2 November 1722.[91]

There are no other documents kept in French military archives detailing the fates of these two small children.

The only way to alleviate the suffering of Irish families, at least for a while, was through almsgiving from the exiled king of England and then from the French king himself once the Stuarts were forced to abandon Saint-Germain-en Laye. The rules of the Jacobite court were different since, unlike the French, the pensions it provided could be passed on to daughters. For instance, a woman named Catherine Croly whose parents had been receiving a small annuity before their deaths obtained 150 *livres* to compensate for this financial as well as personal loss. It was the death of the Queen of England in 1718, and not her parents', that put an end to this scheme. This is why the 'Sieur de Lacy ... at the age of ninety-two' entreated that on his death his officer's pension of 500 livres be passed on to his two daughters who were 'the sad remains of his large family' which had included 18 boys 'from the same marriage of whom fourteen died in the service of the legitimate king in England'. His request was granted.[92]

Official records show that widows could personally appeal to French authorities for help. Thus, the wife of a dead officer called MacMahon came to Versailles in October of 1729 to meet d'Angervilliers to obtain a survivor's pension. She failed to convince the Minister of the urgency of her situation but, ironically, was run over by a *mousquetaire du roi* rushing out of the palace with an urgent message, which forced her to stay in bed to heal her injuries and allowed her to get a small stipend. Yet the sum had only been offered thanks to

---

91   SHD, Administrative Archives, Older Section, Personal files, Colomb O'Donnell, Jean, 22 December 1723.

92   MKWP COFLA, copy of SHD, Older Archives, correspondence section, A1 volume 2515, film n°353, p.1357.

the generosity of the French royal family who at the time was celebrating the birth of the Dauphin.[93]

Women would also send copies of the complex genealogies established by their late husbands to prove their links to the nobility and often underlined the sacrifices made by their families in the service not just of the Stuarts, but also of the Bourbons. Sometimes this strategy backfired, as in the case of Hélène Morony, the wife of a lieutenant attached to Bulkeley's. Her husband already had benefited from a 540 *livres* bonus, slightly more than the average gratification then in existence, and her request was rejected, even if the colonel supported her claim. The files pertaining to Irish officers held in French archives do not always contain the answer from military or civilian authorities, but in Morony's case, d'Angervilliers noted on the side of the paper a terse 'a voucher of one hundred and fifty livres as alms on the condition of never appearing again'.[94]

Childless women of the Brigade could survive by becoming nuns, even if most of them did not have any dowry to offer the Church. Yet even then, payment still rested on the reputation and services of relatives who had died in the service. This was the case for 'Demoiselle O'Keeffe' in 1780. As she was no longer able to pay the Cordelières convent in Paris for her lodging out of her 200 *livres* gratuity, and she asked to have it increased. Born in Besançon in 1734, she was entitled to an extra grant of about 30 *livres* from the authorities because of 'her father's record of service as a captain in the Irish Regiment of Clare', but did not receive any help to settle the arrears of payment for the years 1777 and 1778. Her written claim emphasised, as usual, the number of her kinsmen who had died 'in the service of France'.

Others chose to return to Ireland, as did Jeanne Creagh circa 1714, 'a close relation to the late Archbishop of Dublin' who had until then helped her subsist alongside her brother. She chose to ask for money for her journey back to the island, as she no longer had any support from the Stuarts, her family – her brother had died during the War of the Spanish Succession – or the Irish clergy in France. Reduced 'to the last degree of poverty', she listed her relatives who had served in French armies or fleets and had died as well as her connection to the Catholic Church of Ireland to obtain a gratuity. In the end, she received a voucher for 200 *livres* 'to return home'.[95] As for 'Marie Hacquet, aged twenty-two, daughter of Nicolas Hacquet', a Jacobite veteran, going back to Ireland was also the preferred solution. In her request, she emphasised that she had 'never bothered the court', as a show of restraint designed to contrast with her overly demanding competitors constantly bombarding Versailles with demands. Yet her claim also rested on the many deaths in her family incurred by the wars. Her father, two uncles and her only brother had died in the service of both the Stuarts and Louis XIV.[96]

Peacetime for the 'Wild Geese' in the eighteenth century was a constant struggle which, though less deadly than a war, was just as exhausting. Surviving required money, energy, and interpersonal skills; scarce commodities for poor and isolated Irish soldiers. But by the 1720s and 1730s, Irish regiments had become fixtures in the French army and enjoyed a

---

93 MKWP COFLA, copy of SHD, Administrative Archives, Older Section, Personal files, Ancien Régime, Edmond MacMahon.
94 MKWP COFLA, copy of SHD, Administrative Archives, Older Section, Personal files, O'Donnel.
95 SHD, Administrative Archives, Older Section, Personal files, Ancien Régime, Jeanne Creagh.
96 SHD, Administrative Archives, Older section, Personal files, Thomas Hackett.

far better reputation than their predecessors. Irishmen either still in the army or forced to leave managed to integrate French society relatively more easily than previously understood while Irish officers struggled to maintain their prerogatives thanks to recruitments and patronage. Illegal enlistments in Ireland were still perceived as a threat by both the British crown and British society, though Ireland's relative calm during the first three Jacobite risings in Scotland seemingly defanged that menace. Be that as it may, the Irish Brigade continued to serve the Bourbons even after France no longer faced European coalitions. In the mid–1720s, Pierre Claude de Guignard, a French officer and an author specialised in military matters, favourably compared the Irish soldiers serving the French kingdom to their famous Swiss counterparts, writing that the reductions of their regiments in the first decades of the eighteenth century were only due to their casualties and not to administrative needs and called for their preservation within the French army:

> These precious remnants [of the Irish regiments] should be preserved as the testimony of the inviolable fidelity of this Nation for the interests of an unfortunate Prince, whose disgraces have raised their courage rather than lowered it. ... Although the party they have taken is very laudable, it has often thrown them into an unfortunate ... misery. Everyone knows the marks of confidence which His Majesty has given to these Officers on the most important of occasions; this fact alone is a greater form of praise than anything I could say about them: for example, M. the Duke of Barvik [Berwick] has been made a Peer & Marshal of France; M. Dillon a Lieutenant General, commander in chief of the Army of Dauphiné; M. de Lee a Lieutenant General, chosen by preference to command & defend the important fortress of Lille; M. Routh is a *Mestre de Camp*, chosen to be second in command in Béthune, & several other examples are sufficient to render their fidelity immortal for ever, & to show that in France the rewards of the Sovereign are accorded to true merit, without distinction of Nations.[97]

---

97 Pierre Claude de Guignard, *L'Ecole de Mars: ou mémoires instructifs sur toutes les parties qui composent le corps militaire en France, avec leurs origines et les différentes maneuvres auxquelles elles sont employées* (Paris: Simart, 1725), vol.1, p. 717.

3

'In Hoc Signo Vinces'[1] – The Irish Brigade and the Battle of Fontenoy

The Irish in the French service have frequently signalized themselves, and turned the scale of the war, when the French themselves durst not stand their ground, of which Fontenoy is a late instance.[2]

The War of the Austrian Succession (1740-1748) did not have a major impact on European history since it did not solve the tensions that existed within the continent, but it provided the Irish Brigade with the opportunity to fight the British army both in Flanders and in Great Britain itself. This conflict directly derived from the War of the Spanish Succession since Charles VI, the last Austrian Habsburg Emperor, wanted to avoid the fate of the Spanish branch of his family by keeping the Austrian monarchy united after his death. To secure the position of his heir, he produced a 'Pragmatic Sanction' in 1713 which, when he died in 1740, benefitted his only daughter, Archduchess Maria-Theresa. Yet the agreement was widely rejected and war became inevitable as candidates to the Viennese throne gathered their troops. France and its allies, Spain, Bavaria, Saxony and Prussia, faced Austria, Piedmont, Hanover, the United Provinces and Great Britain on battlegrounds strewn from Flanders to northern Italy. Once again faced with the prospect of a European continent dominated by a Catholic power, London had to intervene to secure its commercial and imperial ambitions. The war first flared up in northern Italy and in Silesia, a rich eastern German province, while the 'Pragmatic Army', a combination of British, Hanoverian, Dutch and Austrian forces, operated in the Austrian Netherlands to counter French manoeuvres against the Holy Roman Empire's possessions in Flanders.

---

1   'With this sign thou shalt conquer'. This motto appeared on most flags of the Irish Jacobite regiments up until their disbandment in the 1790s. It is a religious reference to a mystical episode allegedly experienced by Roman Emperor Constantine I before the Battle of the Milvian Bridge (312 AD) in which his victory closely followed his conversion to Christianity.

2   James Buchanan, *The Complete English Scholar. In Three Parts. Containing a New Method of Instructing Children and Perfecting Grown Persons in the English Tongue and of Learning Grammar in General Without the Help of Latin, Etc.* (London: A. Millar, 1753), 'Of Ireland' pp.396–398.

By then, the Irish Brigade had been fighting for the French for two generations. It was first mustered on the northern frontiers of the realm for a projected invasion of the British Isles before joining Louis XV's armies in Flanders. Led by the *Maréchal* de Saxe, the French defeated the allies' armies officially commanded by the Duke of Cumberland, George II's second living son, at Fontenoy on 11 May 1745. Cumberland was helped by Prince Waldeck representing the Dutch and Field Marshal Königsegg sent by the Austrians. Louis XV's forces were blockading Tournai when the Pragmatic Army endeavoured to raise the siege by attacking their positions from the rear. De Saxe left enough troops to maintain the siege of the Belgian city and went to the south-east to face the allies with about 52,000 men around the small village of Fontenoy whose houses were transformed into bastions supported by earthworks. After the Dutch failed to take the French fortified positions, Cumberland charged the centre of de Saxe's line with 15,000 infantrymen despite the firepower deployed by the redoubts. As Cumberland's regiments penetrated deeper into the French camp by forming a dense column, de Saxe coordinated his counter attacks using the Irish Brigade, the Régiment de Normandie and the Régiment Royal-Vaisseaux on the French left wing with the cavalry units from the *Maison du Roi*. He eventually managed to shatter the ranks of the British and Hanoverian troops, who withdrew with heavy losses.

Today, the intervention of the Irish Brigade on the French side is almost universally considered as the major turning point of the battle. Any military history book, academic paper or encyclopaedic entry devoted to Fontenoy published since the nineteenth century either in Great Britain or in France has had to mention the part played by the Irish on 11 May 1745. Albeit based on undeniable historical facts, this situation requires however a re–evaluation using eighteenth century sources since contemporary witnesses of the battle did not consider the Irish Brigade as the sole reason behind either the French victory or the British setback. Besides, even when Irish Picquets landed to help the Young Pretender in Scotland in the autumn of 1745, the French still struggled to recognise the potential of the descendants from the 1691 refugees living in their midst, while the British had a hard time accepting defeat at the hands of Jacobite forces. Feeling somewhat slighted by both camps, members of the Irish community living in France started to write down their own history to cement the importance of their own military past. Fontenoy soon replaced Cremona as the epitome of the Irish fighting spirit and was eventually transformed thanks to a rewriting of the battle itself into an Irish victory.

'Your King in fields of blood':[3] French viewpoints on Fontenoy and the Irish in 1745

The Irish Brigade in the early 1740s
France enjoyed a relative period of peace from 1715 to 1740, but Irishmen still joined the French army filling the gaps left by grizzled veterans in Jacobite regiments. Conflicts did erupt with Spain from 1719 to 1721 and in Poland and Italy from 1733 to 1738, but none of these directly threatened the realm. In 1734, during the War of the Polish Succession, the French authorities reissued the royal decree forcing any foreign nationals from the British

---

3   Voltaire, *La bataille de Fontenoy: poème* (Paris: Prault, 1745), p.3.

Isles to immediately join the ranks of the Irish Brigade or be sentenced to the galleys.[4] This was done even though France and Great Britain were still technically allied nations. The news exasperated the British and the decree was soon replaced by one actually reducing the number of men per company in each Irish unit.[5] In the meantime, in Ireland itself, the late 1730s and early 1740s were marked by a series of bad crops leading to a major famine in 1740 and 1741 that drove many young Irish Catholics to seek a living abroad. These newcomers were welcomed in the regiments which also resorted to decrees to maintain their Irish characters by attracting Irishmen still serving in other regiments of the French army:

> The Captains of the Irish Regiments shall likewise continue to take from French Regiments, the English, Scottish & Irish soldiers who have enlisted therein; whether their enlistment was prior or subsequent to the present one, by paying thirty *livres* for each private to the captain of the company in which he is enlisted, & this in accordance with the decree of the first of July 1721 derogating in favour of the Irish captains from that of the sixth of April 1718.[6]

Similarly, Irish deserters could benefit from a form of immunity but only if they returned to the ranks of one of the regiments of the Brigade.[7] By 1741, there were five Irish regiments of foot numbering a total of 2,550 men, each composed of a battalion of 510 men divided into 17 companies of 30 men. By May of 1741, each battalion saw its headcount increased to 685 men. Local archives in western France allow researchers to track down the arrival of these new recruits entering the country via Nantes.[8] In October of 1744, their presence combined with a reduction of the number of companies within each battalion from 17 to 13 – with one grenadier company and 12 fusilier companies; the latter equivalent to the 'hatmen' of British regiments – allowed Louis XV to reinforce the Irish Brigade by creating a brand-new infantry regiment. The decree specified that the king 'wanted to show his satisfaction of their service by offering them the means to continue even more usefully in the future'. Under the tutelage of the *Maréchal* de Noailles, it took the name of a former major in Dillon's Regiment, Count Thomas Arthur Lally de Tollendal, who became its colonel. All of these regiments were supposed to be exclusively composed of 'nationals', that is Irishmen:

> His Majesty grants fifty *livres* for the enlistment of each of the four hundred and forty-five men who will remain to be raised to complete this regiment of six

4   *Ordonnance du Roy pour obliger les Anglois, Écossois et Irlandois qui sont en France de prendre parti dans les régimens [sic] irlandois qui sont au service de Sa Majesté* (Paris: Imprimerie royale, 2 November 1734).

5   *Ordonnance du Roy portant réduction des compagnies d'infanterie françoise et irlandoise, obliger les Anglois, Écossois et Irlandois qui sont en France de prendre parti dans les régimens [sic] irlandois qui sont au service de Sa Majesté* (Paris: Imprimerie royale, 25 April 1736).

6   Pierre de Briquet, *Code militaire ou compilation des ordonnances des rois de France* (Paris: Prault père, 1741) Vol.3, pp.382–383.

7   *Ordonnance du Roy pour admettre les Irlandois qui ont déserté des troupes de Sa Majesté à profiter de la dernière amnistie, en s'engageant dans les régimens [sic] de leur nation* (Paris: Imprimerie royale, 25 November 1734).

8   Angers Municipal Archives (AMA), EE 11, p.111, 18–20 October 1744 and p.112, 14 May 1744.

hundred and forty-five men, and moreover fifty-one *livres* fifteen *sols* five *deniers* for clothing, and fifteen *livres* of gratification per man if the companies are complete for the review of April of next year, 1745. The armament composed of a musket and a bayonet will be delivered in kind for these four hundred and forty-five men from the royal magazines.[9]

Meanwhile, the war slowly expanded and the French decided to revive the Jacobite threat to disrupt the British efforts within the Pragmatic alliance. By 1743, James III, the 'Old Pretender', was invited to leave his exile in Italy and his son was chosen to lead an expedition in the British Isles. In 1744, popular French newspapers had a hard time keeping the information to themselves, with *canards* – handwritten newspapers circulating in secret – openly showing the Irish as part of the invasion forces:

> Swiss Guards, French Guards,
> Normandie, Lyonnois, Bourbounois,
> The brave Irish Brigade,
> and the Navy are all ready.
> Sixty-four battalions,
> With lifted spirits,
> By order of the great Bourbon king.[10]

Citing the *Brigade Irlandoise* in such a popular poem implies that most people knew who the Irish were, but 1745 proved that the French still had much to learn about the descendants of the Jacobite refugees. The regiments cited had been gathered under *Maréchal* de Saxe's command in and around Dunkirk and Boulogne. Such a choice of an experienced commander proved that Versailles was actually ready to use the Jacobite menace in a more aggressive way. Louis XV complimented him when he was officially appointed:

> Nothing is more valuable to the success of so just and glorious a purpose than to entrust the command of this corps to a person whose talents, bravery and experience in warfare can command the confidence of both our troops and that of loyal British subjects.[11]

However, bad weather conditions in the Channel, the Royal Navy's activities in the area, and a French clerk from the ministry of Foreign Affairs named Bussy who secretly worked for London,[12] all conspired to postpone and eventually cancel the expedition altogether.

---

9   *Ordonnance du roy, pour la nouvelle composition des cinq régiments irlandois; création d'un sixième régiment; & augmentation de solde aux sergens, haute–payes & soldats* (Paris: Imprimerie royale, 1 October 1744).

10 Edmond–Jean–François Barbier, *Journal de Barbier, Chronique de la régence et du règne de Louis XV: 1718–1763* (Paris: Charpentier, 1857), vol.7, p.212.

11 Jean–Pierre Bois, *Maurice de Saxe* (Paris: Fayard, 1992), p.312.

12 Général Gilbert Forray, *Les débarquements en Angleterre de César à Hitler* (Paris: Economica, 2010), p.144.

The Battle of the Boyne, 1 July 1690, Jan van Huchtenburg (1690-1733). (Rijksmuseum, Amsterdam)

IN HOC SIGNO VINCES

Flag of the Clancarthy Regiment (1692-1698) held at the Invalides in Paris (6647, cote Ba 6). (Musée de l'Armée, Dist. RMN-Grand Palais)

Little is known of the uniforms worn by the first Irish regiments serving in the Sun King's armies. So far, no verifiable records have been found regarding the colours of the facings worn by soldiers once they were refitted by the French. We can only assume that the red tunic was decorated with the usual distinctive colours normally found in the royal army at the time (greens, yellows, whites, and blacks), with blue specifically attached to royal Stuart units. Little bows worn on the shoulders or around the knees helped

to keep a certain sense of individuality in a military world that quickly became regulated. From left to right, the non–commissioned officer and the three hatmen represent types of soldiers that would have been seen on the different fronts of Louis XIV's penultimate war. Muskets, using powder charges hanging from a bandolier worn across the chest, were still the norm, while plug bayonets slowly replaced pikes. (Artwork by the Author)

From left to right: Soldiers of the regiments of Bulkeley, Rothe, Clare, and Berwick, circa 1720. They wear the usual military outfit of the early years of the eighteenth century, consisting of a wide–brimmed tricorn with a cartridge box and other military equipment in natural leather. By then, the legs were protected by tight-fitting leggings. Clare's had yellow facings while Bulkeley's were green and Rothe's (sometimes

spelled Routh or Rooth) were blue. The figure in the bearskin cap is a grenadier from Berwick's Regiment. Grenadiers were sometimes equipped with axes instead of sabres. Source : Pierre Lemau de la Jaisse, *Abrégé de la carte générale du militaire de France* (Paris: Prault Père, 1739), pp.276, 277, 278 and 283. (Artwork by the Author)

From left to right, the first soldier is a horseman from Fitzjames's cavalry unit with a large sabre and a carbine. Skull caps were often worn underneath the cocked hat to provide much needed protection. Next comes a private from Clare's Regiment with the traditional yellow facings. Both are depicted as they would have appeared during the War of the Austrian Succession. The officer to his right belongs to Dillon's

Regiment in the type of outfit he would have worn on the field of Fontenoy. His *hausse–col*, a form of gorget, was a remnant of medieval armour. It first covered the neck before being turned into a symbol of command. The last figure belongs to Lally's Regiment as it would have appeared in the 1750s. Source: La Chesnaye des Bois, *Dictionnaire militaire portatif* (Paris: Gisset, 1758) pp.578-583. (Artwork by the Author)

From left to right: A private from Dillon's Regiment wearing the official uniform for the year 1786: 'Lapels and facings in a light–yellow colour, a red collar, the top of the forearm trimmed with four squared buttonholes, and four large buttons. Yellow buttons' (from *Réglement arrêté par le roi, pour l'habillement & l'équipement de ses troupes : du premier Octobre 1786* (Paris: Collignon, 1786), p.50. Facing him is an officer from Walsh's Regiment with the same cut, except for the blue facings and the yellow collar. The third figure represents the type of uniform probably worn by Irish soldiers in the new Brigade established in the

mid-1790s. Though the correspondence attached to this unit insisted on details such as buttons and lace, precious little is known about the actual appearance of the troops as they left Limerick to go to the West Indies. The final figure is a *voltigeur* (light infantryman) from the Régiment Irlandais. His silhouette no longer belongs to the eighteenth century and his uniform is, down to its smallest detail, entirely based on the French Napoleonic light infantry pattern, except for its green base colour and its yellow, rather than white, piping. (Artwork by the Author)

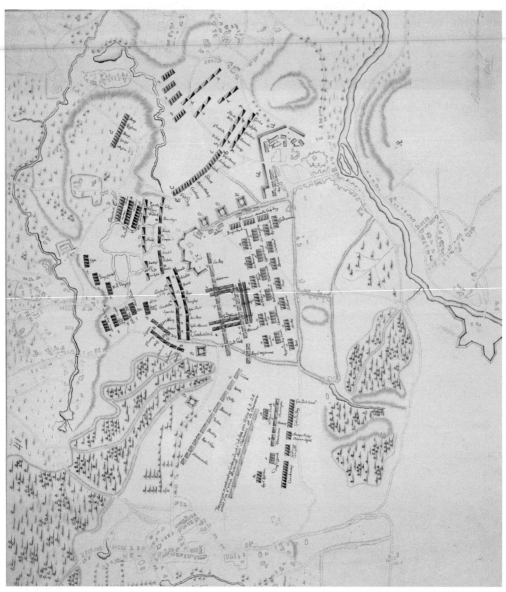

A map representing the positions of the armies at the beginning of the battle of Fontenoy, 11 May 1745, showing the position of the Irish Brigade on the French left. (Rijksmuseum)

The Irish Brigade then reintegrated the larger French army that was to be engaged in conti-nental Europe as it had been during the War of the Polish Succession a decade earlier. The opening stages of the new conflict seemed to smile upon the French as the Pragmatic Army was almost entirely encircled by *Maréchal* de Noailles' forces in western Germany. Though France and Great Britain were not yet technically at war, their forces faced each other in northern Bavaria at Dettingen in the summer of 1743. The Irish Brigade was placed on the first line of the right wing, the most prestigious post,[13] and held the village of Aschaffenburg alongside other French units under the Prince de Tingry's command. Though they were not actively involved, their role consisted in completing the encirclement of George II's army. The battle, which ought to have shattered the Pragmatic Army due to the risks taken by its leaders in their route through Germany, turned into a disastrous French defeat when the Duc de Grammont and the Gardes Françaises disobeyed orders and engaged the enemy under inauspicious circumstances. The Brigade had to wait two years to once again get to grips with a British army.

'The enemies have been quite defeated':[14] Fontenoy in French Official and Personal Battle Reports

As soon as the action was over on the night of 11 May 1745, Louis XV and the Dauphin wrote directly from the battlefield of Fontenoy to reassure their respective spouses as well as the country without singling out one particular unit as being instrumental in the victory. The heir to the throne only stated in his private correspondence that he had witnessed 'privates fighting like lions'.[15] The *Gazette*, the French monarchs' unofficial press office, published a first report about Fontenoy four days after the battle in which de Saxe barely appeared with Louis XV being described as the sole winner of the day, while the *Maison du Roi* was the only French unit actually standing out.[16] After several months in late 1744 during which the king's health had faltered and his very survival was at stake, the happy news from Flanders transformed him into a national hero, the nickname *bien aimé* (beloved) being added to his royal title. The newspaper did not mention the Irish Brigade until the official account of the battle was published at the end of May, but then again it was not cited as an essential component of the French victory against Cumberland's forces.[17]

The victory in Flanders echoed throughout France thanks to solemn processions, *Te Deums* and fireworks organised in Paris and in the largest cities of the realm.[18] The complete defeat of a coalition led by the British in the presence of both the French king and his heir immedi-ately became the most pressing topic of conversations and publications. At the end of May of 1745, the *Gazette* published a list of the names and the ranks of the most important casualties

---

13   Etat des troupes aux ordres de Mr. le Maréchal de Noailles au camp de Stockstatt, 19 au 27 juin 1743, cited in Chevalier de Malbez, *Campagne de Mr. le maréchal de Noailles en l'année 1743* (Paris: Picard, 1892), p.64.

14   Letter from Louis XV to Marie Leszczynka his wife, 11 May 1745, cited in M. Fs. Barrière, *Mémoires du Duc de Richelieu* (Paris: Firmin Didot frères, 1858), vol.2, p.99.

15   Jean–Biaise Desroches–Parthenay, *Mémoires historiques pour le siècle courant, avec des réflexions & remarques politiques & critiques* (Amsterdam: Etienne Ledet, 1745), pp.547–548.

16   *Gazette* (Paris: Galerie du Louvre, 15 May 1745), p.253.

17   *Gazette* (Paris: Galerie du Louvre, 29 May 1745), p.281.

18   *Mercure Historique et politique*, vol.46, p.18.

Maurice de Saxe (1696–1750). Hyacinthe Rigaud, 'Maurice de Saxe, Duc de Curlande et de Semigallié,
Maréchal de France'. (Anne S.K. Brown Military Collection)

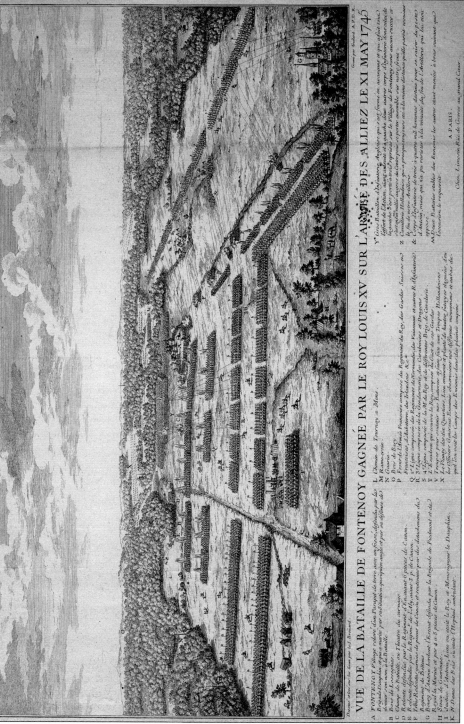

A map of the Battle of Fontenoy, 11 May 1745. S. Brouard, 'Vue de la Bataille de Fontenoy Gagnée par le Roy Louis XV sur l'Armée des Alliez le XI May 1745'. (Anne S.K. Brown Military Collection)

within the French army where the Irish appeared alongside other royal troops.[19] Surprisingly, given the usual antagonistic portrayal of the enemy in such publications, the story issued in June of 1745 in the same *Gazette* paid homage to the English whose 'infantry closed ranks and formed itself into a column before resuming its charge and the fearless bravery with which it fell upon the French troops equally deserves praises from both armies'.[20] After the *Maison du Roi*, entirely composed of cavalry units, the next French troops to be openly praised were the soldiers and officers of the Régiment de Normandie, one of the oldest infantry regiments in service at the time. Then, the well-timed intervention of four artillery pieces against the front of the Anglo-Hanoverian column appeared. Soon, knowing who actually took the initiative of diverting these guns became a subject of endless discussions. They had originally been kept in reserve and positioned to protect the King's retreat in case of a defeat.

The Irish did appear but were clearly kept in the background of what amounted for most commentators to a French victory won almost singlehandedly by Louis XV. The official French report of the battle mentioned the Irish alongside the Gardes Françaises, Gardes Suisses, the Régiments de Normandie and that of Royal-Vaisseaux as having charged 'with fixed bayonets' but without singling out the Brigade as decisive.[21] Before the first cannon shots were heard on the battlefield, the position occupied by the Irish was not deemed as vital to the French plan:

> The Irish Brigade, composed of 6 Battalions, had its right supported by the left of the Swiss Guards: this Brigade had in front of it Barry's wood, but could however see in the open at a musket's range and the second Redoubt, which was in front of its fifth battalion, was defended by the second battalion of the Régiment d'Eu, with 4 pieces of cannon. This redoubt proved eventually useless.[22]

Personal correspondences and memoirs written by French protagonists of 11 May 1745 usually give more details about the battle and the involvement of the Irish on that day. One that was published anonymously in Amsterdam in 1745 does cite the Irish as belonging to the French troops that were 'cruelly mistreated' by the English only to see their morale boosted by the timely appearance of Louis XV and the Dauphin. Interestingly enough, the author also saluted the English for their 'unwavering fearlessness'.[23] D'Argenson, the French minister for Foreign Affairs, was present on that day and confirmed in his report to the French Queen that the Irish were stationed before the battle to the left of the French positions behind a barricade made of tree trunks that joined two redoubts manned by the Régiment d'Eu. The Minister clearly stated that the other French units such as Normandie and Royal-Vaisseaux were posted behind the Irish, a piece of information confirmed by the Baron d'Espagnac in his

19 *Gazette* (Paris: Galerie du Louvre, 29 May 1745), p.294.
20 *Gazette* (Paris: Galerie du Louvre, 29 May 1745), p.274.
21 Anon., *Relation de la bataille de Fontenoy, Et de la Victoire que l'armée du Roy, commandée par Sa Majesté, a remportée sur l'armée des Alliez* (Paris: Pierre Valfray, Imprimeur du Roy, 1745).
22 Z***, *La conqueste des Pays–Bas par le roy, dans la campagne de 1745, avec la prise de Bruxelles en 1746* (The Hague, Publisher unknown, 1747), pp.12–13.
23 Desroches–Parthenay, *Mémoires historiques pour le siècle courant*, p.555.

Journal des campagnes du Roi. The baron described the Anglo–allied army as a 'monstruous phalanx composed of many nations and which seemed like a hideous hydra'.[24]

D'Argenson's description of the enemy's attack corroborated the official reports published in France, in that his account depicted the Dutch battalions as incapable of storming the French right wing due to the heavy bombardment of their lines. His narrative insisted on the Anglo-Hanoverian attacking the centre and the left of the de Saxe's forces head on. D'Argenson indicated that the counter-attack prepared by the *Maréchal* was supposed to be conducted on both sides of Cumberland's column once it had entered the French camp, but the French regiments fighting closer to Fontenoy actually moved too quickly and received the full force of the British salvoes, while the Régiment Royal-Vaisseaux and the redoubts positioned on the left blocked the advance of the Pragmatic column. De Saxe decided to break the stalemate that followed by sending in the Irish Brigade, closely followed by Normandie and Royal-Vaisseaux, in yet another counter-attack. D'Argenson mentioned the fact that the Irish had captured an enemy flag and cited them, alongside prestigious French royal units such as the *Maison du Roi*, the *Gendarmerie* and the *Carabiniers*, as being particularly deserving of praise.[25]

De Saxe himself admitted in one of his letters that he was 'in a critical situation for almost an hour'[26] when the Anglo-Hanoverian battalions forced their way inside the French perimeter and plainly confirmed that he was the one who ordered the attack from the Irish Brigade, Normandie, Royal-Vaisseaux and what was left of the Gardes Françaises and Gardes Suisses, a piece of information he confirmed in the official battle report written on 13 May 1745, stating that the 'Irish Brigade, that was leading, went over there with as much audacity as possible'.[27] With the help of the French cavalry, he 'saw this body of Englishmen and Hanoverians destroyed in an instant'.[28] Louis XV wrote directly to the *Maréchal* de Saxe to thank him personally but only mentioned the part played by his cavalry from the *Maison du Roi* and the *Carabiniers* in the final assault.

Other French witnesses, such as Emmanuel de Croÿ-Solre or Joseph-Louis Baron d'Heiss, both cavalry officers engaged once the enemy column was formed, wrote their own accounts of the battle. De Croÿ-Solre stated that the French in the days preceding the battle could not believe the Anglo–Hanoverians would mount a frontal assault on heavily fortified positions. His own cavalry regiment was posted behind the Irish, and he noted that the British and Hanoverians advanced towards the French line in 'the most orderly and graceful fashion'.[29] Contrary to what d'Argenson and de Saxe wrote, his testimony indicated that the French

---

24 Jean Baptiste Joseph Damarzit de Sahuguet, baron d'Espagnac, *Journal des campagnes du Roi en 1744, 1745, 1746 & 1747* (Liege: Publisher unknown, 1748), p.11.

25 L. Dussieux, E. Soulié (eds.), *Mémoires du duc de Luynes sur la cour de Louis XV (1735–1758)* (Paris: Firmin Didot frères, 1861), vol.7, p.167.

26 Maurice de Saxe, *Lettres Et Mémoires Choisis Parmi Les Papiers Originaux Du Maréchal De Saxe* (Paris: Smits, 1794), vol.1, p.227.

27 M. de Lescure (ed.), *Nouveaux mémoires du maréchal duc de Richelieu, 1696–1788* (Paris: Dentu, 1869), vol.3, p. 255.

28 Dussieux, Soulié (eds.), *Mémoires du duc de Luynes*, letter from the Maréchal de Saxe, 12 May 1745, in Anthoin [sic], p.179.

29 Emmanuel de Croÿ-Solre, 'Mémoires du Maréchal de Croy–Solre', *Nouvelle Revue Rétrospective*, 1895, p.13.

Louis XV (1710-1774). (Anne S.K. Brown Military Collection)

reserves on the left were led by the Régiment de Normandie immediately followed by the Irish Brigade and the Régiment Royal-Vaisseaux,[30] proving once again that memories and official accounts of a battle can often be contradictory. The Baron d'Heiss firmly believed the battle had been won by de Saxe's battle plan and personal disposition, but also thanks to the 'eighty pieces of cannon he [de Saxe] knew how to position'.[31] His own attention was focused on the four cannon brought by the British in front of their column, and when he and his men charged forwards; the only cavalry regiment that followed was Fitzjames' while the rest of the brigade had lost its way.[32] According to the Baron d'Heiss's account, each British volley killed or wounded about 10 men in his ranks, leaving certain regiments with only a handful of horsemen. He also saw the Irish Brigade and Normandie attacking Cumberland's column 'with fixed bayonets' alongside French heavy cavalrymen.[33]

Only one anonymous source clearly cited the Irish as being the ones who saved France's army on that day:

> We have just won a great victory, *Monsieur Le Maréchal* de Saxe, with death on his lips, has beaten the King's enemies and forced them to withdraw in disorder, the English under Ath, and the Dutch under Mons. The bad manoeuvre of the Gardes Françaises who, as usual, fled from the first charge, that of some other regiments almost had us lose it. The wise disposition of *Monsieur Le Maréchal*, the value of the Irish Brigade, that of the Régiment Royal, Régiment de Normandie and Les Vaisseaux gave us back the day. The English attacked with astonishing audacity, the Irish received them in the same way. Whilst our Infantry under *Monsieur* de Loewendal charged the enemies, the King's Household, with more impetuosity than order, and the *Carabiniers* pierced their line of infantry which formed a square of about 30 Battalions, and it is then that they fled. It is believed that their loss amounts to 6 or 7000 men, for in addition to what was found on the field of battle, *Monsieur* de Grassin [head of the French light infantry] who followed them, told *Monsieur Le Maréchal* that the villages which were in the rear of their camp are filled with wounded and dead. They have abandoned their artillery. We have already 35 guns and we are after the others and 60 artillery caissons with cartridges &c. ... many officers, especially Irish, of whom 25 of the regiment of Fits James [sic] and about 1500 men have been killed.[34]

30   Emmanuel de Croÿ-Solre, 'Mémoires du Maréchal de Croy–Solre', *Nouvelle Revue Rétrospective*, 1895, p.18.
31   Baron d'Heiss, 'Détail de ce que j'ay vu de la bataille de Fontenoi donnée le 11 May 1745', *Revue Rétrospective*, juillet 1893, p.66.
32   Baron d'Heiss, 'Détail de ce que j'ay vu de la bataille de Fontenoi donnée le 11 May 1745', *Revue Rétrospective*, juillet 1893, p.68.
33   Baron d'Heiss, 'Détail de ce que j'ay vu de la bataille de Fontenoi donnée le 11 May 1745', *Revue Rétrospective*, juillet 1893, p.71.
34   Anon., *From the battlefield near Antoing* [sic], 11th of May 1745, EE Correspondence (critical edition) general editors, R. V. McNamee, N. Cronk, letter editor, T.D.N. Besterman, Digital correspondence of Voltaire, letter n°: D.app.70.

According to contemporary sources, the Irish attacked the Anglo-Hanoverian column twice. The first assault was without any effect on the allies as stated by one French officer from the Régiment de Normandie who wrote that the Irish were repulsed before his own unit helped them get back to the fray.[35] The *Maréchal* de Saxe's papers published at the end of the eighteenth century described the Irish ferocity during the fighting: 'they … ran like rabid dogs, screaming like savages. They were repulsed ten paces before reaching the ranks and none of them turned their backs'.[36] The Irish then returned for a second and final charge during which they did use their muskets firing at point blank range on the enemy's ranks, as prescribed by official French military tactics:

> … then one must advance at the double quick, and break the silence shouting 'Kill! Kill!' and 'Long live the King!' And then throw oneself eagerly upon the enemy; or after firing one volley right in his belly, use the bayonet, and kill anything that resists, until the enemy flees and one sees that the battle is won … [37]

The *Maréchal* de Saxe went on in another statement: 'the second regiment of English Guards which faced that of Bulklay [Bulkeley] must be almost entirely destroyed, [the Irish] took a standard and two artillery pieces complete with their gun carriages which were posted in front of the battalions.'[38] There is little proof about the Irish actually capturing a British standard on that day. Once the order to charge the column was given, chaos ensued:

> It was approximately one o'clock when all the troops marched on in unison and found themselves fifty paces away from the enemy. Then, walking more lightly, they charged them with such fury that this column was pierced from all sides, the Grenadiers à Cheval gave the first sabre slashes, the Gardes Françaises the first bayonet thrusts, the *Maison du Roi* penetrated it in the same way; the *Carabiniers*, the Gardes Françaises and the Irish found themselves all mingled in the middle of that column composed of thirty battalions and supported by some cavalry; its head and its tail both shattered and found themselves in the greatest disorder imaginable. It was about two o'clock in the afternoon.[39]

The Irish regiments were allegedly attacked by the *Carabiniers* who mistook them for British soldiers because of their red uniforms. According to Voltaire, several Irishmen were killed before voices from the Brigade shouted '*Vive la France*'. Yet, none of the French official

---

35   Lieutenant Ferrand quoted in the *Revue d'histoire rédigée à l'État–major de l'armée*, Section historique, January 1905, n°51, p.504.

36   *Relation de la bataille de Fontenoi* [sic], from P.H. de Grimoard, *Lettres et mémoires choisi parmi les papiers originaux du Maréchal de Saxe* (Paris: J. J. Smits & Cie, 1794), vol.1, p.227.

37   Pierre Claude de Guignard, *L'École de Mars: ou mémoires instructifs sur toutes les parties qui composent le corps militaire en France avec leurs origines, & les différentes maneuvres ausquelles* [sic] *elles sont employées* (Paris: Simart, 1725), vol.1, p.652.

38   SHD, manuscript MR–2061 – 139. *Relation de la bataille de Fontenoy, gagnée par le Roy le 11 may 1745*, M. le Maréchal comte de Saxe commandant sous les ordres de Sa Majesté.

39   M. le comte de Chabannes, 'Projet de relation de la bataille de Fontenoy, gagnée le 11 mai 1745', quoted in Jean Colin, *Les campagnes du maréchal de Saxe* (Paris: Hachette, 1903), vol.3, pp.307–314.

reports published at the time mentioned this incident. Voltaire did write about it in two of his books, though the anecdote only appeared in the 1756 version and was abandoned in subsequent reissues.

An account written in 1745 by a Capuchin monk called Dominique de Béthune, officially translating the views of a Persian noble living in France, did praise the valour of the enemy. The so-called translator was accused of presenting a text deemed to be biased to the Austrian cause, but defended the document as being impartial since he 'followed to the letter the rights of people on which the faith of treaties rests'[40]:

> Each party performed gallantly. The English headed by the Duke of Cumberland fought like lions. The Hanoverians did everything one could hope for due to their natural bravery ... The victory seemed at that moment to declare itself in favour of the Duke of Cumberland, when the Irish Brigade supported by that of Normandie snatched from this Prince the palm his great courage was to bestow upon him.[41]

Other contemporary sources mentioned the fact that Louis XV personally thanked and praised the Régiment de Normandie for its opportune intervention, but nothing was officially written about the Irish, though they did receive medals from the King's own hands on 26 May 1745.[42] Losses among the Brigade during the battle were quite substantial, with one sixth of the Irishmen listed as killed or wounded, but French units like Normandie or Aubeterre lost even more men with a 50 percent casualty rate. Though less often cited as prominent during the assaults than the infantry units, Fitzjames' cavalry regiment was reduced to half of its initial battle strength.

'We know the Bourbons are the heroes of the day':[43] Fontenoy and French Artists
Fontenoy was almost immediately immortalised by French writers, poets and music composers all eager to please Versailles. Most of their writings were solely focused on the battle as a personal victory of the French king, with his son and the *Maréchal* de Saxe closely following as major figureheads, the Irish only appearing in a minor role. Yet this outpouring of words, verses and musical notes led to controversies and disputes as military victories often fuelled jealousies regarding who should be applauded, rewarded and remembered. Two major composers of the French court, François Colin de Blamont, the superintendent of the King's own Chamber Music Orchestra, and Esprit Antoine Blanchard, the deputy conductor of the Royal Chapel at Versailles, proposed rival *Te Deums* celebrating France's conquest as soon as the good news was heard, provoking a serious dissension between the two men that had to be settled by the King's own entourage. Every single artistic production written about the battle had to be approved by Prosper Jolyot de Crébillon, the royal censor of spectacles, and Claude-Henry Feydeau de Marville, the *Lieutenant Général de Police* in charge of the capital's security, before it could be officially printed.

40   Dominique de Béthune, *Le Persan en empire ou correspondance entre plusieurs voyageurs* (The Hague: Communauté des Libraires, 1745), vol.4, foreword.
41   Béthune, *Le Persan en empire*, vol.4, p.1522.
42   Jean–Pierre Bois, *Fontenoy, Louis XV arbitre de l'Europe* (Paris: Economica, 2012), p.111.
43   Louis de Boissy, *La Folie du Jour* (Paris: Clousier, juillet 1745), p.19.

Being the official historian attached to Louis XV since April of 1745, Voltaire penned one of his most famous works in honour of the winners of the battle and was allowed to print it as early as the 17 May 1745. Though working for the king, his poem was actually commissioned by the Duc de Richelieu, which explains the importance given to this officer in subsequent French narratives of the battle. The philosopher evoked the Irish in his verse as allies equal in importance to the Swiss when most of the other poets did not even mention the Brigade's presence, but he made a mistake in the first edition, writing in it that the Chevalier Jacques de Dillon, often referred to as James in other sources, was an officer from Switzerland who needed to be avenged by his countrymen:

> Clare with the Irishmen, invigorated by our examples,
> Avenges his betrayed kings, motherland and temples.
> Wise people & faithful, happy Helvetians,
> Our ancient Friends & our Fellow citizens,
> To Dillon's spirit your hand sacrifices,
> By fire and iron a crowd of enemies,
> Everything falls before us, everything flees our exercise,
> And the Englishman, in the end, fears LOUIS & his own demise.[44]

Similarly, Voltaire in his *Histoire de la Guerre de 1741* misspelled 'Mylord Clare' who led the Brigade on that day writing instead 'Mylord Clark'.[45] The philosopher's poem had to be rewritten six other times to accommodate all the courtiers. Voltaire was usually panned for praising both experienced senior officers and lowly sycophants and for ignoring basic historical facts, earning him the nickname *gazetier* (in other words a small-time journalist) from his many critics. Most of them pointed out that his poem did not put enough emphasis on Louis XV and the Dauphin while at the same time blaming him for having written it to please Versailles more than to add to France's proud literary production.

In the eyes of the philosopher, only officers were worthy of praises, leaving precious little room to the Irish soldiers, which earned him criticisms from one of his old enemies, the Abbé Pierre-François Guyot Desfontaines, who corrected his mistake:

> You barely talk about our brave Irish ... The things you could have said about the Irish, who, ever since they have been serving France, [who have become] French in a fashion, have always distinguished themselves in combat? Did they not acquire glory during the great Spanish war? They can beat the English anywhere, except in their own country, it is their destiny to avenge, under the banners of France, the awful woes their tyrannically oppressed families suffer.[46]

---

44   Voltaire, *La Bataille de Fontenoy*, p.10.
45   Voltaire, *Histoire de la Guerre de 1741* (Amsterdam: Publisher unknown, 1755), vol.2, p.125.
46   Abbé Pierre–François Guyot Desfontaines, *Avis sincères à M. de Voltaire: au sujet de la sixième édition de son poëme sur la victoire de Fontenoy* (Paris (?): Publisher unknown, 1745), pp.7–8.

Another author, Jacques d'Estrées, based in the Netherlands, also noticed the error made about Dillon's nationality but regretted that Swiss and Irish soldiers were praised instead of French military men:

> I would ask him what our Helvetians have in common with the *Chevalier de Dillon*, the Colonel of an Irish regiment in the service of France, to sacrifice the enemy crowd that our efforts have crushed to the spirits of this foreigner … this enemy was not supposed to be sacrificed to the spirits of a foreigner, but to the spirits of the fellow citizens whom we had lost at the beginning of the battle.[47]

Similarly, Pierre Honoré Robbé de Beauveset, one of Louis XV's protégés, identified the blunder made by Voltaire and attacked him head on:

> That the noble Irishman by you be downgraded,
> Of his rich parents may he be disinherited.[48]

Voltaire had actually already mentioned the Irish in some of his previous writings, but rarely to their advantage, especially when he wrote about the 1641 insurrection. His assessment of their military value back in 1691 as it appeared in his book about Louis XIV's reign published in 1751 was rather vexing to the descendants of the Jacobite refugees:

> The Irish, that we saw being such good soldiers in France and in Spain, have always fought badly at home. There are nations that seem to be made to be dominated by another. The English have always had the superiority of genius, riches and military victory over the Irish.[49]

The initial version of that text had an even more controversial take on the difference between the two nations since the English were described as having over the Irish the 'superiority that whites have over niggers [sic]'. As for the arrival of the 1691 exiles, Voltaire showed little sympathy for the Irish described as being only motivated by greed: '… the French fleet was busy … transporting back … the Irish Catholic families who, being very poor on their island, wanted to go to France to live off the King's generosity'.[50]

Voltaire finally corrected the lines of his poem dedicated to the Irish in the following versions of the poem, simply by erasing any allusion to Dillon and extending the role played by the Swiss. And yet he did change his point of view on the Irish as military men when he published his *Eloge des morts de la guerre de 1741* in which the following passage can be read: 'And so, this foreign troop which has become so national and which bears the name of

47 Jacques d'Estrées, *Le Controlleur du Parnasse* (Amsterdam: Wolf and Fleischmans, 1745), p.154.
48 Pierre Honoré Robbé de Beauveset, *Epitre du sieur Rabot, maître d'école de Fontenoy sur les victoires du Roy, 2ème, 3eme, 4eme, 5eme, 6eme, 7eme & dernière édition, Augmentée d'une complainte à L'Apollon de la France, à Fontenoy, 1745*, in *Mélanges de poésies sous le règne de Louis XV* (Paris: Publisher unknown, 1745), pp.6–7.
49 Voltaire, *Le Siècle de Louis XIV* (Berlin: Henning, 1751), vol.1, p.267.
50 Graham Gargett, 'Voltaire and Irish history', *Eighteenth century Ireland*, vol.5, 1990, p.129.

Dillon has seen the children and the younger brothers rapidly succeeding their fathers and elder brothers killed in battle'.[51]

One possible explanation for this change of heart is that the historiographer worked for a while in the months following Fontenoy with Comte de Lally-Tollendal, an Irish officer personally distinguished by Louis XV in 1745 who had been charged with organising a French landing in England to support Charles Edward Stuart. Voltaire was quite impressed with the young colonel and, years later, fought to rehabilitate Lally's reputation after the Irishman was executed on charges of corruption after having lost the French territories of India during the Seven Years War.

Though derided, criticised or envied by other authors, Voltaire was soon followed by many copycats. They would first write in a serious, laudatory tone before turning towards a more satirical style. Most poets agreed with François-Nicolas Guérin, a professor of rhetoric at the Collège du Plessis in Paris, who bemoaned the fact that 'a famous poet has said it all, celebrated it all'. Few dared to say anything contradicting Voltaire's version and Guérin himself exalted both Louis XV and the Dauphin without mentioning anybody else by name, not even de Saxe, a misstep that was corrected in the subsequent version published a year later.[52] The *Maison du Roi* was the most lauded unit, leaving the other troops in the background, while Louis XV encouraged everyone to fight. Maurice de Saxe himself was transformed into a full-blown French subject thanks to his 'rare bravery'.

Elie Catherine Fréron, a staunch opponent to Voltaire, also commended Louis XV, the *Carabiniers* and the *Maison du Roi*, but had a somewhat more nationalistic approach. He had Maurice de Saxe declaring about the French:

> This people, when it wants to dominate with its courage,
> the enemy's outrage,
> only needs a leader
> or the eyes of its ruler.[53]

The French victory inspired countless parodies in which Voltaire ended up as the butt of the joke. His own style was thus parodied in 1745:

> What! Of the present century, the tragicomic,
> epic, political, critical and lyrical author,
> Englishman for thirty years by disposition,
> Turned French again thanks to a pension,
> Finds it fitting that the King should be a victor.[54]

The battle inspired a series of documents which took the form of fake requests written directly from Fontenoy to Louis XV. The first one was published by Jean-Henri Marchand, a

---

51   Voltaire, *Œuvres complètes de Voltaire, siècle de Louis XV* (Paris: Baudoin frères, 1828), p.351.
52   François–Nicolas Guérin, *La Victoire de Fontenoy, Poème au Roy* (Paris: Thiboust imprimeur du Roi, 1745), 11 pages.
53   Elie–Catherine Fréron, *La journée de Fontenoy, Ode* (Paris (?): Publisher unknown, 1745), p.9.
54   Beauveset, *Epitre du Sieur Rabot*, pp.3–4.

lawyer who pretended to be Fontenoy's local priest asking Louis XV to pay for the burial of the many dead left on the battlefield. Soon, imitators appeared giving a voice to the friends and neighbours of the fictitious Belgian priest wishing for the French king to solve their problems and mocking Voltaire's own take on the battle. Attacking Voltaire's poem guaranteed publicity, even when the author actually supported the philosopher's style as did François Dugas Quinsonas who wrote his *Capilotade* under the penname of *Chevalier de Momus* to ridicule the historiographer's efforts while defending Voltaire in his *Apologie du poème de M. de V**** sur la bataille de Fontenoy.*[55]

Though his work was considered quite divisive, Voltaire inspired many of his contemporaries in the way Irish people were depicted. The *Mercure de France* of July 1745 published an *Ode sur la bataille de Fontenoy* written anonymously that showed the Irish once again avenging Ireland as well as France: 'The Irishman* [note in the margin: * Irish Brigade] that sets upon them is not afraid of receiving their fire, he avenges his country, his kings and his God, his honour and that of France'. [56]

The *Maréchal* de Tressan also described the main protagonists of the battle but did not just evoke Louis XV and his *Maison du Roi*, but also the Irish associated with the Régiment de Normandie in the victorious counterattack:

Exiled from a beloved island [note in the margin: The Irish]
Victims of an inhuman fate,
Come defend the motherland
That received you in her heart.[57]

But this positive image was not always shared by other poets. One of them did praise the Irish but mentioned their ferocity, a character trait that had been attributed to the English in Voltaire's work:

Our brave Irish under Clare's command,
Struck fear and dread in the enemy's ranks,
They murder them horribly, I would say barbarically,
If they hadn't avenged their temples and their KING.[58]

In 1768, Jean-Henri Marchand, mentioned above, created a tragi-comic opera entitled *La Bataille de Fontenoy ou l'Apothéose Moderne* to honour de Saxe. In the foreword, he emphasised that the victory was in line with the exploits of the French monarchy, inspiring a Greek author to write a text in the ancient style which happened to fall into his hands. Dillon was

55   François Dugas Quinsonas, *Apologie du poème de M. de V**** sur la bataille de Fontenoy* (Paris: Publisher unknown, 1745).
56   *Mercure de France* (Paris, Guillaume Cavelier, July 1745), p.104.
57   Tressan, Louis–Élisabeth de La Vergne, *Réponse à M. de Voltaire sur son poëme de "La Bataille de Fontenoy"*, par M. L. M. de Tr... [Tressan], *maréchal des camps et armées de Sa Majesté* (Paris: Gandouin, 1745).
58   *Récit du siège de la ville et citadelle de Tournay et de la bataille de Fontenoy par le sieur D**** (Tournai: Jovenau, no date), 11 pages.

cited as one of the victims of the battle and this extract shows Voltaire was still being copied decades after his poem was first published:

> The valiant & faithful Irishman
> Thought himself interested
> In avenging his own quarrel,
> And by hatred strengthened,
> Of our brave French he served the zeal[59]

In terms of iconographic representations, the style adopted in most French paintings was that of the so-called 'commander's battle' in which major protagonists such as kings or generals occupied the centre of the picture leaving actual fighters in the literal background. These paintings, whether modest in size like the miniatures by Louis Nicolas Van Blarenberghe or large like Pierre l'Enfant's compositions, emphasised two major facts: the leading role of Louis XV and de Saxe and the effort made by the royal army as a whole, without highlighting any particular unit. Numerous engravings of the Battle of Fontenoy were published shortly after the French victory, such as Antoine Benoist's *Bataille et défaite de l'armée des alliés dans le champ de Fontenoy*, where the action focused once again on the cavalry and Louis XV. The Irish were only depicted in their supporting position on the left of the French battle line. Illustrated maps followed the same pattern, with the Irish being included without being presented as major players. In more formal depictions, like the royally commissioned paintings of Pierre l'Enfant, the presence of the Brigade was made quite clear. Being Louis XV's official battle painter, he produced two paintings dedicated to the battle. One of them is now on display in Paris' *Musée des Invalides*. This first version, painted between 1750 and 1760, shows the Irish fighting with the British column, the different regiments being identifiable by their uniforms and standards. After Charles Parrocel's death in 1752, l'Enfant took up his former master's task of finishing a series of seven oil paintings depicting the major battles of the Flanders campaign of 1745-1748. In those paintings dating back to 1771, red uniforms do appear on the left-hand side corresponding to where the Brigade stood during the battle, but the action was focused on the central figures of Louis XV dressed in scarlet and Maurice de Saxe in his blue uniform riding horses in front of the general movement of the whole French army counterattacking. Fontenoy was still the subject of iconographic representations in the nineteenth century, but it retained its aspect of a celebration of a personal victory of the king of France over the English or of a French military exploit like Jean-Louis Ernest Meissonnier's or Edouard Detaille's own renditions. French literature, painting and correspondence were largely influenced by Voltaire and generally left the Irish in the background of the story.

In 1746, the Irish Brigade was sent back to the northern province between Calais and Boulogne hoping to be allowed to intervene in favour of Charles Edward Stuart, but apart from small groups of volunteers called picquets that were chosen within the regiments, the Irish mostly stayed quietly in their garrison towns. Meanwhile, the campaign in Flanders

---

59   Jean–Henri Marchand, *La Bataille de Fontenoy, ou l'Apothéose moderne, opera–tragédie en trois actes. Traduite du Grec par un Ciclopédiste* (Chambord: Panckoucke, 1768), p.48.

continued. Though the regiments of the Irish Brigade were not involved in the Battle of Roucoux (1746),[60] with the exception of general officers like Bulkeley and the Duc de Fitzjames,[61] they fought at Lawfeld (1747) where they were reportedly 'entirely demolished'.[62] In the latter battle Dillon's Regiment charged through the village and resisted the counterattack from Cumberland's forces,[63] earning de Saxe's compliments, but once again the casualties among officers were quite high. Colonel Edward Dillon was mortally wounded in the assault alongside hundreds of his men:

> Captains Bourck and Lévis, Lieutenants Charles Kennedy, O'Shiel, Taaffe and Nihell, Ensign Moore and one hundred and thirty-seven soldiers killed or dead as a result of their wounds. Captains Jacques Nihell (from the grenadier company), O'Connor, Calaghan, Jean and Joseph Kennedy, Antoine Bourck, André Mac Donaugh and Fanning; Lieutenants Magennis, O'Reilly, Commerford, Nicolas Bourck and Naylor (of the grenadier company) were wounded, the latter seriously. Cadet Thomas Browne and one hundred and two soldiers were also wounded.[64]

Louis XV insisted on keeping Dillon's Regiment under the command of a member of that family. Edward Dillon was thus replaced by his brother Henry Dillon who at the time lived in England and became the titular colonel.

'A dreadful miscarriage[65]*: Fontenoy and the Irish Brigade as Seen by the British*
The Seven Years War is usually seen as the moment when a truly British form of patriotism started to take root in the United Kingdom. The mixed results of the War of the Austrian Succession, with Dettingen's surprise victory quickly followed by Fontenoy's failure and the fall of the Austrian Netherlands in the hands of the French, were quickly forgotten as the *Annus Mirabilis* of 1759 crowned Britain's efforts against the Bourbons less than 15 years later. By the 1740s, administrating the colonial empire was already more important than winning or losing a battle on the European continent. Besides, Fontenoy was soon overshadowed by Charles Edward Stuart's expedition of 1745 in Scotland and the defeat of the Jacobite threat. Generally seen as a war fought in favour of Hanover's interests rather than Britain's, popular publications often underlined how the Germans were favoured during the

---

60   Multiple spellings exist for this particular battle: Raucoux, Roucoux, Rocourt or even Roccoux.

61   See the Royal Collection Trust, *Ordre de Bataille des Français en 1746*, at <https://militarymaps.rct.uk/war-of-the-austrian-succession-1740-8/order-of-battle-1746-ordre-de-battaille-des>, accessed August 2022.

62   Lawfeld was also spelt Lafelt or Lauffelt. The Irish are quoted as present in *Relation de l'action qui s'est passée au village de Lawfeld entre l'aile gauche de l'armée alliée et les Français le 2 juillet 1747 par un officier étranger*, (SHED – 1V, Article 15, Section 1, n°19) and in *Registres des Lettres de Guerre*, (SHED GR 3 A 123). They also appear in the order of battle kept in the Royal Collection Trust at <https://militarymaps.rct.uk/war-of-the-austrian-succession-1740-8/order-of-battle-1747-1-r-may-1747-ordre-de>, accessed August 2022.

63   Baron d'Espagnac, *Relation de la campagne en Brabant et en Flandres, de l'an M.DCC.XLVII*, (The Hague: Frederic Henri Scheurleer, 1748), pp.109–110.

64   Charles–Joachim–Edgard Malaguti, *Historique du 87e régiment d'infanterie de ligne, ex–12e Léger* (Saint Quentin: Moreau & fils, 1892), pp.53–54.

65   *The Scots Magazine*, vol.7, 1745, p.218.

opening stages of the conflict while the British bore the brunt of the fighting.[66] Similarly, the Scots fighting in the British army were perceived as unreliable troops due to the mutiny of the Black Watch when it learned it would leave to fight in Flanders. Yet this forgotten war paved the way for a slow but steady change of attitude in London regarding not only German allies and Caledonian soldiers, but also concerning the acceptance of Irish Catholics in British ranks. While the formal admission of Irish Catholics was not implemented until the Revolutionary Wars of the late eighteenth century, 1745 proved to be a turning point in the gradual evolution of the perception of Ireland's military potential in the eyes of the English authorities and the English public opinion. To a certain extent, Fontenoy was the first step to the creation of a truly British army.

In the first half of the eighteenth century, both Catholic and Protestant soldiers from Ireland were still forbidden from serving the House of Hanover.[67] The Protestant elements of the island had to be kept there in order not to weaken their community's ascendancy. Able-bodied Protestants were needed to defend the island against a potential Irish rebellion and were therefore technically barred from entering the British Army. Yet Irishmen did serve in the British Army in the 1740s. Books collecting jokes made at the expense of the Irish were not uncommon and some anecdotes appearing in those publications clearly implied that Catholics were present in London's forces:

> Two *Irish* Soldiers, and two *Scots*, being together in an Ale-house; amongst other Discourse, one of the *Scots* happened to admire that one of his Officers should be turned *Catholick*; saying, he knew not any Thing that could persuade a Man to leave the *Protestant Religion* for that; whereupon one of the *dear Joys*, after much Clamour and Hubbub, drew his Sword, and attempted the *Scot*; he in the mean Time, not only defended himself, but worsted the *Irishman*, whilst the other two fairly stood Spectators; At length, the Noise brought the Master of the House into the Room; whereupon *Teague* began to accuse his Brother *Irishman; swearing upon his Shalwashion, hee was an Enemy to Chreesht and Shaint Pautrick, and dat hee vill put de Sweare upon de* Scotchman *for speaking Treason:* Whereupon his Friend, and the other declared, there had not one Word passed about the Government: But *Teague* returned to rave and swear, *Bee de Mash*, (and what else his Education suggested) *hee vill put de fwear upon all of dem; for in fait, if nothing was spoken against de King's Majesty's' Grace; yet vasb dere very great Treasson againsht de Papish.*[68]

---

66   See Anon., *A True Dialogue Between Thomas Jones, a Trooper, Lately Return'd from Germany, and John Smith, a Serjeant in the First Regiment of Foot–guards* (London: B.C., Pater–Noster Row, 1743), p.3.

67   … the Act of 1745 provides, not only that they be able–bodied men, free from ruptures, and every other distemper or infirmity that as by the present laws render them unfit for duty, but that they be not Papists, Irishmen, nor under the age of seventeen nor above forty–five years; allowing them however to be received if they be not under the size of five feet four–inches without shoes. *The Scots Magazine*, vol.7, 'Abstract of the recruiting Act', May 1745, p.231.

68   Mac O Bonniclabbero of Drogheda [sic], *The Irish Miscellany: Or Teagueland Jests: Being a Compleat Collection of the Most Profound Puns, Learned Bulls, Elaborate Quibbles of the Natives of Teagueland* (London, J. Perry, 1746), p.42.

Because of the ambiguous attitude adopted by London towards using men who were clearly seen as potential traitors, the Irish were not celebrated even when accomplishing impressive feats of arms. The Battle of Dettingen provides a good example of this situation: Thomas Brown, serving in Bland's Dragoons, became a national celebrity for having retrieved his unit's standard in the middle of a fierce fight which left him both famous and scarred for life.[69] Yet one publication from 1743, openly hostile to the war and the submission of British interests to those of Hanover, reveals that an Irishman called Darough was first celebrated before Brown's exploit monopolised the public's attention:

> We were entertained a long while with Encomiums on Mr. *Darough*, a brave *Irishman*, in Sir *Robert Rich's* Dragoons; he was painted on Foot and on Horse-back, and had all the Thanks of the Public for having ventured his Life to retrieve the Honour of his Regiment; but all on a sudden, the poor *Hibernian* is stript of all his Glories, to deck out Mr. *Brown*, a valiant *Yorkshireman*, of *Bland's* Dragoons. For my Part, if the Exploit has been done, I matter not by whom, either by a *Yorkshire* or *Irishman;* 'tis enough to please me, that the Hero was one of his Majesty's Subjects, I mean, of these Nations; for, I am not as yet so *Germanized* as to be very anxious about my Brethren in the Empire; I wish them well, but they must forgive me, if I wish my Fellow-Islanders better.[70]

The Battle of Fontenoy did reconcile the English with the Hanoverians and the Scots. As for the Irishmen in the service of France, they were at first left in the background but did appear in British accounts as the battle slowly entered the realm of history.

News of the French victory arrived in Britain in May 1745 just a few days after George II had left the island for his annual summer stay in Hanover. The *London Gazette* published an official account of the 'action around Tournay', as the name Fontenoy did not yet appear, which mentioned the Dutch regiments not carrying out the orders given to them by the generals of the Pragmatic Army. The article also addressed Brigadier General Ingoldsby's failure to take an important French position which could have turned the tide in favour of the allies. The French were just addressed as 'the enemy' and no mention was made of the Irish Brigade, while the Hanoverians were saluted ('the Hanover troops, as well cavalry as infantry, have had their share with us in the dangers, fatigues and loss') as well as the Highlanders.[71] The information was then redistributed throughout England by local newspaper such as the *Derby Mercury* or the *Newcastle Weekly Courant*. The Duke of Cumberland was seen as the hero of the day, while the unfortunate Ingoldsby was nationally shamed.

The violence of the battle shocked most of the British protagonists. One of them, Charles James Hamilton, a young British officer, sent a letter to his aunt back in England describing the attacks, insisting on how de Saxe's hidden guns won the day:

69   See Michael McNally, *Dettingen 1743, Miracle on the Main* (London: Osprey Publishing, 2020), pp.72–73.
70   Anon., *The Triumphant Campaign* (London: J.M., 1743), p.39. See also Anon., *British Glory Reviv'd* (London: J. Roberts, 1743), p.28.
71   *The London Gazette*, edition of the 7 May 1745, issue 8430, pp.6–7.

The Duke of Cumberland (1721-1765), engraving after Thomas Hudson. (Anne S.K. Brown Military Collection)

We have had a most bloody battle with the French. Yesterday we began at 5 in the morning & left off at 2 in the afternoon, all which time the French kept cannonading us; I was forced to be very civil & make a great many bows to the balls, for they were very near me, for both my right- & left-hand men were killed, & all round me there were men & horses tumbling about, but thank God none touched me. We could do nothing but stand there & be knocked on the head, for they had a great many batteries & three times the number of cannon that we had, and besides that they were entrenched up to the ears that we could not hurt them ... The foot were very sadly cut to pieces, for the French put grape shot into their cannon & cut them down just as if they were sheering corn.[72]

It seems the British authorities in Ireland were quite aware of the part played by the Irish at Fontenoy. John Potter, the undersecretary of the Lord Lieutenant of Ireland, wrote in the autumn of 1745 about the possibility of a resurgence of illegal recruitments on the island inspired by the battle:

It is not much to be wondered at that Saxe, who is a foreigner, should advise foreign troops, as he did before the Battle of Fontenoy, what the Irish did there is well known, as also what the Scot Highlanders did on our side, besides it's pretty certain the French will want men against next campaign. I can't entirely disregard this thought, though perhaps there is not much to it.[73]

The British public was made aware of the way the French presented the battle through translations. The text accompanying France's *Te Deum* celebrating Louis XV's victory mentioned above was published in English a few weeks after its use in French churches.[74] Similarly, the official French battle report was transcribed in magazines printed in the United Kingdom.[75] Yet the French were nevertheless denied their victory as the city of Tournai still held and de Saxe's forces were said to have suffered many casualties while the rest of the Pragmatic troops were closing in. The defeat was seen by some in England as a sombre prospect for the war but also as a minor setback in otherwise glowing military records:

And as to the opinion cherished by some *gloomy minds*, that such a shock as this, at the beginning of a campaign, is not to be repaired, and consequently we must expect everything to go against us, at least for this year; if we would think still in the true *British military spirit*, this should appear to have no foundation.[76]

---

72 Charles James Hamilton (3rd Dragoons) to Lady Murray 12 May 1745, cited in *Journal of the Society for Army Historical Research, vol.6*, n°24 (April–June 1927), pp. 94–96.

73 PRONI, T3019/690. Dublin Castle, John Potter, undersecretary, to Robert Wilmot, secretary to the Lord Lieutenant, 1 September 1745. The word 'men' was underlined in the original document.

74 Anon., *The Political Cabinet; or, an Impartial Review of the most remarkable Occurrences of the World, Particularly Europe* (London, J. Roberts, 1745), p.407.

75 *The London Magazine*, June 1745, vol.14, p.346.

76 *The Scots Magazine*, vol.7, May 1745, p.220.

Even though the British were defeated, they found consolation in the reputation they acquired in having tried to force unassailable positions while being shelled for hours and remaining disciplined under fire.[77] Poems started to appear in magazines reminding readers that 'British valour' had been defeated by bastions and guns more than men, an argument repeated in a Dutch account translated in the English press where the Irish were not cited and the French victory was due to concealed guns wreaking havoc on the Pragmatic troops:[78]

> The left wing of the French, after having retired a great way, for fear of coming to engage sword in hand, at length opened, and likewise uncovered two batteries of great guns, charged with cartridges of small shot; which made so terrible a fire in front and flank, that the English infantry were obliged to give way, and to fall upon the second line. if we had only fought against men, I can assure you that the siege of Tournay would have been quickly raised, and that there would not have escaped a third part of the French army; which, as we were eye witnesses, is composed of very contemptible people: but we fought, according to the report of all their deserters, against 266 pieces of cannon, as well battering as field.

The French, particularly de Saxe, were even accused of waging 'war like a *Turk* and not like a *Christian*' especially in the use of cartridge cannon and 'materials not permitted by the Law of Arms', a reference to the supposed poisonous contents of the canister shots.[79] Most occurrences of the word 'Irish' in these publications had to do with smuggled linen between Ireland and France rather than the military connections between the two neighbouring countries and whenever the Irish Brigade was mentioned by name in British publications, it was because the initial source being quoted was French.[80] Lists of casualties, both British and French, were published in periodicals available in England, in which Dillon's name appeared alongside other high-ranking officers whose demise seemed worthy of report.[81] Some poems were published at the time of the battle, but none had the influence that Voltaire's enjoyed on the other side of the Channel. The only works that could bear comparison were those written by Tobias Smollett, a famous eighteenth century writer, who penned several works about the 11 May 1745. They were published by Mary Cooper, an English publisher who operated in Paster Noster Row in London who also had French documents related to the battle translated into English.

Slowly, the Irish started to appear in the British press. At the end of May 1745, the *Gentleman's Magazine* explicitly cited the Irish Brigade as being instrumental:

> Letters from Flanders say, that the Irish troops in the French service, who signalled themselves at Ypres, recovered the day in the last battle, when the French guards ran; but they suffered much as the following list shews:

---

77   *The Scots Magazine*, vol.7, May 1745, p.222.
78   *The Scots Magazine*, vol.7, May 1745, p.238.
79   *The London Magazine*, June 1745, vol.14, pp. 296–97 and 399. See also the *Gentleman's Magazine*, 1745, vol.15, p.422.
80   *The Scots Magazine*, June 1745, vol.7, p.286.
81   *The London Magazine*, May 1745, vol.14, p.234.

Clare's regiment, Lieut-col. O'Neil, killed, Maj. Shortal, wounded, Capt. Lieutenant Shortall, and the captainsTaffey, Mackeligot, and Mac Guire, killed. Capt. grant, Lord Clare's aide de camp, and the captains Christopher Plunkett, Brian O Brian, Creagh, Prosper, Kennedy, Daniel, MacCarty, and John O'Brian, wounded. The lieutenants Edw. Fitzgerald and Mac Namara, killed, Hugh Taffey, Davern, Cha. [chaplain? *chevalier*?] O'Brian, Cornelius O'Neil, and Brian O'Brian, wounded.

Lally's regiment, Col. Lally, Lieut. Col. Higerty, Major Glosco, and the captains Butler and Warren, wounded. Lieutenant Born and the captains Butler and Warren, wounded. Lieutenants Born and Kelly killed; Fitzgerald mortally wounded; Creagh, Wogan, Henesy, Manfield Stack, and Thomas Stack, wounded.

Dillon's regiment, Col. Dillon, lieut. colonel Manners, capt. Kerry, and cha. [chaplain?] Manoury killed, the captains Nickill mortally wounded; Nic. Wogan lost an arm, Cusach, Higarth and Bourk, wounded. The lieutenants Barry and Glosco each lost a leg, Moriarty lost some fingers; Mic Burk and Flannegan, dangerously wounded.

Berwick's regiment. The captains Bourk, Nangle, Anthony, Cook, and Hickens, killed. Capt. Coclong, lieutenants Plunkett, Carroll, Mac Carthy, and Dase, wounded.

Ruth's regiment, the captains Windham, St Leger, and Grace, killed; Christy, and O'Brian, mortally wounded. Lieutenants Tim O Sulivan, Florence Sullivan, Hady, Delany, O Brian, O Honlan, Osburg, and Burn, wounded.

Buckley's regiment, capt. Morgan Mac Swiney his arm broke.

Fitzjames' Horse. Almost cut to pieces, having 25 officers killed, and wounded.[82]

The repetition of similar family names within regiments and within the Brigade itself naturally corresponds to the recruiting strategies evoked earlier in this book.

Most of all, the Irish Brigade emerged in histories of the battle written later in the eighteenth century. They would for instance appear in a simple footnote in 1747 in Samuel Boyse's *An Historical Review of the Transactions of Europe*. The comment was meant for the Irish troops serving James II in the early 1690s and went as follows:

> However ill the Irish troops behaved at home, it has never been denied but they have greatly distinguished themselves in the French and Spanish service. even so late as the Battle of Fontenoy, it is allowed they bore the shock of that dreadful day, and saved the French army.[83]

Ten years after the British defeat in Flanders, William Biggs clearly mentioned the role played by the Irish in his *Military History of Europe*.[84] The famous dialogue involving a French Captain, d'Anterroches, and Lord Charles Hay ('Gentlemen of England, please fire first!')

---

82   *The Gentleman's Magazine*, "Historical Chronicle", 31 May 1745, vol.15, pp.275–276.
83   Samuel Boyse, *An Historical Review of the Transactions of Europe from the Commencement of the War with Spain in 1739* (London: D. Henry and J. Robinson, 1747), p.30.
84   William Biggs, *The Military History of Europe* (London: Baldwin, 1755), p.310.

did not appear before 1756 in Britain when Voltaire's book *L'Histoire de la Guerre de 1741* was translated into English with extracts depicting the major battles of the war appearing in the columns of the *London Magazine*. With the Seven Years War, a slight change can be witnessed in British, especially English, attitudes towards the Irish. One literary magazine, the *Centinel*, thus published a story based on an 'Irish Bull', a joke made at the expense of Irishmen, about an Irish servant fighting his French counterpart for the honour of his female employer. The conclusion is worth quoting:

> We see the value of Ireland in this instance; and should learn to reverence what we are too apt to ridicule. The same spirit that called out this single Frenchman would be terrible to his countrymen in the field. It is unhappy, that the artifice of this people [the French] has found the way to turn their courage in some degree against ourselves. There is no part of the French force that could be terrible to an English soldier but their Irish regiments: they have been signally useful to that people on all occasions, and it is a reproach to our policy that we do not engage them in greater number. I am no native of Ireland who write this, that, Mr. CENTINEL, you can attest for me, but I shall add to their character, that courage is not more general among them than fidelity. We see here the men, from among whom regiments might be raised for the most desperate service: let us use them well, and there is nothing we may not promise ourselves in return. What may not be expected from a corps of men fighting for their country: every one of which would be ready to call out his man to single combat. We are apt to entertain an ill opinion of the lower people of that nation, because we see too many of the worst; and because from our own dispositions, we are ready to drown a thousand instances of virtue under one of vice: but we have here a proof, that all those of the lower class are not the wretches they are represented.[85]

In Britain, the image of these exiles was not always entirely negative, but it still retained a stereotypical vision of the people serving France or Spain as being self-absorbed and obsessed with war. One picaresque novel written by an Irish Protestant offers an interesting mirror image of how the British saw the Irish living in France and how the Irish naturalised in France perceived themselves:

> It happen'd that Captain Magragh of Lord Clare's Regiment, had lately taken Apartments in the same Hotel. This Gentleman thought it his Duty to pay his Respects to the two English Officers, and made them a very civil Visit. They received him in a polite Manner, and in an hour's conversation found out his Rank and his Character. He was of a lively Soldier-like Disposition, and very communicative. His Father had quitted Ireland, and followed the Fortune of King James the Second. He was born in France, but spoke English with a prodigious Irish Accent, tho' he had never been in that Kingdom. He told them of the vast Estate

---

85   *The Centinel*, 'Quid domini faciant?', 6 August 1757, pp. 176–79. The Latin quote is from Virgil and, in its entirety, translates to 'What would the masters do/when their own servants dare such things?'

his Father lost in Ireland, and how near he was, the other Day, of recovering it. He spoke of the War in Germany and in Flanders, and gave them a History of his own Exploits. He mentioned the Valour of the Irish, and without considering the French Policy, seem'd to glory in their being sent foremost on the most desperate Attacks. His Conversation, and the Oddity of his Language, was agreeable enough, and made our Friends desire a further Acquaintance. In a few Days he invited them to a genteel Supper, with two other Officers of the Irish Brigade. The Chat turned on War, and Captain Magragh spoke very eloquently on Sieges and Battles, for he could really speak on little else.[86]

In theatres, the Irish were no longer used as bogeymen and while Teague, the stereotypical Irishman, never really disappeared, there were examples in which a native of Ireland showed his true quality on stage, implying that at heart he was more British than Hibernian. This was the case for instance in Thomas Sheridan's Captain O'Blunder whose brogue firmly anchored him in that theatrical tradition, though his attitude towards a Frenchman in the play, another stock character named Mr Ragou, proved that the Irishman's loyalties firmly lied in the British camp. O'Blunder eventually duelled and killed the Frenchman.[87] Pamphlets published during the Seven Years War about the use of mercenaries recruited in Germany and paid with English money also used the example of Irish soldiers to prove that soldiers of fortune could actually be very loyal as well as efficient:

> Call but to mind the spirited Behaviour of the Irish Brigade! The Severe Duty they sustained and the signalled service they did in the Battle of Fontainoye [sic], leave us surely little room to doubt either the courage or utility of hired forces.[88]

Military histories and biographies started to appear in the mid to late 1750s in which the Irish played a more significant role in defeating Cumberland. A 'society of military gentlemen' published a book about the military history of Great Britain in which the Irish appeared as being in the vanguard:

> All these corps moved at the same time, the Irish, commanded by my Lord Clair, against the front of the column, ... they were all separated from the English column by a hollow hay, they forced through it, firing almost muzzle to muzzle, and then fell upon the English with their bayonets fixed to their muskets.[89]

The anecdote of the Irish uniforms being mistaken by French *Carabiniers* for British redcoats also appeared in this volume, probably thanks to the translation of Voltaire's book

---

86 William Chaigneau, *The History of Jack Connor, now Conyers, part 2* (London: W. Johnson, 1753), p.172.

87 Thomas Sheridan, *The Brave Irishman, or Captain O'Blunder, a Farce* (Dublin: R. Watts, 1754), p.12.

88 John Shebbeare, *An Answer to a Pamphlet, Called, A Second Letter to the People. In which the Subsidiary System is Fairly Stated, and Amply Considered* (London: M. Cooper, 1755), p.17.

89 A Society of Military Gentlemen, *The Military History of Great Britain, from Julius Cæsar to the Conclusion of the Late War* (London: R. James, 1762), p.183.

on the War of 1741 a few years before. Dictionaries specialised in military matters published in England after the 1750s also drastically enhanced the part played by the Brigade. Richard Rolt, an English author specialised in military matters, saw his vision of the Battle of Fontenoy wholeheartedly adopted by the authors of histories and encyclopaedias, though he had been at one point suspected of having Jacobite sympathies:

> This new disposition made an immediate alteration, checked the violence of the British infantry, and gave leisure to the Irish brigade, and that of *Vaisseaux*, to form themselves. Such was the furious bravery of the British infantry, that *Maréchal* Saxe was now reduced to his last, sole, and principal effort, to retrieve the honour of the day: this was in bringing up the Irish brigade; a corps, on whose courage and behaviour, he entirely depended, for a favourable decision of so great, so dubious, and so well contested a battle. The Irish brigade, consisting of the regiments of Clare, Lally, Dillon, Berwick, Ruth, and Buckley [sic], with the horse of Fitz-James, being drawn up, were sustained by the regiments of Normandy and *Vaisseaux*, and marched up to the British line without firing: the British ranks were now prodigiously thinned; the men wearied; and wherever they trod, obliged to fight over the mangled carcasses of their dying countrymen: while their new, and bravest opponents, were fresh for engagement, and prepared for the rough, the savage encounter; an encounter like that on the plains of Pharsalia, where brothers might embrue their hands in fraternal blood, relations sluice out the tide of consanguinity, friends murder friends, countrymen countrymen; and where every dreadful act of war was dressed in more formidable, more awful horrors ! Soon as the Irish brigade advanced, dreadful was the fire, great was the slaughter; for havock seemed here the most delighted with her bloody banquet: the combat was sharp, strong, and bloody; they fought hand to hand, bayonet to bayonet, foot to foot, and blow for blow: but so great was the diminution of the British troops, the attack of the Irish brigade so vigorous, the fury of the French artillery so perpetually brisk, that being now also charged by the Household troops, and attacked in flank by the Carabineers, they began to stagger, nor could they support the violence of so rude a shock; and, about one o'clock, were again obliged to retire to the ground between the village and the point of the wood.[90]

Other comments sporadically appeared in historical writings about the War of the Austrian Succession which helped build a new image of the Irish soldier. This extract from a biography of the *Maréchal* de Saxe published by an English historian in 1758 shows an interesting back-handed compliment about the Irish serving under French flags which was slipped into the text:

> In the pursuit, the French killed several of the Irish, in taking them for parties of the English army, their uniform being very much alike; however, they deserved it,

---

90   A Military Gentleman, *A New Military Dictionary: or, the Field of War*, (London: J. Cooke, 1760), p.32, article 'Fontenoy'

for fighting so bravely in so bad a cause, and being principally instrumental in the success of that day.[91]

Local historians also changed the public's view on the Irish Brigade, as did John Ferrar, an amateur librarian and antiquarian from the city of Limerick. He was himself the grandson of an English officer who had served under William III and, in 1767, his *History of Limerick* devoted an entire chapter to Irish military matters, even though he did not belong to either the Old Irish or the Old English communities of the island. His appendices included a list of all the regiments which had left Limerick in the 1690s and were by then serving in the French army but, most interestingly, he reused information presented in documents published in France a few years before by the Abbé MacGeoghan about the numerical importance of the Brigade. He longed for the Irish to serve the Hanoverian crown:

> What reflections should not this raise in the humane mind, and what Lover of his country would not wish to see some methods contrived to make such brave men serve for, rather than against their country? The Great PITT, found the means of making the rebel Highlanders serviceable subjects, and it must be owned that their bravery hastened the reduction of North America.[92]

Ferrar's works were reprinted on a regular basis and were read by the elite of the Irish Protestant community.

The official outbreak of the Seven Years War in 1756 was accompanied by two important facts regarding the enlistment of Irish soldiers in Ireland: firstly, the illegal recruitment of Irishmen for France was once again strictly punished, and secondly Irish Protestants were no longer officially banned from entering the British Army. By the early 1760s, the Catholic elites of Ireland decided to take the initiative in order to prove to the British authorities that the so-called 'Papists' could actually be relied upon and help in the global conflict engulfing Britain at the time. Lord Halifax, the then Lord Lieutenant of Ireland, showed an interest in having the Irish join the armies of Britain's Catholic allies, such as Portugal, a controversial proposition that never really took shape. Polemicists like Henry Brooke, who had been very critical of the Irish in the years following Fontenoy, had mellowed by the end of the century when it came to accepting the idea of a particular brand of bravery to be found among his countrymen from Ireland.[93]

In 1775, when the American insurgency forced Britain to recruit more troops, both the Prime Minister, Lord North, and the British authorities considered using the will of the Irish Catholic elites to integrate British society on somewhat equal terms with their Protestant countrymen to encourage poor Catholic men to join the army. Saint Patrick's Day was deemed important enough to be officially celebrated in the British Army in the 1780s, which tends to prove that a substantial number of Irish Catholics did enlist. Yet, while the Catholic upper classes had moved closer to the central government purely out of interest, the lower

---

91   W.H. Dilworth, *The Life and Military History of the Celebrated Marshal Saxe* (London: G. Wright, 1758), p.98.
92   John Ferrar, *An History of the city of Limerick* (Limerick: Andrew Welsh, 1767), p.147.
93   Henry Brooke, *The Tryal* [sic] *of Roman Catholics*, (London: Faulkner, 1762), p.187.

classes remained close to Jacobitism. The use of Catholic troops against the largely non-conformist American rebels between 1776 and 1783 was problematic and raised the spectre of a return to Ireland or mainland Britain of large numbers of Catholic men trained in the use of arms. Besides, Ireland's nascent nationalism found a paradoxical way of expressing itself with the Volunteers movement of the late 1770s and early 1780s when some Protestant patriots actually donned either red or green uniforms and called themselves 'Irish Brigades', openly referring to the units serving France at the time.[94]

'It seems that the French are not as aware of the Irish as they ought to be':[95] the Irish and their Self–Perceptions

The Brigade suffered horrendous casualties not only at the Battle of Fontenoy, but also during the rest of the campaign in Flanders, and soon had to fill its ranks with either deserters from the British ranks or recruits from the local Belgian population. As indicated in the previous chapter, officers needed to maintain their companies if they wanted to benefit from the regimental system and they were thus required to remind French military authorities of their career highlights to benefit from the privileges enjoyed by officers in Ancien Régime France. This extract from Charles O'Brien, Viscount Clare's personal file is a good example of the way Fontenoy was presented in a high-ranking officer's military file:

> In 1745 he was present at the Battle of Fontenoy where, as he led the Irish Brigades [sic] and the Vaisseaux, supported by the régiment de Normandie he broke through the enemy who had penetrated between the village of Fontenoy and a redoubt occupied by a battalion from the régiment d'Eu. He dispersed more than 25 English and Hanoverian battalions that had formed a sort of column, took two English standards and captured more than 15 cannon that they had in front of them. His conduct during this action where he received two gunshots in his breastplate owed him praises from the King under whose eyes he fought. His Majesty honoured him the following first of January by naming him as a commanding officer in his order [of the Holy Spirit].[96]

Networking strategies and an effective narrative of the Irish participation in the battle were paramount, and Fontenoy was the ideal symbol to remind the French of the specificities of the Irish community. Obviously, personal correspondence sent by Irish officers to their relatives illustrated their involvement, but most importantly the fact that Louis XV had shown, according to them, some gratitude towards the Brigade. A constant feature was the understandable grief about casualties:

94   Anon., *The Remembrancer, or Impartial repositery of Public Events for the year 1782* (London: Debrett, 1782), part 2, p.285.
95   Anon., *Lettres d'un officier irlandois à un officier françois* (Paris: Publisher unknown, 18 July 1756), p.4.
96   MKWP, copy of SHD, Administrative Archives, Older Section, Personal files, Charles O'Brien, n°228.

… the French cavalry which was meant to support us retreated in disorder when the first shot of the enemy was heard, which caused some confusion in our ranks, but we quickly recovered. The attack was resumed more hotly than before, and lasted thus for nearly two hours, when we broke them completely, they abandoned their guns, which are in our possession, a sergeant of Buckley's took two flags, and Captain Kennedy of Dillon's regiment another one. … It is estimated that of killed and wounded in our brigade there are sixty men. Poor Chevalier Dillon, Colonel O'Nail [sic] Colonel Cairry [sic] and the Lieutenant-Colonel of Fitzjames' regiment are among those killed.[97]

Voltaire's poem and the passage on Dillon's spirit obviously angered the Irish who felt the need to correct him themselves. A short poem was thus written by one of Jacques Dillon's friends about the death of the Irish colonel. While hoping for some literary inspiration, the anonymous author had his verses amended by a Muse telling him that celebrating Dillon's courage and addressing Voltaire's mistake had to prevail over grief:

> Come and paint him surrounded by a loyal troop,
> Whose example, whose soul is a heart full of devotion,
> For their religion, their honour and their laws,
> Who serve their protectors as if they were their sovereigns,
> Guided by duty not by vengeance,
> Say that CLARE & DILLON to their bravery alone,
> by flying into danger owe all their successes,
> If, of their oppressors, proud rivals of the French,
> You also wish to talk about, you can, but take head
> Of the expression and the tone one hazardously uses these days
> Though enemy of a people one must respect it,
> The Happy Helvetian did retract,
> the one adjective accusing him of selling out for a few verses,
> Wiser than him you do not need to apologise,
> Thus, without sharing an eternal glory,
> Do let the Irish avenge their colonel by themselves.[98]

The adjective ('épithète' in the original text) evoked here was a reference to the word 'vicious-ness' attached to the British actions in the poem, a term which shocked readers of the first edition. Voltaire added a note in subsequent versions to explain that he only meant to talk about British privates, as their officers were 'as generous as ours'. The 'Happy Helvetian' referred to both Voltaire himself and his admiration for the Swiss regiments of the French army, in stark contrast with his apparent disdain for the Irish.[99]

---

97   MKWP, 'Letters from Fontenoy', *The Irish Sword*, vol.19, No.78, 1995, p.243.
98   Newberry Collection (University of Chicago), E 5 L92705 v. 03 no.43. *Vers sur le Chevalier Dillon colonel d'un régiment irlandais tué à la bataille de Fontenoy, faits par un de ses amis* (Malta: à l'enseigne de l'Amitié, 1745), 2 pages.
99   Voltaire, *La bataille de Fontenoy gagnée par Louis XV sur les alliées, le 11 May 1745* (Paris: Pancoucke, 1745), 6th edition, p.7.

Another counterattack followed. One of the most outspoken critics of the philosopher's work was an Irishman living in France, a man called Jean (John) Dromgold, who wrote a memoir about the literary shortcomings of the poem and also about Voltaire's disregard for English and Irish soldiers. Although his reply was polite, the Irishman accused him of being a 'formidable enemy' of his countrymen. Dromgold referred to Cremona as the most significant historical moment for the Irish, a memory that Fontenoy had revived:

> On the famous day of Cremona, when this town was, so to speak, wrested from the hands of Prince Eugene, who had taken it by surprise during the night, two Irish regiments distinguished themselves greatly. M. de Mahoni, Captain in one of these regiments, was dispatched by Monsieur de Revel to bring the King the news of this glorious the news of this glorious affair. He discharged his commission as a man of spirit, and omitted nothing of all the details, except the praises which could naturally fall on his little troop. '*Monsieur*,' said Louis XIV, with that air of grandeur and kindness which he knew so well how to blend together, 'you tell me nothing of my Irish, your brave countrymen?' 'SIRE,' replied M. De Mahoni, 'they have followed the example of Your Majesty's subjects.' ... I now dare to tell you, without fear of being denied, that to serve the King, and to die under his eyes, the Irish need no one's example, and that they will not yield it even to the natural-born subjects of His Majesty.[100]

Dromgold obviously reacted to Voltaire because of his mistake about Dillon's nationality. but went further than French critics:

> Would you be so ignorant of the history of the country as to not know that he was Irish? Or, which seems more likely, would it be that, having learned of the Father's exploits, you were so jealous of the Son's glory that, not trusting enough in his vengeance to his countrymen, you charged the Swiss with it? Why should you envy his regiment, and even nearly eighty officers, and four hundred [sic] soldiers of the Brigade, the glory of having died for the King, and for him? ... But who charged you, Sir, to exclude the Irish from being our ancient Friends, and fellow citizens? If attachment and service can merit this title services can merit this title, the Irish can dispute it with the Swiss.[101]

In Dromgold's point of view, jealousy and lack of consideration seemed to explain much about Voltaire's treatment of the Irish. But above all, the Franco–Irish author highlighted two aspects of the Irish presence in France that were to mark most, if not all, subsequent publications about the Brigade. He was one of the first authors to compute the number of Jacobite refugees who arrived in France in 1691, 16,000 men according to him, and he drew parallels between his exiled compatriots and the Jews, evoking the

---

100 Jean Dromgold, *Réflexions sur un imprimé intitulé: La Bataille de Fontenoy, poème: Dédiées à Monsieur de Voltaire, Historiographe de France* (Paris: Pancoucke, 1745).
101 Dromgold, *Réflexions sur un imprimé intitulé.*

biblical diaspora. His inclusion of the anecdote of the interview between Mahony and Louis XIV allowed him, through a dialogue flattering to both parties, to put his compatriots on a pedestal. Even if in doing so he blithely mixed up exiled figures such as the Earl of Roscommon, an author of satirical poetries now forgotten, and Jonathan Swift, the Irish Anglican author of *Gulliver's Travels*, his vision of a literary united Ireland is still interesting to note.

Praised by other French authors for his style, the Irishman's essay earned him a place as a secretary and later as an aide-de-camp to Louis de Bourbon-Condé. What *Lieutenant Général* de Marville wrote about him echoes the problems of survival for Irish people in France discussed in the previous chapter:

> 25 June 1745: *Monsieur* le Comte de Clermont [another title of Louis de Bourbon Condé] left to join the king in Flanders. It is said that a reply to Voltaire's poem had fallen into his hands. He was so pleased with it that he wanted to know the author, saying that a man who had composed such an amusing play must be the most amiable of men in the trade of life. By dint of searching, it was discovered that he was an Irishman, a professor at the *collège* of Navarre. The prince sent his retinue to him, and the Irishman came to the Abbey. He saw a well-put out man, of good appearance and of the best humour in the world; he asked him if he was engaged in holy orders. The Irishman said that he was not, but that he had been obliged to take a pulpit to support his mother, two sisters and two brothers. The Comte de Clermont proposed to him to leave his post and have him as his second squire. The Irishman accepted, and at present he and all his family are housed at the Abbey. The Prince had three suits of clothes made for him and gave him a hundred *louis d'or* to begin equipping himself. His name is Drumgold [sic] and he is an Irish gentleman.[102]

The municipal archives of the city of Troyes have another example of a document highlighting Irish warlike exploits between 1745 and 1746. This epic poem written to praise Charles Edward Stuart was penned by an anonymous author writing 'with an impartial hand' because of his status as a 'chevalier de Malthe françois [sic]'. As expected, the author emphasised the 'zeal and loyalty of the Irish' and his work was prefaced by an Irishman who, unfortunately, only signed with the initials 'G.G.G.'. The inscription in the introduction written in honour of Bonnie Prince Charlie is worth quoting:

> ... if all my nation, scattered in various climes, could effectively unite as it is by its own wishes... You would soon be at the head of an army which all our relatives and compatriots would contribute to increase, an army that a thousand powerful motives concur in rousing, making it invincible.

The Irish appeared as the most valuable assets in the Prince's hand:

---

102 A. de Boislisle, *Lettres de Marville, Lieutenant Général de police, au Ministre Maurepas* (Paris: Champion, 1903), Vol.2, p.100.

With the fearless Gaul dashing off to glory,
A moment of happiness leads him to victory.
By a bloody path he follows it with great gaits;
The Irishman aids him & braving deaths,
They both overthrow this dreadful mass.
..., Yes, my Prince, with the Irish you can do anything
They can do anything for you under these double auspices,
… the faithful Irishman whose valour is to be crowned,
have him triumph in spite of London's stubbornness.[103]

Voltaire revived the literary ire of the Irish once again when his work on the life of Louis XIV was published in 1751. Certain passages displeased an Irish reader, who remained anonymous as he published a reply in the *Mercure de France* in the summer of 1753. He had joined the Irish troops in 1688 and his career had come to a halt with the signing of the peace in 1748. Praising once again Voltaire's work, the officer deplored the fact that he had not acquired a 'more accurate knowledge of Irish affairs'. He first reminded his readers that despite the defeat at the Boyne the Irish 'put up such a good show that the enemy did not dare to trouble them in their retreat', and then went on to describe the first siege of Limerick where 'there were no better bulwarks than people determined to die rather than give in'. Strangely, his description of the Battle of Aughrim gave him the opportunity to attack Patrick Sarsfield, whom he portrayed as the reason behind the Jacobite defeat through his 'treachery' at the head of the cavalry, even though he saluted a few lines later the memory of Lord Lucan, the title given to the very same Sarsfield before he arrived in France. The author then criticized Voltaire, quoting his passage on the Irish 'who had always fought badly at home', explaining that his countrymen, unarmed and outnumbered, had on the contrary shown uncommon bravery and that their leaders, far from taking advantage of Louis XIV's largesse, which they could have enjoyed at a lower cost by staying at home, had sacrificed themselves in the name of the Sun King. He rejected Voltaire's accusations of unscrupulousness on the part of the exiled Irish: 'No, Sir, there was no other motive for almost all the Irish officers to go to France … other than that of uniting their fates to that of their Prince, a motive, if you like, that is romantic'.[104]

In the summer of 1756, a series of letters were published in the French press seeking to explain to the general public that Irish soldiers and their descendants had nothing to do with the enemy across the Channel and had been granted the right to remain in France thanks to their faithful service to the French kings. This series, which was published between July and September of 1756, was written by an anonymous author, probably an officer in the Brigade since he claimed to be 'born in France and to have lived almost always in the midst of Frenchmen'. One passage summed up the grievances of the Irish during the Seven Years War and gave to his community another of its founding texts establishing the greatness of the military history of the Irish Brigade:

103 Archives municipales de Troyes (AMT), Anon., *Essai épique sur les Irlandois, dédié à son altesse sérénissime, Eduard Stuard [sic] Prince de Galles* (Publisher unknown, no date).
104 Anon., 'Lettre à M. de Voltaire sur son Histoire de Louis XIV, par M. ***', *Mercure de France*, (Paris: Chaubert, June 1753), p.145.

For the past sixty-six years there has been hardly a known country where some individuals of this Nation [Ireland] have not distinguished themselves in the profession of arms. The whole Corps has never fought without acquiring glory, and we can defy all our enemies to name a single occasion in which a Corporal & two Irish Fusiliers have shown the least cowardice.[105]

The author was clearly trying to correct French people's lack of knowledge concerning Irish military history:

A number [of the French] confuse them with the English & those who pride themselves on being better educated know roughly that there are Irish regiments that fought well at Fontenoy and Lawfeld, that are strongly attached to the house of Stuart and the Catholic religion, and finally that there is a decided antipathy between the Irish and the English; and that it is to this animosity that Paris and the Provinces attribute all the marks of valour which the Irish have shown in the last war, as if the Irish troops had not behaved with the same distinction under the reign of Louis XIV and had not acquired glory in Flanders, Germany, Italy, Spain, and on all occasions when that Prince thought fit to employ them, whether they were opposed to the English, or had to deal with other enemy nations.

The second letter traced the difficult relationship between the native Irish and the English from the Middle Ages up until the war of 1689-1691 and explained that Ireland and England were two 'distinct and separate nations, subject to the same king' and that the Protestant landlords had plundered the islanders. The author also showed the inexperience of the soldiers raised in Ireland in 1689 before asserting that at the Boyne William III had led 45,000 men against merely 25,000 Jacobites. The siege of Limerick was said to have failed thanks to 'Lord Lucan' and his raid on the enemy's artillery train, and the author then reminded his readers that the Protestant forces had withdrawn in a hurry, but not before burning down their makeshift hospital in front of the Jacobite forces who tried to rescue the wounded. Aughrim was evidently portrayed as a high point in the campaign in which 'the Irish infantry knocked down & defeated the enemy infantry'. The third and final letter focused on the Treaty of Limerick and its consequences, especially for the exiled troops and their families. He ended his demonstration by referring to the most striking Penal Laws, and even highlighted the British desire to appropriate the victory at Fontenoy ('The British sought to console themselves for their defeats by claiming that the greatest victories won over them were due to their countrymen'[106]). The author went on to deny the allied victory at Dettingen before pointing out that the British soldiers were brave only because of the presence of Scots and Irish soldiers in their ranks who counterbalanced the cowardice of the English. The strident nature of the last letter gave an unflattering picture of England but above all insisted on the idea that France ought to maintain when facing such an enemy not

---

105 Etienne Ganeau, *Journal de Trévoux, Mémoires pour l'histoire des sciences et des beaux-arts* (Paris: Chaubert, 1756), *Lettre d'un officier irlandois à un officier françois de ses amis*, p.1879.
106 Etienne Ganeau, *Journal de Trévoux, Mémoires pour l'histoire des sciences et des beaux-arts* (Paris: Chaubert, 1756), p.2163.

just a large fleet but also its 'support and protection to all the Irish who are in her service'.[107] The text ended with the following paragraph:

> It remains for me to tell you, Sir, that all the Irish officers are very keen on fighting England, and that they intend to make the effects of their valour felt by the first Englishmen who will be opposed to them.[108]

In the same vein, the Abbot James MacGeoghegan wrote a history of Ireland in three volumes between 1758 and 1762 where his Jacobite feelings were openly displayed, even at a time when the Stuarts' claim to the British throne was about to disappear altogether. He was probably a chaplain in the Irish Brigade and his book was dedicated to the 'Irish troops in the service of France'. His work is still one of the pillars of the study of Irish regiments and the last two volumes appeared at the same time as relations between France and Britain were improving, leading to his work being censured by the royal authorities because of his remarks against the Penal Laws and the very vindictive tone of his writings. His dedicatory epistle emphasised the Catholic character and the loyalty to the Stuarts not only within the Brigade but among the Irish in general. MacGeoghegan reminded the feats of arms of Irish units on the Continent and the episode of Fontenoy where they 'bravely charged formidable enemies' and contributed 'with so much success to secure a victory, which till then had seemed doubtful'.[109] Reviewing the works on Ireland, he underlined, as others had done before him, what little regard Voltaire had had for the military value of the Irish. On the arrival of the Irish contingent under Justin McCarthy, he only mentioned the existence of Mountcashel's, O'Brien's and Dillon's, as other scholars would do later on. Finally, it is in the conclusion of his prologue that we find the theoretical number of Irish soldiers serving France from 1691 until the Battle of Fontenoy, a figure which is still sometimes quoted as authentic:

> By calculations & research made at the War Office, it was found that since the arrival of Irish troops in France in 1691, until 1745, when the Battle of Fontenoy was fought, more than four hundred and fifty thousand Irishmen had died in the service of France.[110]

In MacGeoghegan's eyes, the Battle of the Boyne, the 'unfortunate success' that forced James II to leave Ireland, almost became a Jacobite victory, with the Irish cavalry 'unwaveringly charged again & again ten times, and in the end, the enemies, stunned by the audacity of the Royalists [Jacobites], halted, reformed in front of them, and then marched again at a slow

---

107 Etienne Ganeau, *Journal de Trévoux, Mémoires pour l'histoire des sciences et des beaux-arts* (Paris: Chaubert, 1756), p.2176.
108 Etienne Ganeau, *Journal de Trévoux, Mémoires pour l'histoire des sciences et des beaux-arts* (Paris: Chaubert, 1756), p.2176.
109 MacGeoghegan, l'Abbé, *Histoire de l'Irlande, ancienne et moderne tirée des monuments les plus authentiques* (Paris, Antoine Boudet, 1758), pp.vi-vii.
110 James MacGeoghegan (Abbé), *Histoire de l'Irlande ancienne et moderne* (Paris: A. Boudet, 1763), vol.3, p.754.

pace to join the King'. The Irish, finally defeated, left for France with 'nineteen thousand fifty-nine' men. His vision of the Irish military exile was idealised to say the least: 'King Louis XIV, of glorious memory, received them with kindness, & offered these voluntary exiles honest terms which they accepted'.[111]

In the years that followed, a few literary references to the Irish appeared, but not to the same extent as the mid-century writings mentioned above. However, there was a clear difference in the way the Irish were treated in the memoirs of the Duke of Berwick. As the natural born son of James II and a high-ranking Jacobite officer who was made a *Maréchal de France* under Louis XIV, Berwick had a direct connection to the Irish Brigade, but between different versions they were remembered in two very different lights. This is how they appeared at the Boyne:

> ...ran after the fleeing Irish, reproached them their cowardice, rallied them, & forced them to make reparation for their fault. These troops returned from their first stupor, got ashamed having abandoned their post and the Duke of Berwick, for whom they had a singular esteem and veneration, & they showed a great desire to return to the fray.[112]

The usual reproach made to the Irish was stated again in the 1778 edition, namely that they were 'better soldiers in France and Spain', but this time it was explained away by the fact that 'King James's troops were new levies, half-armed & little disciplined'. Their arrival in Brest 'in the number of about twenty thousand men' and their participation in the wars of Louis XIV, their 'obstinacy and bravery' completed the picture, whereas the memoirs of 1737 did not dwell on the warlike qualities of the Irish and gave the figure of 14,000 men landing at Brest, although they did not specify the number of those who followed Sarsfield 'some time later'. The rewriting of the history of the Brigade was already underway.

'The proud Scot & the faithful Irish'[113]: The Irish Brigade and the Stuart Expedition of 1745

Though the '45 Rising was to a certain extent an Irish affair in that the expedition relied quite heavily on Irish support, this episode of the War of the Austrian Succession is rarely discussed in the legend of the Irish Brigade, probably due to its ultimate failure. It was, for instance, barely touched upon in the three *Lettres d'un officier irlandois à un officier françois de ses amis* mentioned above. The kingdom of France was still basking in the afterglow of its victory at Fontenoy, yet support for the Stuart cause did not seem to be paramount in Versailles' subsequent war plans. A letter from Charles Edward Stuart to his father shows that the Young Pretender desperately needed auxiliary help from foreign powers to

---

111 James MacGeoghegan (Abbé), *Histoire de l'Irlande ancienne et moderne* (Paris: A. Boudet, 1763), vol.3, pp.742–3, 748–9.

112 Abbé de Margon, *Jacques Fitz-James duc de Berwick, Mémoires du maréchal de Berwik* (sic) (Paris, Paupie, 1737), vol.1, p.56.

113 Anon., *Extrait d'une lettre de la Haye, 30 August 1745* (The Hague: Balthazar Weins, 1745), 2 pages.

transform his early successes in the autumn of 1745 in Scotland into an actual threat to the Hanoverian regime:

> It is of the utmost importance you should send me at least the English, Scottish or Irish regiments that are in the service of foreign powers. Without these troops, I could truth be told maintain myself in Scotland, no matter what happens, during three of four years, but with them I would be invincible. I would even be strong enough to attack the enemy in the provinces where he least expects me. I mostly need some cavalry of which I have little. it will soon be more necessary than it is today.[114]

There had been genuine hope among the Jacobites in the spring and summer of 1745 that the whole Irish Brigade would join the Stuart prince's attempt at reconquering London:

> … it is with pleasure that we have learned that the rumours that had been spread about a considerable embarkation at Brest are unfounded, as well as that of Dunkirk, which others assure us is very real; but that only Irishmen and Scots will embark there. His Most Christian Majesty, not wishing to make enemies of the Protestant Powers, does not wish to interfere publicly in this revolt. On the other hand, the reason for war requiring that he should do as much harm as he can to his Enemies, he would like to support this party; this is why it was imagined at Versailles to dismiss all the Irish & Scots, who are in the service of His Majesty; but by giving secret orders to the Officers on what they should do, which is to go to Dunkirk, where they will find transport ships to take them back to their Homeland … There is nothing more fitting than seeing a seditious, traitorous man helped by Corsairs.[115]

Some reduced officers in the Irish Brigade attached to the garrison towns in northern France also offered to join the expedition.[116] One of them, a *capitaine réformé* from Clare's Regiment named O'Hanlon, illustrates the will of these officers to serve the Stuarts, even at the expense of their own immediate interests within the French army:

> I cannot, Sir, refuse to Mr. O'Hanlon the favour of asking you for a captain's commission established in his name. He is currently at Ghent on the verge of going into England and though he has got a similar commission from the Prince known as the Pretender, he is nevertheless in need of one from the King to protect him from any incident once in England. Besides, he does not pretend that this commission would give him any right to a position in France, nor would it procure him any wages.[117]

---

114 Anon., *A l'auteur des Lettres à un provincial, sur la justice des motifs de la guerre, sur les conjonctures présentes de l'Europe* (Neuchatel: Publisher unknown,1745), pp.13–14.
115 *Mercure Historique et Politique*, vol.n° 119, (The Hague: Frederich–Henri Scheurleer, 1745), pp.464–465.
116 Boislisle, *Lettres de Marville*, vol.2, p.169.
117 MKWP, copy from SHD, Administrative Archives, Older Section, Personal files, Ancien Régime, Capitaine O'Hanlon. Letter from the Maréchal de Noailles, 26 October 1745.

In order not to appear as suspicious in its nature, the commission sent to O'Hanlon did mention a position within an Irish regiment to which was attached a regular pay. This precaution was indeed an absolute necessity but was not always sufficient as illustrated by the case of Francis Townley, a Jacobite English officer serving in the French army and who was arrested in England during the expedition. Though he had been granted a French commission in 1744, Townley was publicly executed on 30 July 1746 as a warning to any other candidate for rebellion.[118]

The victory at Prestonpans in September 1745 encouraged the French to send some help, but the vast sums of money, equipment and the numerous men needed never really materialised. Only a private Irish entrepreneur, Antoine Walsh, offered to help the Stuart prince by providing ships and equipment to go to Scotland though he was suspected of being a front for a French government-backed operation. But a mere 800 soldiers were picked from the Brigade, each of the six regiments forming what were called picquets, temporary units set up for a specific military task and roughly equating to a company in strength. The French passion for odes and poems was still very much alive in the autumn of 1745 when one Irish composer living in France, a Mr Keating, was inspired by the first good news of the Jacobite expedition and favourably depicted his countrymen while addressing Charles Edward Stuart:

See the Irishman, ever faithful,
Either conquering or dying for his quarrel,
From the leopards tearing the bowels
And purging your dear Motherland
From the tigers whose barbarity
Will quench their thirst with your blood.[119]

The Irish Picquets were placed under the command of Lord John Drummond, a Scotsman, and Brigadier Stapleton, an Irishman, and arrived at Montrose on 25 November 1745, while detachments from Berwick's and Fitzjames' Horse were to arrive at Peterhead and Aberdeen at the end of February 1746. Due to the actions of the Royal Navy, only one of the squadrons made it to the shore as the transport vessels were attacked and seized. Hundreds of Irish soldiers never actually had a chance to participate in the Jacobite attempt. This turned out to have dire consequences for the Stuart pretender as those who did join the fight proved immensely useful to the Prince's war effort in Scotland. Being the only ones drilled to fight in European-style battles, they provided the backbone of Bonnie Prince Charlie's expedition.

The Battle of Falkirk in January of 1746 confirmed the fact that the Jacobites had gathered momentum. By that time, the Irish Picquets that did land had fully joined the Pretender's army and served with distinction. They were posted in the second line of battle not out of a lack of respect for their abilities, but, on the contrary, so they could provide support to

118 British Museum (BM), *Satire on the executions of Townley and Fletcher after the Jacobite rebellion, with a view of Temple Bar seen through an arch, 1746*. Etching with hand–colouring.
119 Elie–Catherine Fréron, *Lettres de Madame la Comtesse de ***, sur quelques écrits modernes* (Geneva: Philibert, 1746), vol.1, pp.102–103.

enthusiastic but less well-drilled Scottish clansmen. According to the 'gasconading account' published by the rebels in Bannockburn and relayed with irony by the *Scots Magazine,* their officers were mostly to be praised, 'The Irish officers were of vast use, in going through the different posts of the army and assisting in the various dispositions that were made'.[120]

A letter produced by the Jacobite side and published in France compared the Battle of Falkirk to a 'little Fontenoy' when evoking the effect it had on the British since the government forces were blocked from relieving the siege of Stirling just like the Pragmatic Army had been stopped from helping Tournai several months before. The text obviously emphasised the importance of the Highlanders (designated as 'Mountaineers' in the French text) and did not mention the Irish though the letter was written to a 'retired Irish officer'.[121]

However, the Irish were not always used in the most appropriate manner, leading to unnecessary deaths within the picquets:

> Our trenches traced on a hill to the north of the Castle, by Mirabelle [a French engineer of Scottish origins], advanced very slowly, there being only a mere covering of earth on the hill and we lost a great many men, particularly of the Irish picquets. what a pity that these brave men should have been sacrificed to no purpose, by the ignorance and folly of Mirabelle! These picquets, who behaved with the most distinguished bravery and intrepidity at the Battle of Falkirk preserving always the best order, when the whole of the rest of our army was dispersed, and keeping the enemy in check by the bold countenance which they displayed ought to have been reserved for a better occasion.[122]

In 1746, the Battle of Culloden Moor marked the end of Charles Edward Stuart's hope for even a partial victory in Scotland. The picquet from Berwick's regiment defended a bridge over the River Nairn where it 'behaved itself with distinction' in an action leading to the major battle. The same principle of having the Irish supporting the Jacobite line was adopted for that engagement, except that this time the rear guard had to protect the Scottish Jacobites from being routed once the Highland charge failed to break the British line. While the Highlanders saw their charge countered by Cumberland's men, the Irish Picquets were placed on the left wing of the Jacobite army under Drummond and Stapleton and were forced to protect the remaining troops once defeat was certain: 'The Irish picquets could not resolve to turn their backs and were cut down by the enemy who occupied the centre and could not retire to Inverness where the marquess of Aiguille ordered them to surrender as prisoners of war'.[123]

---

120 *The Scots Magazine,* January 1746, vol.8, p.39.
121 Anon., *Lettre d'un officier du regiment Royal Ecossois, à M. D. ancien capitaine irlandois. Sur la victoire remportée par le prince Edouard, régent d'Ecosse, sur l'armée angloise, commandée par le général Aweley près de Falkirk, le 28 janvier 1746* (Paris: Publisher unknown, 1746), p.3.
122 Chevalier de Johnstone, *Memoirs of the Rebellion in 1745 and 1746* (London: Longman, Hurst, Rees, Orme, and Brown, 1820), p.104.
123 Jean–François de Spon, *Mémoires pour servir à l'histoire de l'Europe, depuis 1740 jusqu'à la paix générale signée à Aix–la–Chapelle, le 18 octobre 1748* (Amsterdam: La Compagnie, 1749), vol.3, part 1, p.125.

The *Gentleman's Magazine* had one eyewitness account delivering information on the demise of the rebel army:

> Last Night one *James Hay*, a Scotchman, who calls himself a Captain and Paymaster of Lord *John Drummond's* Regiment, surrendered himself to the Lord Justice Clerk, and was by his Lordship committed to our Castle. This Man says, that the *French*, viz. *Drummond's* Regiment, the *Irish* Picquets, and *Fitz-James's* Horse, at the Time of the late Battle, amounted to between 6 and 700 Men; that of the first 50 were killed in the Battle, and of the second about 100. He further says that he parted from the Person called Lord *John Drummond* at *Ruthven*, who took the Money belonging to the Regiment from him, and divided it amongst his Officers, desiring every one to shift for himself, as he intended to do; that the Rebels had not received any Pay for some weeks before the battle; that their Magazine of provisions being very low, they were forced to try a battle, that the night before they were extremely harassed by marching and countermarching, and before they could get any refreshment, they were surprised by the Duke's quick march.[124]

The British imposed a fierce campaign of retaliations on the Highlands, while the Irish prisoners from the picquets were treated first and foremost as French subjects who could be exchanged with British soldiers captured in Flanders. Yet one of the Irish officers, Maurice O'Connell, captured three days after the Battle of Culloden Moor, was subsequently 'reduced to the greatest misery possible and was exposed to the cruellest treatments in the six months of his detention'.[125] Documents relating to the Irish Picquets that were captured before they even had a chance to set foot in Scotland give some interesting insights into the Brigade in the mid-1740s. Their officers were all from Ireland, some having officially enlisted as early as 1711 as in the case of James McGrath who declared to be 50 years of age, which would have made him 15 when he officially joined. Most of them were experienced middle aged officers, the sort of men Bonnie Prince Charlie desperately needed. They had been enlisted by other, older Irish officers, more rarely by a soldier, in places like Lille, Cambrai or Valenciennes where the Irish regiments were usually posted in the eighteenth century. They were also arriving in harbours like Bordeaux or La Rochelle. Surprisingly, one soldier was convinced to join at Saint-Germain-en-Laye, proving that the Irish community still had some representatives in the area decades after the deaths of the Stuart monarchs and the departure of their descendants to Italy. All soldiers were Irish, with a few English and Scottish exceptions, and all had enlisted between the late 1730s and the early 1740s, confirming the findings of French local archives previously mentioned. The cavalrymen in Fitzjames' Regiment were generally enlisted around the same years. Most had decided to become members of the Irish Brigade 'purposefully', with reasons varying from visiting a family relative to one who just 'went to see the country of France'. The grounds for enlistment were roughly the same as they had been in the first half of the eighteenth century, though the Stuart cause is never officially mentioned. Some had been 'bred in the regiment' like Andrew Connell, a corporal

---

124 *The London Magazine*, vol.15, p.253.
125 MKWP, Copy of SHD, Administrative Archives, Older Section, Personal files, *Trésor Royal*, Maurice O'Connell, letter to the Count de Saint Germain, 17 October 1775.

of 28 who counted no fewer than 18 years of service, while some claimed to be Frenchmen in order not to be sent back to Ireland where they were 'suspected of some crime'. More interestingly, some assured their captors they had been 'decoyed', in the sense of lured into French service, on a 'forced errand',[126] or were made prisoners and had to join the regiment, as many did in the cavalry unit.[127] In time, the soldiers were either exchanged with British prisoners of war held in France, pardoned on the condition of a permanent banishment from the British Isles or even managed to escape back to France as did Charles Edward Stuart himself.

In the end, the War of the Austrian Succession did not actually benefit either the Bourbons or the Stuarts on the geopolitical stage, but it did mark a watershed in the complex military and cultural relations between Great-Britain, Ireland and France. Fontenoy proved once and for all that the Irish regiments fighting for Louis XV were a force to be reckoned with, but it also marked the decline of the Brigade as its Irish character rapidly began to fade. Fewer Irishmen joined its ranks after 1746 while enlistments of Germans, Belgians and even French soldiers increased. Although Britain tried to ignore its defeat in the Austrian Netherlands, it started to properly notice the military potential of the Irish Catholic population whereas the French still struggled to understand the Irish community that had been living among them for more than 50 years. Similarly, Versailles did not capitalise on the initial success of the Jacobite rebellion in Scotland. There is no denying that Fontenoy and the rest of the campaign in Flanders were resounding French successes, but the real victors in the long term were the British themselves. They managed to capitalise on their own defeat by transforming the Irish Brigade into a British corps fighting for the wrong cause. British popular culture played a pivotal role in making Irish Catholic soldiers more acceptable by turning them into friendly idiots.[128] As for the Irish community living in France, it tried to educate the French about the specific part they played in the royal army, but the losses incurred by the battle irreparably damaged the influence members of the Brigade could muster at Versailles.

126 National Archives (TNA), Kew Gardens, SP36/89.
127 For a more complete analysis of the Irish Picquets, see Andrew Bamford, *The Lilies and the Thistle: French troops in the Jacobite 45* (Warwick: Helion, 2018), pp.30–49.
128 Throughout the eighteenth century, a comedy entitled *The Refusal* was performed both in London and Dublin. It light–heartedly compared a secret dalliance between a 'handsome wench and a young fellow' to 'spreading a bag of gunpowder before a great fire to dry it' to which a character responded: 'Right Sir, – it puts me in mind of the Irish soldier, who, to steal powder out of a full barrel, cunningly bored a hole in it with a red–hot poker'. See Colley Cibber, *The Dramatic Works of Colley Cibber* (London: J. Clarke, 1760), p.87.

4

'Our regiments are in a class of their own'[1] – The Irish regiments at the crossroads of history (c. 1760–1815)

> The Irish brigade has often fought the battles of
> France, and a people whom the narrow policy of
> their own government alienated, have for ages
> been our faithful auxiliaries.[2]

The last decades of the eighteenth century were decisive for the Irish Brigade as its prospects within the French army started to wane. Fontenoy confirmed the Irish soldiers as members of a military elite but doomed the Brigade as it was never able to fully recover its Hibernian character from the casualties suffered during the War of the Austrian Succession. Once the hopes of a Jacobite victory were decisively dashed at Culloden Moor in April 1746, Versailles abandoned its plans to use the Brigade to help restore the Stuarts. France even expelled Charles Edward Stuart in 1748 as per the agreements signed at the treaty of Aix-La-Chapelle and the British Parliament passed a series of Acts in 1746 clearly targeting members of the Irish Brigade. Treasonous behaviour against the crown was condemned with the loss of property in the British Isles leading even, in certain cases, to a death sentence.[3] This did not deter Irish officers from regularly proposing reports on the state of affairs in Ireland and how France could take advantage of the island to foment a new rebellion, though the Bourbons showed little enthusiasm in pursuing such propositions. After the 1760s, most of the soldiers who enlisted in the Irish regiments no longer had any personal ties to Ireland or even the British Isles. Only their officers remained deeply attached to their Irish and Jacobite roots.

---

1   ADML, Walsh–Serrant archives, bundle n°187.
2   John Corry, *The Adventures of Felix and Rosarito; Or, the Triumph of Love and Friendship. Containing an Account of Several Interesting Events During the Late War, Between France and Spain, in the Western Pyrenees* (London, Crosby & Co, 1782), p.5.
3   ADML, Walsh–Serrant archives, bundle n°47.

Even though the Irish Brigade did participate in the Seven Years War on the side of France, it did not provide Louis XV with a major victory nor did it play a central role in the general war effort. Thus, its value as a military force was questioned during the last decades of the eighteenth century, though it still fought for France during the expedition against Corsica in the 1760s and the War of American Independence in the late 1770s and early 1780s. It was still part of the French army when the Revolution broke out. At the end of the Ancien Régime period and up to the French Revolution, Irish officers actually relied on the warlike reputation and loyalty to the Bourbons of their regiments after more than 70 years of service to justify the very existence of the Brigade. From the 1750s onwards, their own efforts as well as that of the Irish community living in France provided the foundations of the myth of the Wild Geese.

However, the French Revolution of 1789 followed by the beginnings of the French and Napoleonic Wars dramatically altered the military relationship established between the two nations. The dual fidelity of the Irish officers to an ancient nobility and to a foreign country marked them out as natural enemies of the new republican regime. Meanwhile, Britain faced with a renewed French threat on its coasts looked eagerly towards Catholic Ireland as a place to enlist more men for its naval and land forces, seeing the Brigade as a useful tool to inspire recruitments. Thus, the Irish Brigade found itself split between its French and British traditions, leading to an unprecedented transfer of allegiance from one state to another. Paradoxically, the legend surrounding the Brigade was used to justify such a change with a new military history narrative in which the Irish fighting for France ought to have served Britain in the first place.

"The blow has been struck"[4] The Decline of the Irish Brigade (1760s–1780s).

In the years between the end of the War of the Austrian Succession and the outbreak of the Seven Years War, the Irish Brigade was regularly listed as part of planned expeditions into Scotland or Ireland. Projects were drawn in 1749, 1752, 1756 and 1759, but all came to nought. The Irish regiments were reduced in size due to the losses incurred by the hard campaigning in Flanders in the 1740s and also due to Louis XV's subsequent military reforms. French military archives as well as local records show that the Irish regiments were frequently rotated between northern France, Normandy and Brittany, with each unit losing soldiers following royal decrees. In 1749, the Brigade's companies went from numbering 50 men to just 35 and were supposed to exclude any soldier who was not Irish, Scottish or English, with the exception of those who at least were the sons of a subject born in the British Isles.[5] By 1753, Clare's, Dillon's, Roth's, Berwick's, Lally's and Bulkeley's had all been reduced to one battalion of 465 men distributed into 13 companies, each still comprising only 35 men. The entire infantry brigade had a grand total of 2,790 soldiers and 360 officers.[6] Roth's, Berwick's

---

4   ADML, Walsh–Serrant Archives, bundle n°189. Letter from Walsh–Serrant with no place or date about the dismissal on his memoir to protect the existence of his regiment.

5   *Ordonnance du roy, portant réduction dans les régimens [sic] d'infanterie irlandoise & écossoise* (Paris: Imprimerie du roi, 1749), 12 February 1749.

6   *Etat general des Troupes françoises* (Paris: Publisher unknown, 1753), pp.300–301.

Dillon's Regiment 1750s. (New York Public Library Digital Collections)

and Lally's also included a provost helped by five *archers* (military policemen) and an executioner to keep the men disciplined. Besides the Brigade, Fitzjames', the sole cavalry unit that remained mostly Irish in its composition, was first reduced to three squadrons on 30 October 1748 and only two by 15 March 1749. All of its former officers were put on half-pay.[7]

When the Seven Years War broke out in Europe in 1756, the Brigade's potential role in a disrupting invasion of the British Isles was renewed, and its troops were mustered in Boulogne to keep London in a constant state of alert. The Brigade's reputation was officially recognised by the highest French authority when the time came to reinforce its ranks:

> His MAJESTY having agreed to the proposal of the Colonels of the regiments of her Irish Infantry, for an increase in the present composition of these regiments, he would have determined to do so all the more willingly, as he has recognized on all occasions the value, zeal and attachment of the troops of this nation, of which he does not doubt that he will receive new proofs in the present circumstances.[8]

---

7   M. d'Héricourt, *Elemens* [sic] *de l'art militaire* (Paris: Gissey, 1753) vol.3, pp.152, 319, 323–324 and 328.
8   *Ordonnance du roi, concernant les régimens* [sic] *irlandois* (Paris: Imprimerie du roi, 1756), 15 July 1756.

Consequently, the number of soldiers in Irish regiments went from 465 to 525, gaining five men per company, before moving up to 705 men per unit in December of 1756 with 55 soldiers per company.[9] In the autumn of 1756 and the Spring of 1757, each captain in the six infantry regiments was given more time to recruit the 15 extra soldiers needed with the usual monetary incentive attached to having a company at full strength.[10] In 1756, Lally's two battalions, numbering a total of 1,080 men, were sent alongside 150 artillerymen and detachments from French regiments to French possessions in India in order to fight the British, while the remaining five regiments stayed in Europe.[11] The names of the senior and junior officers of the regiment were still of Irish extraction, with, for instance, those onboard the *Centaure*, a 60-gun warship, armed *en flûte* with 28 guns to accommodate the troops:

> Mr Dillon, lieutenant-colonel in Lally's,
> The Chevalier Geoghegan, first captain in Lally's and his company,
> Murphy, captain with a lieutenant-colonel commission and his company,
> Allen, captain and his company,
> Butler, captain and his company[12]

Yet their men had different origins. In December 1756, more than five hundred recruits, formerly from Fischer's light infantry battalion, had arrived at Brest to join Lally's ranks, implying that a large proportion of the Irish troops sent to India were actually either French, Flemish or German.[13] These men fought with Lally's at Pondicherry until the entire unit was captured in January 1761 and officially disbanded once the soldiers returned to France the following year.

After 1757, the Irish Brigade was sent to participate in the German campaign of the French army but was not present at the battles of Hastenbeck or Rossbach. It returned to France to protect the coasts from British landings. The Irish were stationed in Brittany and Normandy when, in 1758, the British tried to capture Saint Malo and failed, and again in August 1758 when London turned its attention towards Cherbourg. 7,000 British infantrymen disembarked and were faced by Clare's Regiment, reinforced by local militias and French detachments.[14] The local French commander, *Maréchal de Camp* Raymond, lost his nerves and let the British first camp on the coast and then take Cherbourg without any form of resistance. Clare's was the only military unit that retired in good order and had been

---

9   *Ordonnance du roi, portant augmentation dans les régimens irlandois & écossois* (Paris: Imprimerie du roi, 1756), 20 December 1756.

10 *Ordonnance du roi, pour proroger jusqu'au mois de décembre prochain, le complet des compagnies de fusiliers des régimens irlandois* (Paris: Imprimerie royale, 1756), 15 October 1756 and *Ordonnance du roi, pour proroger jusqu'à la revue du mois de juin prochain, le complet de l'augmentation réglée dans les régimens [sic] d'infanterie irlandoise & écossoise* (Paris: Imprimerie royale, 1757), 1 April 1757.

11 *Réglement pour le traitement du régiment irlandois de Lally, destiné à passer aux Indes orientales* (Paris: Imprimerie du roi, 1756), 19 October 1756.

12 ADIV, C1173, *Etat des dispositions des troupes sur les vaisseaux du Roy et de la compagnie des Indes ci après*, November 1756.

13 See SHD, GR1 Yc 271, Légion de Conflans, 1758–1776.

14 See Jean–Thomas Voisin La Hougue & Vérusmor, *Histoire de la ville de Cherbourg depuis 1728 jusqu'à 1835* (Cherbourg: Boulanger, 1835).

prohibited from engaging the British by Raymond himself as the enemy's fleet bombarded the shores and would have destroyed the entire unit. The British eventually left the city after having ransomed the local population.[15]

Thereafter the Irish regiments remained to guard the north-western provinces of France as well as serve in a form of psychological warfare since they could in turn be used to launch a reprisal raid in the British Isles.[16] In February 1759, Dillon's was sent back to Brittany to replace French units stationed there, and was closely followed by Rothe's and Berwick's.[17] On Saint Patrick's Day in 1759, a great mass was ordained by the officers of the regiment of Clare, with half the regiment and the flag being blessed by the clergy of the city of Vitré.[18]

In 1759, Clare's, Dillon's and Rothe's were all ordered to serve under François de Chevert in northern France to prepare for a possible invasion of the British Isles which did not materialise with only one French privateer, François Thurot, incidentally himself a descendant of an Irishman settled in France after 1691, managing to land a blow against the British. He captured the port of Carrickfergus in Ulster after having successfully evaded the enemy's fleet.[19] Later the same year, Versailles once again toyed with the prospect of a major French landing against London. *Maréchal* Conflans was supposed to lead an expedition force where the Irish Brigade would have been a great asset, but the project foundered after the disastrous Battle of Quiberon Bay in November 1759 mangled the French navy.

Getting more recruits for the Brigade was still a major concern for its senior and junior officers. One would think that desertions from the British ranks would have made it easier, especially since the Seven Years War often offered ample opportunities for covert Irish Catholics enlisted in the British Army to join their brethren on the French side. However, the reality was more complex. To start with, prisoner exchanges could be affected by such enlistments. When a few British deserters offered to join Clare's right after the Cherbourg expedition, the French authorities declined the opportunity:

> At Versailles, 29 October 1758.
> M. *le Maréchal duc* de Belle-Isle to *Monsieur le duc* d'Harcourt,
> I have received, Sir, the letter which you did me the honour of writing to me on the 24th of this month, on the subject that among the English soldiers who deserted or were taken prisoner during the raid on Cherbourg, there are five or six who want to take part in Clare's regiment. The King, to whom I have reported this, has indeed agreed to the idea, although it would be much more useful to us to exchange these prisoners for French soldiers who are presently in England. As for the proposal to have the surplus of these English prisoners transferred to Blois to be joined to those who were taken at Saint-Cast, it would seem to me to be very appropriate to

---

15   Gazette (Paris: Chaubert, 1758), p.142
16   ADIV, Commission intermédiaire des Etats de Bretagne, C3815, official marching orders, 1758.
17   ADIV, C3815, official marching orders, 16 April 1759.
18   ADIV, fonds Bourde de la Rogerie, 5J 72, *Registre historique du prieuré de Notre Dame de Vitré*, 17 March 1759.
19   Though his ships returned to France after a few days of occupation, he was killed during the naval combat when the Royal Navy finally caught up with his small squadron. None of the soldiers onboard his six men–of–war were from the Irish Brigade.

make this this arrangement, and if you would be willing to send me the list of these prisoners, I will send you the necessary orders in consequence. I have the honour to be, etc.[20]

A series of documents held in the local archives of eastern Brittany also illustrate the difficulties encountered by French authorities in maintaining Irish units. The letters detail the arrival of 64 Irishmen who left the British Army in North America after the taking of Fort Oswego near New York in 1756. The Irish first joined the French and were later shipped back to France to bolster the ranks of the Brigade. When they arrived at Brest in November 1757, the officer in charge of their well-being was immediately confronted with logistical problems with half of the men falling sick and not enough money to pay those 'unpaid volunteers'. Soon, ill treatments at the hand of French officers led to desertions and the remaining Irish soldiers ended up being imprisoned in Brest to make sure they would eventually join the companies most in need of recruits. Eight other Irish soldiers who had joined the French in Québec also asked to enlist in the royal army. One of them, a man called Walter Nugent, had already enrolled with the *Compagnies Franches de la Marine* and had to be reclaimed by the Irish Brigade since foreigners were not officially accepted in French troops.[21] Such a large number of Irish soldiers available for enlistment became a rarity in the second half of the eighteenth century.

As the war entered the 1760s, the numbers of men per company in Irish infantry regiments were increased:

> Irish & Scottish Infantry: Each Regiment of Irish & Scots is a Battalion of 70 men in thirteen Companies, one of which is of Grenadiers of forty-five men, & twelve of Fusiliers of fifty-five men, not including Officers. Each Company, either of Grenadiers, or of Fusiliers, is commanded by a Captain, a second Captain, a Lieutenant & a second Lieutenant. That of Grenadiers is composed of two Sergeants, three Corporals, three *Anspessades* [equating to chosen man or lance corporal], thirty-six Grenadiers & a Drummer. That of Fusiliers of three Sergeants, four Corporals, four *Anspessades*, forty-three Fusiliers & a Drummer.[22]

The Irish garrisoned in the west of France left some traces of their passage, not all them positive. A close scrutiny of the surviving evidence within local archives provides evidence that, for instance, the Irish officers of Rothe's Regiment were accused in 1758 of misbehaving against the *étapier*, the civilian clerk in charge of receiving and lodging regiments whenever they moved from one place to another, leading to a complaint being filed against them. Likewise, in 1759, the commissioners in charge of regiments' lodgings sent a letter to the Duc d'Aiguillon to put an end to the brazen attitudes of Irish officers 'who choose on their own volition new lodgings or even go to another parish on their own accord', even though

---

20 Célestin Hippeau, *Le gouvernement de Normandie au XVIIe et au XVIIIe siècle d'après la correspondance des marquis de Beuvron et des ducs d'Harcourt* (Caen: De LaPorte, 1863), vol.1, p.246.
21 ADIV, fonds Bourde de la Rogerie, 5J 72, 1758.
22 Montandre–Longchamps, *Etat Militaire de la France pour l'année 1760* (Paris: Guillyn, 1760), pp.193–194.

Régiment de Lally 1757. Plate n°113 from the manuscript *Troupes du Roi, Infanterie française et étrangère, année 1757, tome I.* (Paris – Musée de l'Armée)

the *étape* was organised along strict lines by French military and civilian authorities.[23] Even if it should be noted that the Irish were not the only ones whose behaviour was questionable – the same documents list problems caused by French units, with for example the officers of the Régiment de Marbeuf damaging a Breton rectory they deemed unfit to house them – one anecdotal element tends to prove that the Brigade still harboured rather rough characters. A series of anonymous hand-painted pictures was published in 1757 depicting French troops at the onset of the Seven Years War. Nowadays held at the *Musée de l'Armée* in Paris, it portrayed every single unit in a rather positive way, with soldiers either playing cards, mounting guard or courting pretty ladies. The only example in the lot showing a soldier stealing the livelihoods of French peasants was the illustration for Lally's Regiment.[24]

In any case, though the soldier depicted definitely belonged to the Brigade, he was not necessarily Irish. Bulkeley's illustrated this fact in the early days of 1760 when, while stationed in Brittany, it was beset by a series of desertions. Twenty-seven men from the entire regiment – no fewer than 10 companies lost between two and six soldiers each – were condemned *in absentia* to be shot by firing squad. The vast majority of the culprits were of Dutch, German, Austrian or Belgian extraction, and those recruits that actually hailed from the British Isles were not just Irish, but also came from Scotland and England. The French regimental system, ever since 1716, provided a physical description of each and every soldier serving in its ranks so that they could easily be spotted as deserters or bounty jumpers. One of the runaways was thus physically described: 'Jean Cahill, a native of Waterford in Ireland aged thirty-three, five feet three inches, bright blond hair, wide forehead, grey eyes, long nose, slightly marked by smallpox'.[25]

In 1762, as the war was winding to a close, the Brigade was once again faced with the prospect of reforms. It kept five regiments on active duty and integrated what was left of Lally's in their ranks after it had returned from India, alongside the two Scottish regiments of Royal Ecossois and Ogilvy. Surviving when wars ended still required efforts. The same year, the French military hierarchy ceased to accept the practice of having reduced officers accompanying Irish troops in officers' brigades attached to each regiment as it had been habitual at the beginning of the eighteenth century,[26] but at the same time also recognised the presence of women in Irish regiments as a relatively normal occurrence acknowledged in official documents:

> HIS MAJESTY being desirous of treating favourably those married Foreigners who wish to serve in the Regiments of Irish Infantry, shall during the war, & so long as they serve in the field only, give one *sol* per day with a ration of bread, to their wives, who shall be required to remain at the Assembly Quarters of the Regiment; His Majesty intending that this payment shall no longer be made when they leave the Assembly Quarters, or their husbands are no longer in the Regiment.[27]

23   ADIV, C3815, official marching orders, 1759.
24   Anonymous, *Musée de l'Armée*, Paris, 1757.
25   ADIV, C1107 1760-1787 military matters.
26   *Ordonnance du roi, concernant les régimens d'infanterie irlandoise* (Paris: Imprimerie du roi, 1762), 21 December 1762
27   *Recueil des nouvelles ordonnances militaires* (Metz: Collignon, 1767), p.11.

In the meantime, Britain raised regiments in Ireland for its own forces in increasing numbers because of the renewed threat of a French invasion. Because of the Penal Laws, these new troops could not call upon Catholic recruits. To this effect, Thomas Waite, the undersecretary to the Chief Secretary for Ireland, mentioned in one of his dispatch that 'Lord Forbes' regiment'[28], the 76th Foot, needed more men from the island to become a fully-manned unit, albeit with the usual caveats attached to such an enterprise in a country that still applied strict legal prohibition against 'papists': 'Colonel [Forbes] is to be stationed at Armagh for the purpose of reviewing and examining the recruits as they are raised with the strictest orders not to allow any but able–bodied men and Protestants'.[29] However, the area had been 'so thoroughly gleaned' that Forbes' regiment was allowed to enlist throughout the whole kingdom to reach its recruitment objectives. Interestingly, its colonel had one request which reveals the ambiguous nature of the exercise considering the unspoken competition with recruiters from France:

> His Lordship this morning desired he might be permitted to paint the Irish Harp upon his drums and to exhibit it upon his colours, in aid of the recruiting service, and said he had no doubt but [the regiment?] should very soon feel the good effects of it... My Lord Lieutenant... seemed to be of the same opinion with My Lord Forbes as to the use of the above devices or of any others to distinguish the regiment to be Irish. The Scotch have their royal [sic] with the crown and thistle. If it was to be called the English Irish Brigade in opposition to that in the French service, such a distinction would probably not only fill the corps very soon, but forever animate men to do well.[30]

During the second half of the eighteenth century, Irish officers and members of the Irish community living in France slowly grew disillusioned with their adopted motherland. In truth, the Irish had every right to be disappointed in their French hosts. After all, the French still seemed to struggle in the second half of the eighteenth century with understanding the presence of a community originally born in or with family ties to the British Isles. The Irish living in their midst were considered as somewhat alien even several decades after their landing in Brittany and after three major wars fought on the same side. When the Seven Years War unofficially broke out in 1754, Irish traders who had been residing in places like Nantes, Saint Malo, Bordeaux or even Marseilles all felt the need to prove their loyalty to the Bourbons by sending official letters to Versailles once royal decrees forcing any British male subject found on its territory to join the Irish Brigade were published. Irish Catholic merchant Antoine Kelly explained 'that he followed King James II to France and fears that he might be treated as an English subject forced to leave the kingdom according to the king's orders'.[31]

---

28   George Forbes, 4th Earl of Granard, was raising the 76th regiment at the time.
29   PRONI, T3019/3085, Waite, Dublin Castle, to Wilmot. Kildare, 4 January 1757.
30   PRONI, T3019/3085, Waite, Dublin Castle, to Wilmot. Kildare, 4 January 1757.
31   AMM, Series EE 127/2, military matters, 13 February 1756.

Meanwhile, in Ireland itself, the British authorities in the mid–eighteenth century were well aware that French ships were still smuggling Irishmen back to France.[32] By that time, Britain was both openly looking for experienced military men and was reinforcing its legislative arsenal against possible rebellions in Ireland by prohibiting enlistments or recruitments within the British Isles for service to a foreign state. This Act provided the means for London's authorities to deprive Irishmen in the French army of the last remnants of their possessions in the native land by confiscating their estates. It forced some Irish officers to break, at least officially, any bonds with France:

> Mr John Warren... was an officer in the French service which he quitted in consequence of the Act of Parliament, but came over a few days too late he is under the protection of Mr Nugent, one of the Lords of the treasury who has promised to obtain a pardon for him in Ireland where his eldest brother has an estate of £1,800 a year. Another brother of Mr. Warrens' is aide de camp to the Prince de Soubise, a colonel by brevet, or has a company in Ruth's [Rothe's] regiment. Mr John Warren had some injustice done [to] him in France with respect to his rank, is disgusted with the French and has been heard to say that he would fight up to the knees in blood rather than suffer the French to make a conquest of England and Ireland, but he is a friend to the Pretender's interest, is sensible, has about eight or nine hundred pounds and proposes to purchase a company in the Dutch service.[33]

Once the attempt against the British Isles was abandoned and the threat of a British expedition on Brittany was removed, the Irish were sent back to Germany. Seven pickets from all the Irish regiments distinguished themselves at the siege of Marburg in February 1761 where they victoriously resisted an attack from the Hanoverians.[34] According to a contemporary newspaper, food shortages drove numerous deserters from the Hanoverian and Hessian regiments to join the Irish. These newcomers kept their old red uniforms but were given white cockades as a symbol of their new allegiance.[35] The war also marked the end of Fitzjames' cavalry regiment. As the only Irish cavalry unit that had survived the reforms of the first 50 years of the eighteenth century, it participated in the Battle of Rossbach where the French and Austrian forces were routed by the Prussians. According to Frederick the Great's own memoirs, two Austrian cavalry regiments vainly tried to repulse the Prussian onslaught and were abandoned by their French allies, with the notable exception of the Irish cavalry unit led by Colonel Thomas Betagh which charged to protect their fleeing comrades.[36] It paid a heavy price as the regiment was almost wiped out when Prussian hussars counter charged them. One of Betagh's kinsmen was wounded during the fighting but distinguished himself in the retreat. He received the Order of Saint Louis for his efforts. In April 1767, he became an infantry brigadier and served as one of the senior officers in Clare's. Fitzjames' was officially disbanded, putting an end to the presence of Irish cavalry

---

32 PRONI, T3152/725, 294.33, Letter from Duncannon, 23 June 1755.
33 PRONI, T3158/1471, 13 December 1756, 'list of Popish and disaffected persons now in London'.
34 *Mercure de France*, April 1761, p.199.
35 *Gazette de Vienne* (Vienna: Trattner, 14 January 1761), vol.5.
36 Frédéric II de Prusse, *Œuvres Historiques (1740–1763)* (Paris: Hachette, 1872), vol.2, p.174.

in the service of France. By 1762, the Irish foot regiments were once again sent to northern France to get ready for yet another project of invasion, which was ultimately halted by the peace treaty of Paris. The Irish were sent to their usual garrison duties.

With the return of peace, the threat of military reforms reappeared, compounded with a loss of influence at court after the deaths of Lord Thomond in 1761 and Charles Edouard de Rothe in 1766, two senior Irish officers who had led Irishmen to victory in the 1740s. In 1766, Rothe's Regiment became Roscommon's after Robert Dillon, the ninth Earl of Roscommon, became its colonel. It was transferred in 1770 to the Comte de Walsh–Serrant, an Irishman whose family had helped Charles Edward Stuart back in 1745 and who had obtained lands in western France that granted them nobility. Walsh had been Roscommon's acting colonel since the late 1760s.[37] Franco-Irish relations were also marred by the scandal attached to Thomas Arthur Lally Tollendal's loss of France's Indian possessions. Lally, who had distinguished himself at Fontenoy and served as colonel of his own regiment, was accused of having betrayed the king's interests in the subcontinent, of being corrupted and eventually of having lost Pondicherry to the British. Although he had resisted against thousands of troops with barely 800 men, the disastrous state of the colony and his abrasive nature had earned him very little sympathy from his colleagues who immediately turned on him once the French prisoners arrived in Britain. This led to a lengthy trial in France ending with his conviction. While he was interrogated by a French court, Lally complained that 'after fifty years of service and five wounds received while serving France, he was treated like the vilest criminal'. His plea did not save this *lieutenant général des armées du roi* and *grand croix de l'ordre de Saint Louis* who was sentenced to death and executed almost immediately after having tried to commit suicide.[38]

By 1765, the head of France's government under Louis XV, the Duc de Choiseul, conducted a major overhaul of the entire French forces as the army desperately needed change. In a report directly written to the French monarch, Choiseul, though himself surrounded by Irish nobles, openly expressed the idea that the Irish Brigade was part of a military tradition which was had outlived its usefulness:

> The five Irish battalions that are kept in your service are, strictly speaking, just a pension that you give to Irish families established in France ever since 1688 [sic] as the regiments are nothing, but Your Majesty's greatness had to retain officers whose fathers had served France with distinction.[39]

In the late 1760s, Bulkeley's and Roscommon's participated in the expedition sent to conquer Corsica. They both arrived in the island in March 1769 with the second French expeditionary corps under the Comte de Vaux, with Roscommon's returning to mainland France in September 1770 and Bulkeley's in January 1771. They were both stationed at Corte.[40]

---

37 François Edme de Montandre–Lonchamps, *Etat militaire de la France pour l'année 1768* (Paris: Guyllin, 1768), p.265.
38 *Le nouvelliste suisse, historique, politique, litéraire* [sic] *et amusant* (Neuchâtel: imprimerie des éditeurs, 1766), May 1766, pp.125–129.
39 *Journal des Savants*, 'Mémoire de Monsieur de Choiseul remis au Roi en 1765' (Paris: Imprimerie nationale, April 1881), p.250.
40 *Mercure Historique et politique*, vol.167, p.517.

During that period, Irish officers produced documents about the importance of maintaining the Brigade.[41] Walsh–Serrant produced a report summarising the exploits of the Brigade in order to convince Versailles not to disband the Irish troops, emphasising the importance of the Franco–Irish friendship ('and thus politics wants to see France, the protector of the Irish in the previous century, keeping them as friends for ever'). Most importantly, Walsh–Serrant warned his potential readers of the type of message sent to Britain and to the Irish living in France every time an Irish regiment was disbanded:

> Every variation in the Irish troops in his service, and particularly the disbandment of the cadets, the disbandment of the Fitzjames regiment, and the reduction of the number of officers, has given rise to prejudices which the English Government has used; and it is well known how much and with what expressions it has made this reform in the Irish infantry and the destruction of the Fitzjames regiment resound throughout the British dominions ... The slightest diminution of the opportunities which would remain for the officers of this nation by a new reform or incorporation would complete the extinction of the credit of the subsisting Irish regiments – a new form would even be destructive of this credit in that it would be a discouraging example of instability and would carry to Germany the service of a nation which is already so welcome and so famous there.[42]

The 1760s and 1770s saw a rise in the publication of documents related to the status of the Irish serving France. As Irish regiments faced mergers, the Irish, the French and the British all tried to take ownership of the Brigade, with Britain openly courting the idea of an Irish Brigade serving under its flag. Private correspondence proved this with, for instance, Frederick Hervey's visit to France in the late 1760s. Hervey, who was to become the Church of Ireland's Lord Bishop of Derry, took advantage of his Grand Tour to visit Irish seminars in France to probe what Irish Catholics living on the continent thought about a new type of oath he had devised which would foster religious and, ultimately, political tolerance. Hervey believed that Catholics living in France and those living in Ireland did not have a 'common way of thinking both in point of politicks [sic] and religion'. His memorandum also mentioned a visit to an Irish regiment in France where a significant change in attitudes both among the Irish officers and a representative of the Church of Ireland could be noticed:

> The second voyage confirm'd the discoveries of the first: He pursued them even to the Island of Oleron where he found an entire Regiment of Irish officers: Among the whole corps there were about two dissenting voices... It may not be unreasonable to add that at the eve of a French war such a law would be doubly usefull – as it would deprive that nation of the only troop which could make an Irish invasion practicable and as it would furnish our Sovereign with a set of officers perfectly well acquainted with the enemy's Coasts and Sea Ports.[43]

---

41   NLI, Positive Microfilm n°155, 1771.
42   ADML, Walsh–Serrant Archives, bundle n°47.
43   PRONI, D1514/1/5/8, Draft memorandum by the Bishop of Derry on a Catholic oath, December 1770.

In parallel, in 1770, a French journalist exiled in Brussels called Augustin-Pierre Damiens de Gomicourt wrote in a newspaper published in Paris – which had a fictitious London address – that Britain considered officially recruiting Catholic soldiers for its armies. He then quoted an Irishman of his acquaintance:

> Never, said an Irishman to me yesterday, could the English do better. The late Duke of Cumberland experienced their bravery at the Battle of Fontenoy. It was in part to the Irish brigades that France owed its victory. Let the English take a disinterested look at all the countries of Europe, they will see the case made for my brave compatriots. The best officers of the troops of the [Holy Roman] Empire are Irish: there are at least twelve of them among the best generals of the King of Spain. What prejudice blinded the English when they thought that they could be betrayed by the Irish Catholics, especially by those who, having remained in their homeland, have property, wives and children who are always answerable for their loyalty! Besides, should not the British Ministry feel that by admitting Roman Catholics into the military of the nation, it would weaken that of our neighbours? For how many of those who are now in its service would hasten to abandon it, if they were assured of finding employment in that of their homeland![44]

In parallel, French authors started to echo the image of the Irish Brigade spread by members of the Irish community as early as the 1760s in geography and history manuals but still retained Voltaire's opinion of their worth outside of their native island:

> It has been remarked that the soldiers of this Nation are brave, indeed well-disciplined in foreign countries, but quite different in their own. The Irish troops in the service of France, have acquired much glory on the various occasions on which they have been employed.[45]
>
> The Irish brigade showed enough, that the country, which [a soldier] adopts, always becomes dearer to the soldier than the one where he was born.[46]

As we saw, the Jacobite community living in France also helped reshape the memory of Irishmen who had come to France in the 1690s, once again attacking Voltaire as the main antagonist of an Irish-driven narrative. The memoirs of the Duke of Berwick, the natural born son of James II, were reprinted in 1778 and explained away the lacklustre fighting spirit found in Irish troops during the Williamite war:

> It appears, from Maréchal de Berwick's account and from the above relation of the Battle of the Boyne, that all those who have hitherto given us general or particular

---

44 Auguste Pierre Damiens de Gomicourt, *L'Observateur Français à Londres* (Paris: Lacombe, 1770), pp.102–104

45 Jean–Joseph Expilly, *Description historique–géographique des Isles britanniques ou des royaumes d'Angleterre, d'Ecosse et d'Irlande* (Paris: Prault, 1759), p.387.

46 Claude–Louis–Michel de Sacy, *L'honneur françois, ou histoire des vertus et des exploits de notre nation, depuis l'établissement de la monarchie jusqu'à nos jours* (Paris: Costard, 1772), p.450.

histories of the Irish war, have copied very imperfect and faulty Memoirs: M. de Voltaire, among others, when he wrote: King James did not help in Ireland the secours sent by Louis XIV … The French fought at the Battle of the Boyne: the Irish fled. Their King James having not appeared during the fight, either at the head of the French or of the Irish, was the first one to withdraw. … If the Irish proved to be better soldiers in France and Spain than they appeared in that war, would it not be because King James' troops were newly raised, half-armed and poorly disciplined ones?[47]

Despite Voltaire being once again fiercely criticised regarding his vision of Irish history, he was also instrumental in the rehabilitation campaign of Lally led by the colonel's illegitimate son, Trophime Gérard Lally. It is worth noting that this was one of the philosopher's last combats for justice, though he was far more cautious than his young protégé regarding the late colonel's temperament.[48] Young Lally wrote a book in 1779 which turned his father and the Brigade into heroes by revealing how the colonel had, on his own initiative, reconnoitred the positions around Fontenoy before the battle and had persuaded de Saxe to change his plans to win against Cumberland. The Irish Brigade was obviously at the centre of this new narrative:

As for the details of that famous day, they are all known. It is known that the Irish troops decided the victory; that several of their Chiefs sealed it with their blood; that my father had the good fortune to make a special contribution. We know the advice he gave in the most critical moment, which he first communicated to Lord Clare & the Normandy Brigade, which he then addressed to one of the Generals running from rank to rank, & which was adopted. It has not been forgotten that he addressed his soldiers: "Remember that it is not only against the enemies of France, that it is against your own enemies that you are going to fight, & do not fire a shot, until you have the point of your bayonets on their bellies". It is known that at once he charged, while singing, on the flank of this famous English column, and penetrated so far, that a great number of his Soldiers were killed by the French Carabiniers'. [49]

On the other side of the Channel, English popular culture had started to change the general opinion regarding Irish military men in Britain, with for example a character like Major O'Flaherty created by Richard Cumberland in two of his plays in 1771 and 1785. O'Flaherty represented both the international careers of Irishmen fighting abroad and a newly found respect for the Irish as one of his most quoted lines underlined his noble nature:

---

47   Jacques Fitz–James, Duc de Berwick, *Mémoires du Maréchal de Berwick, écrits par lui–même* (Paris: Moutard, 1778), pp.460 and 462.
48   Voltaire, *Précis du Siècle De Louis XV* (Geneva: Publisher unknown, 1769), vol.12, p.364.
49   Trophime Gérard de Marquis Lally Tollendal, *Mémoire produit au Conseil d'État du Roi par Trophime–Gérard, comte de Lally-Tollendal … dans l'instance en cassation de l'arrêt du 6 mai 1766, qui a condamné à mort le feu comte de Lally son père* (Rouen: Besongne, 1779), p.33.

Look, friend, I am a soldier, this is not the livery of a knave; I am an Irishman, honey, mine is not the country of dishonour.[50]

Thirty years after Fontenoy, most of the soldiers and officers of the Brigade who had served at the battle were either dead or retirees, but if the new captains and lieutenants still retained a close link to the Irish community, the rank and file replacements rarely did. The 1770s witnessed a larger number of non-Irish soldiers joining the ranks. Health certificates written by the regiment's surgeon offer an idea of the changes that occurred at the end of the Ancien Régime:

We, the undersigned surgeon major of the Military Hospital of Avesnes and surgeon major of the Irish Infantry Regiment of Dillon, certify that the named Antoine Prudeaux, sergeant in MacDermott's company in the said regiment, is suffering from variable rheumatic pains which are felt more particularly during changes in the weather, which, combined with his advanced age, make it absolutely impossible for him to continue to serve the King. In witness whereof, we gave the present certificate made in Avesnes this 11 August 1784.[51]

A few years before the Revolution, if an Irish officer wanted to obtain a pension for himself or guarantee his children's future by securing a position in a military academy, he had to prove that his aristocratic roots went back four generations. Not being able to rely on connections in Ireland made things more difficult, but a form of solidarity existed among Irish officers:

I send you a certificate to get it signed from four of the most antient officers of the regiment who know my family best in order to present it to court to have my poor children whom I am not able to provide with an education worthy of a good gentleman, placed in the military school by the favour of a friend in great credit with the minister to whom it was represented beforehand that it was very hard for an Irish gentleman to provide himself with his titles of nobility from home, especially when they were not rich, the minister returned for answer that an attestation of nobility signed by four of the most ancient officers of the regiment should be sufficient and he should take upon himself to give it the force it required to be received without any further difficulty.[52]

This type of situation had its limits. When obtaining new commissions in the slimmed down regiments proved harder, personal connections trumped any form of Irish solidarity. Thus, Walsh in his personal correspondence underlined the fact that 'We [the Irish] are not a corps when it comes to favours, only when it comes to the service in the army'.[53] He did

50   Richard Cumberland, *The West Indian* (Belfast: Henry and Robert Joy, 1774), p.64.
51   Note from Surgeon–Major Legros 8 November 1784, Florida State University Digital library, French Revolution Collection on Camille Desmoulins, Lucile Duplesis and Arthur Dillon 1702-1876, at <http://purl.flvc.org/fcla/dt/3180314>, accessed August 2022.
52   ADN, Correspondance du Capitaine Dillon à Cambrai (circa 1778).
53   ADML, Walsh–SerrantArchives, bundle n°187.

regularly travel to Versailles to meet either ministers or the king himself to plead for his cause, emphasising the fact that he did it wearing his uniform, a quasi-obligation for any officer in the last decades of Ancien Régime France. Yet Walsh's faced a dire situation. In 1775, the four regiments of Bulkeley, Clare, Dillon and Berwick were merged into two regiments, each composed of two battalions.[54] Dillon's joined Bulkeley's and retained its name, Berwick's was merged into Clare's but kept Berwick's as a regimental name. The same year, Walsh's was supposed to be merged with the Régiment Royal Italien, and then with the Légion du Dauphiné which had welcomed the remains of the French Corsican regiment. This new unit consisted of mounted dragoons and foot soldiers. All the Irish, Scottish and English soldiers originally belonging to Walsh's were supposed to join the two remaining units of the Brigade, while all other nationals were redirected towards the Légion.[55] Walsh–Serrant was furious at the new organisation and the fact that the other Irish units had been preserved ('As you might believe this does make me retch knowing that my regiment is being passed over by Berwick's').[56] Official steps were taken by the Irish military community to halt the proceedings, as shown in this extract from a personal letter written by Count de Walsh–Serrant to his father:

> It has come to my attention, my dear Papa, that the brave and loyal countrymen, chevalier de Nugent, Redmond, Wall, D'arcy, Drummont, Gordon, chaplain of the Scots, O'Neill chaplain of the Irish, had a petition sent and delivered directly to the King signed by them telling the Conseil d'Etat about how our incorporation was harmful to the political existence of the Brigade and they have enclosed my two memoranda which I gave to one of those mentioned above and all the other documents that were made on this subject. As for me, I shall personally write to the King. This is where our business is at the moment, that is to say in the gravest danger.[57]

In the end, after a gruelling campaign of lobbying at Versailles, Walsh's regiment was reinstated:

> 14 May 1776.
> In the name of the KING.
> HIS MAJESTY, deeming it useful for the good of his service, to create a third regiment of Irish Infantry, both to give to this nation marks of the satisfaction which It has of its services, and to place the Officers who were previously incorporated in the Légion du Dauphiné, or placed at the continuation of the two regiments of Irish Infantry preserved in virtue of the Ordinance of April 26, 1775, ordered & orders as follows:

---

54 *Ordonnance du roi, concernant les régimens [sic] d'infanterie irlandoise* (Paris, Imprimerie royale, 1775), 26 April 1775.
55 *Ordonnance royale pour mettre la Légion corse sur le pied des autres légions françoises, sous le nom de Légion du Dauphiné* (Paris, Imprimerie royale, 1775), 26 April 1775.
56 ADML, Walsh Private Archives, bundle n°189.
57 ADML, Walsh Private Archives, bundle n°187.

ARTICLE ONE.

THIS regiment will bear the name of Walsh, His Majesty having indeed agreed to accept count Walsh-Serrant to command it; & will be composed, as well in Officers as in Under-Officers, Grenadiers, Fusiliers & Chasseurs, as it was regulated by the Ordinance of last March, concerning the French & foreign Infantry. The said regiment will resume the rank it occupied in the Infantry, after the regiment of Berwick, formerly Clare, and before that of Enghien.

... It is His Majesty's intention that in the future only Irish, English or Foreign soldiers will be admitted within its ranks: very expressly forbidding to the Officers of the said regiment to receive in it, under any conditions, any man born in Alsace, in Lorraine or in any other province of his dominions; enjoining the Commissioners of War who will have the police of the said regiment, thereafter, to have issued on the spot, absolute leave to those who are born in any province of his kingdom, & who are engaged in the said regiment; declaring, in such a case, His Majesty, any engagement contracted by a man of these provinces, null & void, unless he is originally English, Scottish or Irish.[58]

As these twists and turns undermined the already strained Franco–Irish relations, there were rumours in the summer of 1777 that officers from the Irish Brigade were willing to abandon their loyalty to France to join the British and protect Ireland:

The Bishop of Cloyne [Charles Agar] told me in confidence that offers have been made on the other side, by all the Irish officers in the French and foreign service, to throw up their commissions, enter into the King's service and raise 10,000 Catholics for the defence of Ireland, and it is said that Lord Kenmare [a Catholic Lord] has the promise of a regiment.[59]

In December of 1778, Walsh's two battalions went through Quimper in Brittany where they were inspected by the *commissaire des guerres* in order to receive the proper amount of food for the whole regiment. The unit amounted to 1,104 men with 176 absentees (1 deserter, 4 dead, 168 sent elsewhere by orders of the local French governor). The names of the captains were definitely linked to Ireland (O'Dunne, Galmoy, O'Neill, Sarsfield, Roche), but the patronyms of the soldiers registered as sick in the town's hospital, with Francis Joseph Bouquet, Michel Stadelbauer or Dieu Donné Delvaud, to name but a few, clearly show that at that stage Irish and even British men had disappeared almost altogether from the ranks.[60] The same could be said about Berwick's where, in Conway's company alone, two soldiers, Johannes Schmitz and Jacob Simon, both clearly German subjects, were respectively reported as sick in the hospitals of Paimbœuf and Vannes. Another proof of the lack of Irish soldiers around that time lies in the names of deserters from the Brigade, like Denis Martin Maufrais who was judged for such an offense in April 1778. A native of the French village of Bleury, near Chartres, Grenadier

---

58 *Ordonnance du roi, portant création d'un régiment d'infanterie irlandoise* (Paris: Imprimerie royale, 1776), 14 May 1776, pp.1,2 and 4.
59 PRONI, D2707/A/2/3/45, 17 August 1777.
60 ADIV, C943 1778–1780, Régiment de Walsh, Etat des hommes dudit régiment à l'hôpital du lieu le 19 décembre 1779.

Maufrais was sentenced to eight years of prison for having failed to return from a furlough as prescribed. The official document was signed by the regiment's officers, all of whom had Irish origins.[61] Out of the 10 court martials held in Brittany by Dillon's regiment for the year 1778, none involved soldiers hailing from the British Isles but rather included men from Lorraine, Luxembourg, and what is nowadays Belgium and the western German states.

As part of the royal army, the Irish Brigade was involved in the French efforts to help the American insurgents against Britain's forces in North America and the West Indies. Walsh's and Dillon's both served in the taking of Grenada in July 1779, in which the Irish troops made a frontal assault on the British positions, and the siege of Savannah in the autumn of the same year. Two picquets from Walsh's served onboard the *Bonhomme Richard*, a former French merchant ship turned into a man-of-war in the service of the American Continental Navy. Edward Stack, an Irish lieutenant, led a detachment of soldiers who poured musket fire and grenades onto the deck of the HMS *Serapis*. Ultimately this naval combat led to the sinking of the *Bonhomme Richard*, but the British ship was itself captured by the Americans.[62] Though units from the Irish Brigade participated in the siege of Savannah, they did not prove as decisive as they had been back in 1745. Men from both Dillon's and Walsh's attacked the British forces encamped at Savannah as part of a three-pronged attack that ultimately failed, with, for Dillon's alone, a ratio of one casualty out of every three men actually involved in the fighting.[63] After Edouard Dillon, the regiment's second or deputy colonel, led the difficult retreat through the swamps surrounding the city, he was rewarded with a full colonelcy. This enraged other French officers who, though they recognised he had 'followed the traces marked by his family's blood', bitterly complained that his premature advancement went against normal practices within the Bourbon army.[64]

After the war, the Brigade once again struggled to maintain its recruitments. Documents held in the Walsh family archives in western France give a summary of the number of men enlisted in Walsh's in 1784. They specify that the three main recruiting depots for that unit were situated in Strasbourg, Liege and Paris.[65] Another document, listing promotions and punishments within the regiment, showed that by 1786 its rank and file were unquestionably filled with a mixture of German, Belgian and French soldiers. The differences in the spellings of the names when compared with Vincennes's archives make identifying individuals quite difficult, but not impossible:

> Galmoy's Waylau [Whylane Daniel] drummer 15 canings for getting in a fist fight with Pitschly.
> Barry's Pitschly [Pidjely André] drummer 15 canings for getting in a fist fight with Waylau.
> Barry's Hogan [Hogan Patrick] 50 canings in 2 settings for letting three of his comrades scale up the ramparts to slip out.

---

61   ADIV, C1107, 1760–1787, courts martial from Dillon's Regiment.
62   David Murphy, *The Irish Brigades, 1685–2006, A gazetteer of Irish military service, past and present* (Dublin: Four Courts Press, 2007), p.14.
63   W.S. Murphy, 'The Irish Brigade of France at the Siege of Savannah, 1779', *The Georgia Historical Quarterly*, vol.38, No.4, December, 1954, p.316.
64   ADML, Walsh–Serrant Archives, bundle n°189.
65   ADML, Walsh–Serrant Archives, bundle n°47, 1 September 1784.

Labie [Laby Jean Baptiste] 50 canings for having scaled the ramparts.
Vosterpan [Vostrepen François] 25 canings for the same.
Albrecht [Albrechts Jakobus] 25 canings for the same.[66]

By 1786, Walsh's received 132 men from the Régiment de Salm Salm who had no ties to Ireland and were, according to an official report kept by the Irish colonel, exercised for eight days to be taught 'the words of command', since officers in the Brigade used 'the English language'.[67] Yet the same Irish regiment still boasted enough young Irishmen in its ranks to fill vacant officer commissions in the late 1780s.[68] Though the French military hierarchical system specified that seniority prevailed over any other factor, Irish officers were willing to waive that right to benefit one of their own, either to please a higher-up patron or to recognise the importance of a particular member of the community:

> I, Jacques Tobin, provided with a *cadet-gentilhomme* letter on the 1st of June 1779 and second lieutenant on the 25th of May 1780, willingly consent and accept to give Laurent O'Riordan the rank I have above him given to me by the 12th July 1784 decree and agree to see him achieving the rank of second lieutenant before me.[69]

In September 1787, Walsh's had 1,110 men. It had lost 22 men (one deserter, 13 reformed, four dismissed and four struck off from the lists) and still had 27 men listed as 'absentees' as they were recruiting for that unit.[70] The regiment had a total of 173,687 *Livres* in its coffers. Up until June 1789, members of the Irish community tried to join the Brigade as officers, as did a man called O'Daly: 'Alexandre Claude Louis O'Daly of Douglas, aged 31, served ten years, ten months and twelve days in the Gendarmerie from which he received a certificate and has been ever since a volunteer in the Irish Brigade'.[71]

By 1789, all three remaining Irish regiments were led by *Maréchaux de camp propriétaires*, meaning their colonels both held the rank of a general officer in the French army – the equivalent of that of a major general – and possessed their own regiments. In the mid–1780s, the Irish Brigade continued its nomadic existence between different localities situated for the most part in northern and western France. In 1784, Dillon's was in Avesnes, south-east of Lille, Walsh's was stationed in the Norman town of Blay and Berwick's served on the island of Oléron off the city of Rochefort on the Atlantic coast.[72] By 1788, Dillon's was at Calais and Berwick's in Boulogne.[73] In 1788, Walsh's was at first in Brittany before being sent to the Isle de France (Mauritius) in the Indian Ocean.[74]

---

66   ADML, Walsh–Serrant Archives, bundle n°47 and SHD, matriculation registers from the infantry regiment of 'Walsh irlandais' (1755–1786) GR 1 Yc 1065.
67   ADML, Walsh–Serrant Archives, bundle n°47.
68   ADML, Walsh–Serrant Archives, bundle n°47.
69   ADML, Walsh–Serrant Archives, bundle n°47. Written on the island of Oléron, 19 February 1786.
70   ADML, Walsh–Serrant Archives, bundle n°47.
71   ADML, Walsh Archives, bundle n°47, *Mémoire pour un brevet de sous–lieutenant*, Bouchain, 19 June 1789.
72   M. de Roussel, *Etat Militaire de la France pour l'année 1784* (Paris: Onfroy, 1784), pp.300, 301 and 307.
73   M. de Roussel, *Etat Militaire de la France pour l'année 1788* (Paris: Onfroy, 1788), pp.278, 280 and 286.
74   Archives Nationales Outre–Mer (ANOM), COL E 390, ark:/61561/up424kemfjgx, Walsh, comte, major du régiment de Walsh à l'île de France, 1788.

Dillon n°90 (1779). Plate n°166 in *Uniformes militaires des troupes françaises sous Louis XVI*. (Musée de l'Armée)

The Irish Brigade and the French Revolution

The events of 1789 broke the military routine of the last years of Ancien Régime France and forced the Irish to choose between their loyalty to the Bourbons and their allegiance towards their adopted motherland. The French immediately resented the presence of foreigners among the royal troops sent to quell the first signs of unrest and fairly soon the Irish Brigade was considered in the same negative light as the Swiss or the German units that had remained loyal to Louis XVI. With the declaration of war against Austria and its allies in 1792 and the death of Louis XVI in 1793, Irish military men began to split into two factions, those willing to defend the French monarchy at all costs and those siding with the new French republic. This tumultuous period offered a third option illustrated by Daniel Charles O'Connell's own choice. As the last commanding officer of the old Irish Brigade, he became one of the first colonels of a new Irish contingent serving London.[75] By the early 1790s, the Irishmen who opted to stay in France gradually lost most of the Jacobite symbols attached to their units whose regimental names were soon replaced by mere numbers. Dillon's became the 87eme Régiment d'Infanterie, Berwick's the 88eme and Walsh's was turned into the 92eme. Caught in the middle of a ferocious duel between Great Britain and France, the Irish saw their fidelities tested as both countries offered military opportunities.

The chaos created by the Revolution affected directly former members of the Irish Brigade. Some Irish officers that had risen in the French military hierarchy joined the new regime. For instance, Arthur Dillon participated in the Estates General of 1789 as a representative of the French colonial interests in the West Indies and became a *lieutenant-général* when the war broke out in 1792.[76] To counter the French perception that foreigners were potential oppressors or traitors, Dillon wrote a long text to the French *Assemblée Nationale* to revive the narrative of a loyal Brigade fighting not just for the Bourbon kings, but for France:

> Few persons are acquainted with the details of these regiments, & we thought it would be useful to place at this moment, before the eyes of the representatives of the nation, the rights which the Irish have to its esteem. It is the unfortunate portion of a brave & faithful people, whom the greatest & most generous nation in the universe can justly be proud of, who come to claim on this day of its justice the confirmation of the honourable title of French citizens, which they have obtained for more than a century by their unfailing fidelity, & by the rivers of blood which they have shed for the country which adopted them ... [The Irish regiments] were, we dare say, invincible phalanxes.[77]

Yet, since Arthur Dillon had close links with Camille Desmoulins and his wife Lucile and was a Frenchman of Irish origins, the Revolutionary Terror saw him as a potential member of the counter-revolution movement. He was guillotined on 13 April 1794.

---

75 John G. Gallagher, *Napoleon's Irish legion*, Carbondale, Southern Illinois University Press, 1993, p. 5.
76 Arthur Dillon, *Lettre du Lieutenant–Général Arthur Dillon au ministre de la guerre* (Paris: Imprimerie nationale, 1792).
77 MKWP, COFLA, Arthur Dillon, *Observations Historiques sur l'origine les services, et l'état civil des officiers irlandois au service de la France* (Paris: Demonville, 1794) pp.2 and 19.

Dillon's cousin, Théobald, became one of the first generals of the young Republic. Sent north to face the Austrians, he was massacred by his own men in Lille following a defeat. Just like his relative, Dillon was still considered as a foreigner who had betrayed France for having ordered a retreat. One eyewitness, a close friend of Dillon's, published a testimony in which he described the chaos that ensued the French rout and how Dillon was brought back to Lille. According to this author, hundreds of men who had not been involved in the fighting against the Austrians attacked the general who was killed by one fatal musket shot. What happened next was even more brutal:

> He was dragged out of the cabriolet, thrown to the ground, his body was stepped on: he was beaten with rifle butts, his body pierced by more than a thousand bayonets; I saw several of them bent in two. He was already being dragged towards the lamppost [to be hanged], and I heard neither words nor groans from him. ... French soldiers, with weapons at the ready, were dancing around their general's corpse they were burning ... Several persons assured me, in such a way that I could not doubt it, that they sent soldiers to carry his legs and parts of his body which the fire had not consumed to other soldiers who guarded the citadel, so that they might have their share of the feast.[78]

The members of the Irish Brigade who joined the Prince de Condé's army in his effort to counter the Revolution were favoured as they represented the elite of the former royal army. Former colonels of the Brigade like Walsh–Serrant and Dillon were thus welcomed by the Comte de la Chapelle as *maréchaux de camp* in the royalist forces gathered in western Germany.[79] In response to a proclamation reaffirming the Brigade's fidelity to the Bourbons, Louis XVI's two brothers, princes Louis Stanislas Xavier de France and Charles Philippe d'Artois – respectively the future Louis XVIII and Charles X – issued an official answer in which the Irish narrative was plain to see:

> LETTER from the Regiment of Berwick to Monsieur and Monseigneur Comte Artois of 23 July 1791.
> The officers, non-commissioned officers, Grenadiers and Soldiers of the Irish Regiment of Berwick, filled with the sentiments of honour and fidelity which are hereditary in them, beg Your Lordships to lay at the feet of the King the devotion which they make of their lives for the support of the royal cause, and the oath to employ with confidence their weapons in the most perilous occasions.

Monsieur's reply to the letter of the Berwick Regiment, 28 July 1791:

> I have received, Gentlemen, with true compassion the letter you have written to me: I will send to the King, as soon as I can, the expression of your feelings for him. I tell you in advance that it will ease his pain, and that he will receive with pleasure from

---

78   Anon., *Relation de l'assassinat de M. Théobald Dillon, Maréchal–de–camp, commis à Lille, le 29 avril 1792, par un témoin oculaire* (Paris: Migneret, 1792), p.7.
79   ADML, Walsh–Serrant Archives, letter from Bingen 28 July 1792.

Theobald Dillon's death. Isaac Cruikshank, 'Gallic Perfidy, or the National Troops Attachment to their General after their Defeat at Tournay' (1792). (Anne S.K. Brown Military Collection)

you the same mark of fidelity that James II received, a hundred years ago, from your forefathers: This double epoch must forever form the motto of the Berwick Regiment and it will henceforth be seen on your flags [Motto of the flags of the Berwick Regiment: 1691 Semper et Ubique Fidelis: 1791], and all faithful subjects will read in it their duty and recognise in it the model they must imitate. As for me, Gentlemen, you ought to be persuaded that the action you have just taken will remain engraved in my soul for ever and that I will consider myself happy every time I can give you proof of what it inspires in me for you.

Signed Louis – Statislas [sic] -Xavier.

Reply from Monseigneur le Comte d'Artois:

Your letter, Gentlemen, is dictated by the same sentiment which guided your conduct: the flags of Berwick are and will always be on the path leading to honour, and we will march at their head. Thus, we shall lead you to the feet of our King, and there we shall renew together the oath which we have never failed to take. The memorable example which you have just given to the French Army will be consecrated by fame, and promises us in advance an assured success. The feelings which you inspire in me, Gentlemen, are engraved in the depths of my heart: I would try in vain to express them indeed; but I hope to prove to you soon that I am worthy of your esteem and your confidence and of the blood from which I come.

Signed Charles Philippe.[80]

Individual courage was still the hallmark of the Brigade. One Irish officer, a man called O'Kane, paid the ultimate price when faced with the Republicans:

One even more odious execution, had outraged the Condéans [royalists exiles]: the lieutenant O'Kane, an Irish gentleman and a former officer in Dillon's regiment, was seriously wounded and had been taken prisoner. Republican hussars discovered him in a thicket, unconscious. They came to take him, placed him on a wagon, tied up like a common criminal, and threw him into one of Wissembourg's prisons. There he was made to appear and a few days later he was taken to some sort of a military tribunal, where he was asked if he was a royalist sympathiser. Mr O'Kane could have invoked his foreign nationality and thus survive; he did not deign to stoop to the slightest argument, and was sentenced to death without any protest on his part. He was taken to the execution ground, and as his wounds prevented him from standing, was placed on a chair. With his arms crossed and his head held high, he faced the fire of the platoon of Paris volunteers, who could not help but admire his bravery.[81]

---

80 The Newberry Library, Chicago, USA, Newberry French Pamphlets Collection, n°4935.
81 René Bittard des Portes, *Histoire de l'armée de Condé* (Paris: Dentu, 1896), p.123.

By the early 1790s, Berwick's barely counted 200 men and soon enough the 'armée de Condé' proved no match when faced with the gigantic forces of the French republic. Yet the Irish Brigade did not disappear entirely.

'A most extraordinary measure':[82] The Irish Brigade in the Service of Britain (1794–1798)

Britain, in a surprising reversal of circumstances, welcomed the former members of the Irish Brigade on its soil to fight the new French regime. Many of these Irishmen had joined the émigré forces in the Légion de Damas or had gone to serve abroad when French revolutionaries threatened their lives, proving that for those who had made that choice, allegiance laid firmly with the forces of conservativism. As early as 1793, the Comte de Walsh-Serrant wrote to the British Prime Minister, William Pitt, offering to recreate the Irish Brigade in the French service, but this time to serve the House of Hanover.[83] This first offer was rejected; other proposals included sending Irish Catholic soldiers to the West Indies to quell slave revolts and counter French manoeuvres in the area. Afterwards, a secret correspondence was established between Walsh–Serrant and the Court of St James about exploiting the insurrectional situation in Vendée. In September 1794, while living in Germany, Walsh–Serrant received a letter in French from the Home Secretary, William Bentinck, Duke of Portland, informing him of the British government's intention of restoring the Brigade:

> The King desires to… give the Catholic subjects of this realm a diligent testimony of his affection and trust has determined to re-establish the troops formerly known under the name of the Irish Brigade and since you were a colonel of one of these regiments composing that corps, His Majesty has ordered me to offer you in this new Brigade the same rank of colonel you enjoyed in the old one. His Majesty's intention is that this Brigade should be now composed of four regiments, three of which he ordered me to offer to the colonels (or their representatives) who commanded the three units that composed the Brigade when it was serving His Most Christian Majesty and the fourth one to Monsieur O'Connell formerly a senior officer in the service of France and most certainly well-known from you and all the Irish gentlemen who served in this corps.

Former officers of the Brigade were supposed to serve and the regiments would be officially part of the British Army. Commissions were not supposed to be sold or bought and Portland explained in great details to Walsh that the regiments no longer belonged to their colonel proprietors and only had an 'annual existence'. The new brigade would be sent 'to serve in His Majesty's West Indian colonies or any other of His Majesty's possessions outside of his two kingdoms of Great-Britain and Ireland as he sees fit'. Recruitment was to take place in Ireland among the Catholic population.

---

82   Francis Plowden, *A Short History of the British Empire in 1794* (Londo: G.G. Robinson, 1795), p.301.
83   See Ciarán McDonnell, 'A "Fair Chance"? The Catholic Irish Brigade in the British Service, 1793–1798', *War in History*, 2016, vol.23(2), pp.150–168.

The Brigade was reborn and still relied on its old networks for its reputation and officering. However, its Ancien Régime's status had dramatically changed, not just in terms of allegiance, but also in the way the regiments were to be organised as armies became national entities rather than private enterprises. Plus, former generals in the French army had to abandon their rank and to accept being reduced to mere colonels in order to be admitted in George III's army, since Catholics in the 1790s were not allowed to reach higher echelons. Surprisingly, the British accepted the idea that once the French revolution had been defeated and the Bourbons had been restored, the Irish Brigade would return to France:

> I have now exposed to you all the circumstances that I deemed necessary to help you determine if you would accept His Majesty's gracious offers, I only have to add that if, after due consideration, it appeared to you more suitable not to avail yourself of them, His Majesty's natural kindness will dispose him to interpret the motives which will have determined you in the most favourable manner, and I can even assure you that in the very case that you accept the proposal which I am charged to make to you, and that the War is over or even during its duration, you will be of the opinion to leave the service of His Majesty and to return to that of His Most Christian Majesty, that you will find the King disposed in the same way to grant you your leave and to consider this measure with his customary kindness.[84]

This decision provoked the ire of British observers. Francis Plowden, an English Catholic who benefited from the Relief Act of 1791, wrote a history of the British Empire in 1795 that tackled the subject of the Revolutionary Wars against France, allowing him to criticise the British government's decision of reviving the Irish Brigade the previous year. Plowden questioned the very notion of allegiance when discussing the promise made by the Duke of Portland of a return of the Brigade to France under a Bourbon rule:

> Can there be a more flattering and honourable reward to the long-tried loyalty of the Irish nation to the reigning family of our beloved Sovereign, than to invite them to risk their lives in a calamitous war, under penalties and disabilities, from which he cannot dispense them, and soothe them with the flattering prospect of retiring into the service and pay of the French Monarch, for the avowed purpose of supporting the claims of the Family of Stuart against his Majesty, to whom they have sworn and proved their allegiance?[85]

Plowden also emphasised the 'inconsistencies' in the official policies applied by Pitt's cabinet regarding Catholic enlistments and advocated putting an end to the Test Act that prevented Catholics from entering the British Army. His book questioned the legitimacy of allowing 'subsidised troops' who had 'ever been signalised in the eyes of all Europe for their intrepidity, spirit and conduct … ready to seal their principles with their blood',[86] fight for Britain

---

84   ADML, Walsh–Serrant Archives, file n°40.
85   Francis Plowden, *A Short History of the British Empire during the year 1794* (London: G.G. and J. Robinson, 1795), pp.306–307.
86   Plowden, *A Short History of the British Empire*, p.302.

when a whole section of the British population was forbidden to do so. Similarly, Plowden estimated that the promises of freedom of worship that were made to the Irish joining this new Irish Brigade would not last beyond the end of the conflict itself, considering that their status would not allow them to benefit from pensions once wounded or retired. Plowden's work was heavily criticised for being partisan by literary reviews of the time, especially since his last argument about the Irish Brigade fighting to keep the Stuart cause alive no longer held any potency with regard to the death of the James III in 1765 and that of Charles Edward Stuart in 1788.[87]

In October 1794, the British government accepted Daniel Charles O'Connell and Henry Dillon's proposal of establishing several Catholic units under the command of former members of the *Brigade Irlandaise*. However, Dillon's enthusiasm in recreating the Brigade was met with caution:

> Sir, I have the honor [sic] of your letter of this day's date, acquainting me with your having taken proper means to obtain a list of the officers who served in the regiment that bore the name of your family, and desiring to know my opinion of a button for the uniform of the Irish Brigade & if you are to be presented to the king on Wednesday the 22nd instant in the uniform of that corps. I cannot, Sir, but applaud your zeal, in having lost no time in endeavouring to restore to the service of their own country the gentlemen of whom you have obtained a list. As to the other two points, I apprehend that nothing can be done with respect to either of them until the gentlemen to whom I had his Majesty's orders to offer the command of the regiments have signified to me their intentions of accepting or declining it.
> I am, etc.
> Written and signed, Portland[88]

Portland doubted the former colonels would be willing to lead these units,[89] but the possibility of meeting George III in the uniform of the newly formed Brigade was a promise he certainly could not make since the British monarch had been the one blocking any measure helping the Catholic cause in the 1790s. Former officers of the French Irish Brigade were interviewed to obtain commissions in the new units and candidates for a colonelcy were rejected.[90] Meanwhile O'Connell clearly used the Brigade's reputation of fierce loyalty to convince the British government that relying on it could ultimately be beneficial to London while Europe was engulfed in the French wars. Pitt's administration finally accepted the scheme, but had to consider the Protestant Ascendancy's reluctance in accepting large numbers of Catholic soldiers serving under Franco–Irish Catholic officers. Parliamentary debates also made recruiting more complicated as the Protestant Dublin Parliament resented the idea of Catholic tenants learning how to use firearms, even if they were sent to fight as far away from their native island as possible. Recruiting men in Ireland also proved quite

---

87 *The Monthly Review*, vol.17, pp.285–286.
88 PRONI, T2905/22/18, Portland to Henry Dillon, 7 October 1794.
89 PRONI, T2905/22/21, Portland to Lord St Helens about the re–constituting the Irish Brigade, 10 October 1794.
90 PRONI, T2905/22/20 and T2905/22/20. 9 and 7 October 1794.

difficult since other possibilities started to appear for young able-bodied Irishmen willing to serve. The British army, navy and locally raised Irish militias after 1793 all competed to obtain the best men, leaving few recruits for the new Brigade.

Ironically, the new regiments were partly raised in Limerick, more than a century after the departure of the first 'Wild Geese'. One document from 1796 details the procedure that had to be followed to get Irishmen into these new units:

> Limerick 15 July 1796
> Recruiting instructions for Ensign W[illiam]. P. Creagh
> Mr Creagh will send a weekly return of the men enlisted by him so that it reaches headquarters before Saturday in the week. He will be allowed for any man payed at Headquarters fifteen pounds, five pounds of which will remain in the colonel's hands till the man passes muster to answer for the remainder of his Bounty his debts or any deficiency in his necessaries will be kept by the colonel if the recruit deserts... No recruit will be approved of if not sound and healthy and in every respect within the king's regulations. None therefore shall be admitted under 5 feet five inches if between 18 & 36 years of age: growing lads when well-made will be received at 5 feet three inches. If any recruit proves to be a deserter and is claimed as such the colonel will allow no more for that man but the sum that he really stands in to Mr Creagh... the men under size and age will not be allowed but from twelve to fourteen pounds.
> Count Walsh–Serrant[91]

Finally, in July 1795, the new Irish Brigade was officially announced. Six new regiments were formed that were to be entirely recruited in Ireland. The names of these units (General Duke Fitz-James' – former Colonel to Berwick's – Colonel Henry Dillon's, General Walsh–Serrant's, Colonel Viscount Walsh's) reflected a direct lineage between the most prestigious regiments serving the Bourbons and the new Brigade, with the remaining two, General James Conway's and General Daniel O'Connell's, were led by former senior officers of the Brigade. The Brigade was supposed to be attached to the Irish Establishment but had to be paid by the English based on 'the number of effective men'.[92] The regiments were scheduled to be ready for embarkation from Ireland by September 1796.

British popular culture revamped Irish stereotypes to remind the general public of their loyalty when faced with an external threat. O'Flaherty reappeared in British theatres as the war against France flared up and was the inspiration for a poem published in 1797 in Ireland in which he reminded the readers of Irish fidelity:

> Oh! by Saint Patrick you are too long-winded,
> Tho' 'pon my soul you're very tender minded,
> Why this palaver, and this fine inditing,
> To teach our Irish boys the art of fighting?

---

91 ADML, Walsh–Serrant Archives, bundle n°189.
92 J. Debrett, *The Parliamentary Register or History of the proceedings and debates of the House of Commons* (London: Debrett, 1796), vol.43, p.443.

Who better far, than beef and claret, love it,
Show but the foe, and we will instant prove it.
As for the ladies, may kind heav'n bless 'em,
And no French frizure ever comb, or dress 'em,
Whilst Dennis arm'd with his old friend shillelah,
In love, or war, will never flinch or fail ye,
And in your cause to his last breath will labour,
With grateful thanks for this support, and favour.[93]

Yet accepting an Irish Brigade recruited exclusively among Catholics still posed many problems. The officers from the old Brigade were not necessarily experienced for the ranks promoted to by O'Connell or Walsh, while political and cultural obstacles made recruiting even more intricate. In the end, three out the six regiments were fused together in order to reach their nominal strengths, the remaining three staying in Ireland to complete their recruiting campaigns. When the French republican fleet appeared off Bantry Bay in 1796, the members of the new Irish Brigade clearly declared their loyalty to the British crown.[94] The lack of medical supplies and trained personnel sent alongside the regiments combined with the West Indies' climate proved fatal to a large number of recruits as soon as they arrived in the Caribbean islands in July 1796.[95] Though quickly reduced in numbers by tropical diseases, the Irish regiments were used to fight against Toussaint Louverture's men in what is now Haiti, suffering relatively few casualties. It is worth noting that, in spite of the dire situation in which these units were placed, the soldiers remained loyal to their commanders with no signs of mutiny,[96] though the relationship between the officers and the men was thought as flawed by British observers:

> It is well known, that the French soldiers at that time, were of a docile disposition and easily disciplined; consequently, they required none of those coercive means to form them into soldiers, or to preserve their military acquirements, which often are indispensably necessary in the British service. It thence followed, that the officers of the regiment were intrusted with the command of men, with whose characters and habits, they were totally unacquainted; and who required a system to be adopted very different to that, in which they had been educated. the men of this regiment, were principally composed of recruits of all ages, constitutions, and characters; and enlisted from the very lowest class of the people in Ireland. it was therefore not likely that these troops, should be reduced to a state of good order, or military uniformity by officers, who in carrying on command had been accustomed to make use of gentle rebukes, slight confinement, or at most, mild corporal punishment.[97]

---

93   Edward M. Mandeville, *Miscelleanous poems* (Waterford: John Veacock, 1798), p.151.
94   Philipp J.C. Elliott–Wright, *The Officers of the Irish Brigade and the British Army, 1789–98* (PhD, University of Leeds, 1997), p.270.
95   William Lempriere, *Practical observations on the diseases of the army in Jamaica* (London: Longman, 1799), vol.1, pp.206–218.
96   Elliott–Wright, *The Officers of the Irish Brigade and the British*, p.268.
97   Lempriere, *Practical observations*, vol.1, pp.206–207.

Between July 1796 and March 1797, two out of five men in the 1st Regiment of the Irish Brigade actually died because of tropical diseases, while half the soldiers of the 3rd Regiment died under similar circumstances.[98] While Conway's, Dillon's and Walsh–Serrant's were quickly losing men, the administration and finances of the Brigade proved immensely difficult to manage. The customary system of regimental agents that existed in the British Army baffled the former French officers who found themselves in financial difficulties once their own intermediary died unexpectedly in the autumn of 1797. There was also the problem of the difference in value between Irish and English pounds sterling.[99] Soon enough, London decided to reduce the regiments without informing directly the Irish colonels. Walsh-Serrant learned from Henry Dillon that the British authorities had made their choice regarding the future of the Brigade when the latter wanted to respond to the solicitations of one of his friends concerning the posting of a young ensign within one of the regiments.

Dillon received a letter from the headquarters spelling the future of the Brigade:

Horse Guards, 31st October 1797
Sir,
Having lay before Field Marshal the Duke of York your letter of the 31st instant, I am commanded to inform you in answer that his Majesty's pleasure been [sic] that the different regiments of the Irish Brigade should be forthwith reduced. It is not in his Royal Highness power to comply with your demand in favour of Mr Rivals,

The two Franco-Irish officers immediately wrote a letter to Henry Dundas, the Secretary at War, to complain about this situation:

[We] beg leave to represent to you that the 2nd and 3rd regiments who are at Santo Domingo [are] nine hundred or [a] thousand effective men together and who by a former order which must be executed ere now were to be drafted and to form between themselves only one regiment at the choice of the commander in chief there after inspection and the state in which they will stand respectively at the inspection are in very good order with the most able officers and in the greatest alacrity to serve in that country as in any other. To reduce the said regiments immediately would be a loss to the service.[100]

Nevertheless, by the end of 1797, the three battalions did have to merge together into a single unit, a move mirrored by the three battalions stationed in Ireland before they were shipped off to Nova Scotia in late 1797:

MacMahon says to me in his letter 28 September last that he was then with seven companies under his command that the regiment was 712 me strong including all the three companies who were detached in the bay of Honduras, that general White had ordered all the detachments of colonel Dillon's regiment to be collected from

98   Lempriere, *Pratical observations*, vol.1, pp.210 and 214.
99   ADML, Walsh–Serrant Archives, bundle n°189, letter from Walsh-Serrant, 1800?.
100 ADML, Walsh–Serrant Archives, Correspondence, bundle n°189.

the outpost the next day at Port au Prince to be drafted in our regiment what will make it very near to 200 men stronger.[101]

The year 1798 marked the official end of the new Irish Brigade whose remains were dispersed within other British units while its officers were put on half-pay. In keeping with a form of tradition in the French Irish Brigade, former officers of the newly raised troops of 1794–1798 found employment in other units in Britain. Some even returned to France and achieved remarkable careers, though little is known of the fate of individual soldiers. In the end, the Irish Brigade established to serve the House of Hanover did not prove itself on the battlefield for lack of financial resources and men. Though this sort of situation was the lot of many newly raised corps at the time, it should be noted that two major obstacles combined to stop the experiment: the Protestant Ascendancy's hostility to the emergence of a Catholic force and the fact that the Brigade's own founders had lost any illusions about London's willingness to capitalise on the military past of the French-led Brigade. British authorities obviously could not use it due to the political and cultural dangers attached to such an historical connection.

The 1796 and 1798 expeditions

The French Revolution had inspired Irish Presbyterians and Anglicans to form the Society of United Irishmen in 1791, an association dedicated to political reform in Ireland which was outlawed by British authorities when its republican and insurrectionist ideals were made more apparent. The enthusiasm of Theobald Wolfe Tone, one of their founders and their representative in Paris, persuaded the French to intervene directly in Ireland. Eager to avenge the émigré attempt at Quiberon Bay in 1795, the French Directory established new plans to land troops on the island. But misunderstandings between these uneasy allies quickly made the situation more complicated.[102] Tone wrote two memoranda in favour of immediate intervention to help create an independent Irish republic and the French appointed General Hoche to lead such an operation. From the spring of 1796 two other Irishmen, Arthur O'Connor and Lord Edward Fitzgerald, wrote reports which were carefully consulted by the French republican authorities. Surprisingly, these remained intent on helping the Stuarts reconquer Ireland, but fairly quickly Republican ideals replaced Jacobite ambitions.[103] Yet Paris awaited a successful rising on the island before it committed any troops to the operation, while the United Irishmen wanted the French to land before any revolt could actually take place.[104] With tens of thousands of Frenchmen gathered for the occasion, this was the most serious effort ever attempted, but the United Irishmen advo-

---

101 ADML, Walsh–Serrant Archives, Correspondence, bundle n°181, London, 28 November 1797.
102 See Marianne Elliott, *Partners in Revolution, the United Irishmen and France* (New Haven: Yale University Press, 1982, 1990).
103 Charles Petrie, 'Ireland in Spanish and French Strategy, 1558–1815', *The Irish Sword*, vol.6, No.24, 1964, p.161.
104 Sylvie Kleinman, 'Tone and the French expeditions to Ireland', Pierre Serna et al. (eds.), *Republics at war, 1776–1840* (Basingstoke: Palgrave MacMillan, 2013), p.91.

cated a landing in Galway and were unaware that the French had chosen Bantry Bay in the south of the island. In truth, the Royal Navy ultimately failed to stop the French from trying to reach Ireland, and local loyalist forces were left alone to defend the island. Ironically enough, lack of resources in a French navy depleted by the Revolution, contrary winds and the decision not to land troops made by Hoche's second-in-command, the future *Maréchal* Grouchy, all contributed to stop the project in its tracks.

A few months later, the idea of forming a unit made up of Irish prisoners and deserters in France was revived, but there were few candidates found in Breton and Norman prisons, much to Wolfe Tone's disappointment. He had imagined a predominantly green hussar's uniform for a regiment of mounted scouts who would have served once a foothold had been successfully secured in Ireland, thus leaving aside the traditional red of Jacobite units. Similarly, the proposed colours under which the Irish were to rally once the invasion succeeded was a green banner adorned with a harp topped by a Phrygian or Liberty cap and surrounded by shamrocks inscribed with the motto 'Erin Go Bragh' ('Ireland for ever').[105] It was based on a suggestion made to the French legislature by the United Irishmen themselves in a message sent to Paris on 14 July 1798.

There were still hopes of forming the 1er Régiment de Volontaires Irlandais before embarking from Brest, but the risk of revealing the invasion plan and the official ban on foreign troops in the Republican army put an end to the matter. Hoche's own death in September 1797 dealt a fatal blow to any serious effort at an expedition. Bonaparte, tempted for a moment by a British adventure, finally chose to go to Egypt, much to the French Directory's relief. General Humbert, who had served under Hoche, led a second expedition from La Rochelle in 1798 which, however, also ended in failure, except for the 'races of Castlebar' where 6,000 Irish militia men fled before the modest French forces barely numbering 800. Contrary to the rumours spread in Ireland at the time, Humbert had not landed with 10,000 men, but with only a few veterans from the Italian campaigns. He did, however, bring with him large quantities of weapons, ammunition and uniforms. A few British officers had been drafted in 1796 under General Harty to supervise volunteers once in Ireland, an idea that was revived two years later.

Relations between the French republicans and their Irish counterparts were far from friendly, though the Directory's instructions were filled with romantic notions about the amicable relations between the two nations:

> You must also maintain the most exact discipline among your troops, so that they serve as an example for the Irish troops. Do tell your comrades-in-arms that they must consider the Irish as brothers, as citizens persecuted by a ferocious government, enemy of all free men, and that, as they fight for the same cause, they must be united by the same bonds and the same feelings.[106]

---

105 Bibliothèque des Champs Libres, Rennes, *Hommage des Irlandais Unis de *** [sic] au corps législatif de la République française* (Paris: Imprimerie Nationale, Messidor An VI, 1 July 1798).

106 Archives de la marine, Campagnes, vol.4, 1798, quoted in Edouard Guillon, *La France & l'Irlande pendant la Révolution: Hoche et Humbert, d'après les documents inédits des archives de France et d'Irlande* (Paris: Armand Colin, 1888), p.369.

Instead of being joined by United Irishmen from the cities as planned, the French who actually landed in Ireland found themselves supported by peasants from County Mayo. Contemporary accounts emphasised the way the French openly despised these Irishmen who seemed more interested in the prospect of new clothes and free food than in the liberation of their island. It is true that such negative accounts published after the expedition were influenced by the tensions that existed between former French members of the expedition.[107] One of them, *Capitaine* Jobit, was even openly opposed to Humbert and described the people of Connaught in unfriendly terms.[108] The Irish, for their part, refused to submit to harsh French discipline. However, the United Irishmen continued to portray France as a loyal ally, with any negative view of its intervention related to a form of propaganda spread by agents working for Dublin Castle.[109] In the end, Humbert was defeated at Ballinamuck (County Longford) in September 1798. In a manner reminiscent of what had happened in 1746, his own soldiers were made prisoners of war while his Irish allies were summarily executed,[110] leaving bitter memories in Irish folklore.[111]

The Légion Irlandaise (1803–1815)

After the strategic failure of his Egyptian expedition, Napoléon Bonaparte returned to France in 1799 and, for a time, turned his attention towards Ireland. The short peace brought about by the Treaty of Amiens of 1802 had damaged the relations between the United Irishmen and France since Paris was willing to exchange Irish republicans against French *émigrés* living in the British Isles. But as soon as war was rekindled in 1803, secret contacts between French authorities and Irish rebels exiled on the continent were renewed. Thomas-Addis Emmet, elder brother of Robert Emmet, a United Irishman who had vainly tried to rise against the British in 1803, became one of these conspirators. New projects involving French troops sent to attack Britain appeared on a regular basis up until the disastrous Russian campaign of 1812, and yet landings in Ireland were by then barely considered as a diversionary operation in an all-out assault against the British Isles. In the early years of the nineteenth century, the relationships between Ireland and France were tense as the republic, soon to become an Empire, clearly pursued its own interests rather than Ireland's. Even Robert Emmet had actually warned his countrymen against France in his famous gallows speech:

> Were the French to come as invaders or enemies, uninvited by the wishes of the people, I should oppose them to the utmost of my strength. Yes! my countrymen,

107 John Cooney, 'Two French Revolutionary Soldiers in Rebel Ireland', *Etudes Irlandaises*, n°13–2, 1988, pp.101–07.
108 Jean–Louis Jobit, *Journal de l'expédition d'Irlande,* Nuala Costello, *Analecta Hibernica*, N°11, 1941, p.19.
109 Ultan Gillen, 'Le Directoire et le Républicanisme Irlandais', In Pierre Serna, *Les Républiques sœurs* (Paris: PUR, 2009), pp.327–28.
110 See Pierre Joannon, 'Les soldats perdus de l'armée d'Irlande', *Revue historique des armées*, n°253, 2008.
111 See Guy Beiner, *Remembering the year of the French, Irish folk history and Social Memory* (Madison: Wisconsin, 2007).

I should advise you to meet them upon the beach with a sword in one hand, and a torch in the other. I would meet them with all the destructive fury of war. I would animate my countrymen to immolate them in their boats, before they had contaminated the soil of my country. If they succeeded in landing, and if forced to retire before superior discipline, I would dispute every inch of ground, burn every blade of grass, and the last entrenchment of liberty should be my grave.[112]

Bonaparte, by then First Consul, showed little enthusiasm at the idea of recreating an Irish unit within the French army;[113] eventually, however, a Légion Irlandaise, an Irish Legion, was officially formed on 31 August 1803, four months after hostilities had resumed with Britain and after Emmet's failed rebellion. The new unit was based on the same principle as other foreign troops fighting for France at the time, such as the Polish legions of the 1790s and early 1800s. Simultaneously, Irish refugees who had escaped their native island after the 1798 and 1803 rebellions proved unsuccessful started to arrive in France.[114] They were first gathered and organised in Brest in the winter of 1803 under the titular orders of the *adjudant général* MacSheehy who had been living on the continent since the end of the eighteenth century.[115] The small unit, at first barely more than 30 men, was then increased to a paper strength of five companies of 120 men each. They received uniforms based on the one worn by the French light infantry of the time, but in a green colour instead of the traditional blue, and were presented a green flag adorned with Irish harps on 5 June 1804. One side was decorated with the motto 'Freedom of conscience and Irish Independence' while the reverse one had a dedication 'From the First Consul to the United Irishmen'. The colours' finial at the time was a simple spearhead.

The Irish remained in the Breton town of Morlaix for several months before moving to other parts of Brittany. Soon, they found their provincial posting rather tedious and numerous brawls began to erupt within the ranks or with the local population. Relations among members of the Légion Irlandaise were difficult since republican-minded United Irishmen carried on feuds initiated on the island. This situation was made even more complex when former members of the Irish Brigade belonging to the aristocracy started to join up as these two groups did not agree on the future of Ireland in the event of London's defeat.[116]

Nevertheless, the idea that the Irish belonged to a form of elite still seemed relevant in France. When the Empire was officially declared in December 1804 and the French army received its new regimental colours with eagles added as finials, the only foreign unit on which the same honour was bestowed was the Légion Irlandaise. The new standard had one side decorated with the inscription 'Napoleon I, Emperor of the French, to the Irish Legion'

112 R.R. Madden, *The Life and Times of Robert Emmet* (New York: Haverty, 1868) pp.188–189.
113 Nicholas Dunne–Lynch, 'La Légion Irlandaise au service de la France, 1803–1815', in Nathalie Genet–Rouffiac, David Murphy (ed.), *Franco–Irish military connections, 1590–1945* (Dublin: Four Courts Press, 2009), pp.189–218.
114 Trevor Parkhill, 'The Wild Geese of 1798, émigrés of the Rebellion', *The Irish Sword*, Vol.19, No.2, 2003, pp.118–135,
115 SHD, Sub-series GR XH 14–16 and XH 16b–d.
116 Brian O Cuiv, 'The Wearing of the Green', *Studia Hibernica*, No.17/18, pp.107–119.

while the reverse was adorned with the motto 'Independence of Ireland', a clear acknowl-edgement of the republican ideals of 1798 and 1803.[117] The ambivalence between repub-lican and imperial ambitions led to renewed difficulties among the Irish that sometimes amounted to duels. One of them proved deadly when an oath of allegiance to Napoleon had to be taken by all the members of the Légion. The death of one of the Irish officers cost MacSheehy his post and when the Légion Irlandaise appeared in an official French publica-tion in 1805, the names of the senior officers were no longer entirely linked to the island as an Italian *chef de bataillon* had to be appointed to discipline the Irish:

LÉGION IRLANDAISE, In Brest's Camp
General Staff

PETERZZOLI	Battalion commander
Blac-Kwell [sic]	Battalion commander
Gaillot	Quartermaster
Couasnon (captain)	Major
Mendeville (captain)	Major
Raymond	Surgeon and deputy major
Saint-Leger	Under deputy major
Larippe	Under deputy major

Captains.

Fitz-Henry. Masterson. Galhagher. Macguire. Thyrell. Aherne. Corbet (W.). O'Meara. Derry. Corbet (T.). Ware. Barker. Lawless. Mac-Sheehy (P.). Markey. Mac-Neven. Sweeny. Mauann. Tennent. Omealy. Mac-Sheehy (B). Lacy. Dowdall. Burgen (P.)

Lieutenants.

Powell. Fitz-Henry (J.). Burgess. Reac. Allen. Gibbons. Dupouget. Martin. Mac-Mahon.

Oreilly. Cummins. Mougenot. Morrison. Murray. Byrne. Saint-Leger.

Second-Lieutenants.

Lambert. Reilly. Kelly. Parrotte, Egar. Landey (R.). Macdermotte. Gibbons, Landey (P.).

Scheridan. Thyroux. Osmont. Gillmer, Amorand. Douling Cambell. Swenton. Devreux. Reynolds.[118]

Most of the officers lacked military experience as they often owed their positions to the political supports they claimed to have back in Ireland and their purported ability to use these in order to recruit men in case of a successful landing.[119] These captains and lieuten-ants were supposed to be promoted to higher ranks once in Ireland and as soon as their recruiting promises had been fulfilled. To achieve this goal, Paris accepted some flexibility

---

117 John G. Gallaher, *Napoleon's Irish Legion* (Carbondale: Southern Illinois University Press, 1993), p.41.

118 Antoine–Julien–Pierre Palasne de Champeaux, *État militaire de l'Empire français pour l'an treize: dédié à l'Empereur, d'après son autorisation* (Paris: Leblanc, 1805), pp.104–105.

119 John G. Gallaher, 'Irish Patriot and Napoleonic Soldier: William Lawless', *The Irish Sword*, vol.18, No.73, Summer 1992, p.257.

in the internal organisation of the unit, but French senior officers were far from impressed by these Irish troops. One of their senior supervisors, François-Xavier Donzelot, wrote about his reservations regarding their actual military value:

> If, on the other hand, this corps does not fulfil the functions for which it was set up, will the French government form a national regiment ... similar to those which existed before the Revolution? If this is the government's intention, then there should be strict guidelines and admission to the Légion should correlate with this aim.[120]

The unit was part of the massive invasion of the British Isles planned for the following months. In the spring of 1805, reports had already appeared in the British press of a new expedition directed against Britain as a *régiment irlandais* was rumoured to be onboard the fleet ready to embark from Brest. The news was immediately repeated in several French official newspapers.[121] However, the defeat of the Franco-Spanish fleet at Trafalgar and the Austrian and Russian threat to the East put a stop to this project. The Légion was stationed at Alençon in Normandy for six months before being sent to Berlin after the 1806 campaign.[122] Now that invading Ireland was no longer a viable project, the unit had to grow from a small battalion to a full regiment which implied enlisting more men. The French tried to reinforce its ranks with former Irish rebels who had been sent to Prussia after 1798 and were captured after the Battle of Jena in late 1806. But besides the 200 Irishmen thus recruited, the vast majority of these new *légionnaires* were Prussian or Polish nationals. Besides, most of the Irish found in Prussia had actually served as sailors in the Royal Navy and did not necessarily make good infantrymen.

By 1807, one battalion had been sent to the Netherlands to protect Antwerp from British interventions:

> Notices received from the Baltic tell us that the enemy is gathering a considerable force there. The first Irish battalion has arrived in Antwerp; it is about 1200 strong. This beautiful body of troops wears a green uniform and helmets decorated with large feathers. Their flag has a golden harp with an eagle.[123]

It stayed there for several months at Flushing (nowadays Vlissingen), suffering from the effects of a local disease akin to malaria. The Légion also found itself in renewed financial difficulties and desertion rates augmented accordingly. In 1808, a second battalion was formed to be sent to Spain. To fill up its ranks, several attempts at incorporating Irish prisoners of war in a manner reminiscent of what had happened in the 1740s and 1750s occurred, but difficulties immediately emerged. According to one of the few official

120 Gallaher, *Napoleon's Irish Legion*, p.58.
121 *Journal de Paris*, n°228, 8 May 1805, p.1, *Journal des Débats et Décrets*, 7 May 1805, p.2, *Courrier des Spectacles*, 7 May 1805, n°3004, p.7.
122 *Gazette de France*, n°3235, Saturday 29 November 1806, p.1.
123 *Journal de l'Empire*, 8 August 1807, p.1. The helmets mentioned here were actually shakos.

newspapers published in the French Empire, the tense relationships between Irish, Scottish and English soldiers among those recruits inevitably led to violence:

> There are few Frenchmen in the auxiliary corps of the English army; there are many Englishmen in the French auxiliary corps. The Irish regiments today number up to 3,000 Englishmen or Scotsmen who have been recruited from the prisoners' depots; we do not count in this number the Irish prisoners who have taken service in France; they are Catholics and the most just indignation animates them against the intolerant government which oppresses their country. The animosity which exists between the English and the Irish is such that we have been obliged to remove 1,800 English or Scots recruited in the depots of the prisoners of war from the corps where they had been joined with the Irish, because they were fighting every day.[124]

Another explanation for letting the English and Scottish go was that Napoleon thought the very existence of the Légion offered London the dangerous possibility of refusing prisoner cartels, a feeling he expressed in 1810 in one of his letters to his Minister for War, Henri-Jacques Clarke, himself the son of a former *aide–major* in the Irish Brigade before the Revolution and an advocate of the Légion:

> I have been informed that English prisoners are being enlisted for the Légion Irlandaise. Give orders that all those that were hitherto enlisted be sent back among the prisoners and that none shall be enlisted in the future. I would rather have them remain prisoners because they answer for my prisoners in England and, besides, most of them desert.[125]

Nevertheless, Clarke managed to convince the Emperor to keep an Irish unit within the French *Grande Armée*. The minister was himself quite convinced by the narrative that made the Légion the direct descendent of the 1691 refugees:

> To sustain the existence of this corps … I had carefully gathered into it the United Irishmen and the former supporters of the Stuarts. This corps is a sort of scarecrow for England, which has always been worried about it; and this is all that remains of this army that came to France after the capitulation of Limerick![126]

Both battalions were fused together on the 13 April 1809 to form the Régiment Irlandais. The unit was then engaged in the Peninsular War where many British prisoners pretended to be Irish so they could avoid captivity in France, only to desert as soon as possible afterwards:

---

124 *Journal de l'Empire* (Paris: Imprimerie de Lenormant, 18 August 1810), p.1.
125 Napoléon 1er, *Correspondance de Napoléon 1er* (Paris: Imprimerie impériale, 1856), vol.20, p.553, Napoléon to Clarke, 14 July 1810.
126 Eugène Fieffé, *Histoire de Troupes étrangères au service de France* (Paris: Librairie Militaire, 1854), vol.2, p.185.

ALEX WILLS soldier in the 1st Regiment of the Irish Legion, aged 21 years, was born at Sunderland, served three years and a half to the sea out of that Port, was taken in the Active of Sunderland, Win. Canne Master, by the Le Prospers Privateer of Dieppe, and carried into Tripole [stc] was Prisoner there eight days, and three days in Dieppe, was then marched to Sanlouis and continued-there a Prisoner for four years and nine months — made two attempts to escape but was taken both times—latterly was fifty days on Bread and Water, and that he was Induced to enter into the Irish Legion Solely from the Perishing and Starving condition he was in — he remained in the Corps till taken at the surrender of Flushing.[127]

Between 1809 and 1810, when Napoleon's European power was at its highest, the Régiment Irlandais had a total of five battalions, with two stationed in Holland while a third one was created to serve in Spain alongside the other two battalions already fighting in the Peninsula.[128] In August of that year, the British attacked Walcheren and forced the French forces there to surrender after a fierce resistance. Though most of the officers of the Régiment Irlandais were former Irish rebels, they were considered as French prisoners of war and, as such, were not treated as proscribed men. A few officers managed to escape and one of them, William Lawless, saved the eagle from falling into British hands, which earned him the rank of *chef de bataillon* as well as Napoleon's personal esteem. Yet the vast majority of the men in these troops were former deserters from other foreign units who had little to no relationship to Ireland's military past in the service of France.[129] Even so, despite the widely disparate origins of these troops, one French general, Jean Thomières, delivered a speech in front the Régiment Irlandais right before the Battle of Bussaco in 1810, reminding them of the role played by the Irish Brigade at Fontenoy 65 years earlier, proving that the rewriting of Irish military history had succeeded in France as well and was part of the military tradition of an Irish unit serving that country, regardless of its political, historical or ethnic affiliations.[130] Sometime earlier, it had performed extremely well during the siege of the Spanish town of Astorga where one of its drummers continued to beat the charge even after losing both legs. The poor man received a *Légion d'honneur* for his bravery.

Subsequently, the battalions in Spain merged and participated in the retreat from Portugal before being sent to Holland to recuperate. By 1811, the Régiment Irlandais had become the 3eme Régiment Étranger, though Clarke insisted on keeping the adjective 'Irish' attached to the name of the unit, a habit adopted by most of its officers. Due to Clarke's personal connection to the Brigade, he felt personally committed to the preservation of this unit and kept a watchful eye on the careers of the senior officers he put in place, often against the advice of other Irish officers and the French military hierarchy. For instance, the minister

---

127 P.R.O. Adm. Med. Misc., 61, cited in *Notes and Queries*, January 9, 1926, p.25.
128 Victor Belhomme, *Histoire de l'Infanterie en France* (Paris: Charles Lavauzelle, 1893–1902), vol.4, p.438.
129 Jacqueline Reiter, "'Day after day adds to our miseries": The private diary of a staff officer on the Walcheren expedition, 1809: Part 2', *Journal of the Society for Army Historical Research*, vol.96, No.387 (Winter 2018), p.246.
130 Miles Byrne, Fanny Byrne, *Memoirs of Miles Byrne, chef de bataillon in the service of France* (Paris: Bossange, 1863), vol.1, p.109.

appointed Daniel O'Meara, a former member of the Irish Brigade, to lead a battalion of the Régiment Irlandais in Spain due to family connections among Irish descendants in France, a decision clearly reminiscent of eighteenth-century practices. This irked the former United Irishmen still present in the unit who were firm believers in more meritocratic promotions.

Between 1811 and 1812, Napoleon was aware that London's full attention was focused on Spain at the expense of Ireland's own defences and seriously considered reviving a Franco-Irish military cooperation, but since the links between the exiled United Irishmen in France and those who had remained in Ireland or had fled to America had been severed in 1803, any hope of instigating a new rebellion in the island vanished. By the end of the Napoleonic Wars, the regiment listed only five per cent of its rank and file as Irish, with United Irishmen constituting a minority within a minority while descendants from Jacobite families remained relatively relevant. For instance, Théobald Dillon's son became one of its battalion commanders at the end of 1811, and officers with Irish familial connections were still commissioned in French regiments formerly belonging to the Brigade.

At the end of Napoleon's reign, the 3eme Régiment Étranger proved its worth in the German campaign of 1813 when it was almost wiped out, its eagle being saved by an Irish officer named Hugh Ware. The Légion performed relatively well compared to other foreign regiments serving in Napoleon's pan-European forces, but contrary to what had happened with the Irish Brigade, it did not provide a major victory for the French that would have cemented its reputation and protected it from being disbanded. The unit was recreated on 9 June 1815 when the Cent Jours brought back Napoleon to Paris under the title 7eme Régiment Étranger, but it did not participate in the final campaign against the Seventh Coalition or at the Battle of Waterloo. Eventually, the Légion was officially disbanded on 20 September of 1815 by Louis XVIII who had returned to Paris for the second time, much to the bitterness of the Irish veterans.[131] With the exception of individual enlistments of Irishmen in the French Foreign Legion in later decades of the nineteenth century, this was the end of the military connection between France and Ireland.

By the 1760s onwards, the Irish regiments no longer represented a valid threat against Britain and were thus treated in France as a mere military tradition within the royal army. Nevertheless, a certain mystique surrounding the Brigade started to emerge. Though the French to a certain extent failed to understand the specificity of the Irish community, Britain saw an opportunity in appropriating the regiments' memory. Ireland and the Irish became central components of the British war machine set up against Napoleon's France in the early nineteenth century. By definition, British popular culture could no longer depict the Irish as a threat since they composed up to 30 percent of the forces engaged against the French, even if British military authorities still struggled with the lack of discipline displayed by Irish troops. The exchange of militias from Ireland to Britain and from Scotland, Wales or England to the sister kingdom visibly improved the reputation of Irish soldiers in the eyes of the public. This could be seen in publications centred around British military history like Major Charles James' *Military Dictionary* which, in the 1810s, not only painted the Brigade

---

131 Thomas Bartlett, 'Last flight of the Wild Geese? Bonaparte's Irish Legion, 1803–1815' in Thomas O'Connor & Mary Ann Lyons (ed.), *Irish Communities in early–modern Europe* (Dublin: Four Courts Press, 2006), pp.160–171.

in glowing terms but also saluted its role on the field of Fontenoy, a defeat rarely mentioned in British military histories of the day:

> Irish Brigade, (*la Brigade Irlandaise*, Fr.) A body of men who followed the fortunes of James II and were formed into regiments under the monarchy of France, in whose service they uniformly distinguished themselves, particularly at the Battle of Fontenoy. when the British, having originally gained the day, were finally defeated by their intrepidity.[132]

By the 1810s onwards, official British Army recruitment instructions insisted that officers should no longer question men being drafted about their religion:

> Commanding Officers of Regiments are to be particularly attentive, that no Soldier professing the Roman Catholic Religion shall be subject to any punishment for not attending the Divine Worship of the Church of England, and that every such Soldier be at full liberty to attend the Worship of Almighty God according to the Forms prescribed by his Religion, when Military Duty does not interfere.[133]

By the late 1880s, English historians cited the Irish Brigade as instrumental in the French victory of the previous century, quoting both Henry Grattan, an Irish politician from the ruling Anglo-Irish Protestant class, and a supposed reflection by George II whose origin cannot be traced to any reliable eighteenth century source but does appear in Francis Plowden's history of Ireland published eighty years prior.[134] As the nineteenth century was ending, Irish regiments had become a fixture of the British Army and had proved immensely useful in conquering and protecting the Empire:

> Amongst the most gallant troops of the French army was the Irish Brigade. This force, consisting of some five Fontenoy. regiments, was composed of Irish exiles, Jacobites to a man, and full of deadly hostility against England and the English Government. A portion of this brigade had in the earlier part of the battle helped to defend Antoine against the Dutch. The remainder had been comparatively inactive, and on account of their freshness were chosen to head the final charge on the English and Hanoverian column. The Irish Brigade is said to have advanced to the tune of "The White Cockade". This is the badge at the same time of the House of Stuart and of the House of Bourbon, which befriended the Stuarts. Shouting in their own language, "Remember Limerick and Saxon treachery," the exiles rushed upon the English column, which contained many of their own kin. There was all the fury of civil war in this deadly struggle on foreign soil. This was the charge

---

132   Charles James, *An Universal Military Dictionary, in English and French* (London: Egerton, 1816), fourth edition, p.406.

133   Henry Calvert, Adjutant General's office, Horse Guards, *General Regulations and Orders for the Army* (London: Clowes, 1811), p.84.

134   Francis Plowden, *An historical review of the State of Ireland from the invasion of that country under Henry II to its union with Great Britain* (London: Egerton, 1803), Vol.1, p.291.

which decided the fortune of the day, and it is with truth that in later days a great Irish orator (Grattan) remarked, "We met our own laws at Fontenoy. The victorious troops of England were stopped in their career of triumph by the Irish Brigade, which the folly of the penal laws had shut out from the ranks of the British army. King George is said on hearing of the Irish bravery to have exclaimed, "Cursed be the laws which deprive me of such subjects!"[135]

---

135 Edward Ellis Morris, *The Early Hanoverians* (London: Longmans, 1886), p.138.

Conclusion: 'History changed by a bard'[1]

> We fought for the royal Stuarts that reneged us against the Williamite and they betrayed us.
> We gave our best blood to France and Spain, the Wild Geese. Fontenoy eh?
> ...but what did we get for it?[2]

Though the nineteenth century was essentially shaped by Britain's political, military, economic and cultural clout, it was marked in Ireland itself by a strong desire to rewrite history, especially when military matters were concerned. Europe saw a sharp rise in the publications of nationalistic narratives alongside military memoirs devoted to the dynastic conflicts of the eighteenth century and the Napoleonic era, and Irish personalities like Daniel O'Connell, a Catholic lawyer who pushed for the religious emancipation of his co-religionists, called for Irish writers to step forward and publish their own version of the past. Incidentally, O'Connell's uncle had been one of the last colonels of the French Irish Brigade and served as one of the first military leaders of the one formed by the British in the 1790s. As the Jacobite defeat of 1691 had deprived the Irish Catholic community of what it perceived as a meaningful place in history, the Irish Brigade and its exploits in the service of France embodied everything that was needed to provide the island with relatively recent military glory. Though O'Connell always emphasised that his desire for repealing the 1801 Act of Union had to rely on peaceful meetings and lawful actions, his speeches often referred to the Battles of Cremona and Fontenoy as perfect examples of what could happen again, should the Irish decided to unite their efforts against Britain. These not-so-veiled threats were so common in the 1830s and 1840s and O'Connell and his supporters so eager to see the Irish as the best soldiers in the world that it was even parodied by *Punch*. At the time of the Liberator's arrest, the magazine imagined what Queen Victoria would say on a visit to the jailed agitator:

> Don't talk too much about killing and eating us: don't lead poor hungry fellows on to fancy they can do it. The Irish are strong men, and won every battle that ever was fought. That is very well. From Fontenoy upwards, we give them all to you. I have no objection to think that Cæsar's Tenth Legion came out of Tipperary; and that it was

---

1   'History changed by a bard', from the 'The Battle of Fontenoy', a review of William Joseph Corbet's poem read by J.M. Bellew, *The Shamrock*, Saturday, 13 January 1872.
2   James Joyce, *Ulysses* (Oxford: Oxford University Press, 1998), p.316.

three hundred of the O'Gradys who kept the pass of Thermopylæ. Nevertheless, have no more of that talk about bullying John Bull.[3]

As the first centenary of the Battle of Fontenoy loomed in the mid-1840s, antiquarians, writers and historians started to produce more work centred on the Brigade. Young Ireland, a nationalist movement of young intellectuals led by Thomas Davis, John Blake Dillon and Charles Gavan Duffy, thought that O'Connell's approach to autonomy was not radical enough and relied on a glorified Irish past to achieve their dream of independence. They encouraged and gathered such publications in their newspaper, *The Nation*, which soon collected poems and essays referring directly to the Brigade and the role of the Irish in military history. The Young Irelanders also turned to a publisher called James Duffy in order to spread throughout the country their low–priced books dedicated to Irish history and literature where Davis' poems on Fontenoy and the Brigade were central pieces.[4] Meanwhile, a Catholic author like Matthew O'Conor, who had already saluted the Brigade in a previous history of Ireland published in 1813,[5] went even further in his posthumous work which was entirely devoted to Irish military history.[6] Duffy also published reprints of Charles Forman's pamphlet from the early eighteenth century.[7]

Once O'Conor died, another Irish historian, James Cornelius O'Callaghan, took up his mantle. Duffy published his *Green Book*, a collection of essays centred on Irish history in which this Irish lawyer emphasised the importance of Irish Catholics in not just foreign but also domestic military histories.[8] In 1847, his editing work on the *Macarie Excidium*, a Jacobite narrative of the war of 1689–1691 originally written in Latin, was also focused on making sure the Battles of the Boyne and Aughrim were not entirely claimed by the Protestant Ascendancy. In a letter to the *Nation*, the lawyer wanted to 'coffin' the 'revivals' of Irish history as seen by 'men of anti-Catholic notions'.[9] His political and historical *magnum opus* took him more than 25 years to write, but his *History of the Irish Brigades* failed to find a publisher in Ireland, in spite of the growing demand for a comprehensive work on the subject. His book was finally made available thanks to a Scottish publishing house in the early 1870s and explored in excruciating details every single unit and personality attached to the Brigade. Though considered a major source on the topic, O'Callaghan's propensity to indulge in long meandering footnotes made reading his material more complicated.[10]

Yet O'Callaghan's work cemented the idea that the Irish Brigade proved Britain was not invincible and that a glorious military past could be the sign of a successful Irish political

3   *Punch, or the London Charivari* (London: Strand, 1844), vol.6 & 7, p.248.
4   Thomas Davis, *The Poems of Thomas Davis: Now First Collected: with Notes and Historical Illustrations* (Dublin: J. Duffy, 1846), 232 pages.
5   Matthew O'Conor, *The History of the Irish Catholics from the Settlement in 1691: With a View of the State of Ireland from the Invasion by Henry II to the Revolution* (Dublin: Stockdale, 1813), vol.1, p.230.
6   O'Conor, *Military History of the Irish Nation*.
7   Charles Forman, *A Defence of the Courage, Honor, and Loyalty of the Irish Nation* (Dublin: Duffy, 1844).
8   John Cornelius O'Callaghan, *The Green Book, or Gleanings from the Writing–desk of a Literary Agitator* (Dublin: Duffy, 1845).
9   *The Irish Monthly*, vol.18, p.417.
10 O'Callaghan, *History of the Irish Brigades in the Service of France*.

future away from London. A few years after O'Callaghan's death, an Irish nationalist who took refuge in France because of his political ideas, John Patrick Leonard, translated Arthur Dillon's speech in front of the *Assemblée Nationale* during the French Revolution, reinforcing once again the posthumous reputation of the Brigade.[11] Irish Nationalist newspapers throughout the nineteenth century regularly reprinted in their columns anecdotes and poetical works about Irish military achievements in the service of the Bourbons while artists, called elocutionists, recited poems and ballads about Fontenoy accompanied by stirring music. Their regular tours around Ireland, Britain and America transformed the Brigade's major figures and battles into household names.

During the American Civil War, the creation of an Irish Brigade was clearly inspired by the exploits of its eighteenth-century European ancestor with a motto referring to 11 May 1745 clearly displayed in New York during one of its first parades.[12] Meanwhile, in France, the presence of the Irish in the French army was treated as a mere historical curiosity and the victory at Fontenoy did not enjoy the same historical legacy. Historians and historical painters' production in the nineteenth century most readily centred on the Revolutionary and Napoleonic periods rather than on the last years of the Ancien Régime. Artists specialising in historical paintings like Horace Vernet or Ernest Meissonier both gave their version of the Battle of Fontenoy in which the French army, de Saxe and Louis XV were the main protagonists. In these thoroughly-researched displays of historic military uniforms, the Irish were nowhere to be seen. As the battle itself slowly faded in the background of history, some French authors rejected the idea that the Irish had won the day for France,[13] but the 11 May 1745 never became more than an anecdote in French history books with Voltaire's imagined dialogue between Lord Charles Hay and *Capitaine* d'Anterroches mentioned above. The episode was used by the republican French school system to distance the new regime from that of the French monarchy' supposed disdain for the lives of its servants.

For the British, the presence of Irish soldiers in their official military history still posed a problem, even after a century of Irish soldiers loyally serving the crown. Military historians from the late nineteenth century like John William Fortescue would criticise the lack of discipline displayed by the Irish in the Peninsular War under Wellington and still saw the Irish Brigade as the epitome of a traitorous behaviour that could not resist proper British discipline:

> The Irish Brigade, which consisted of six battalions, was made up not of Irish only but of Scots and English also, desperate characters who went into action with a rope round their necks, and would fight like devils. Yet, even in this second attack the British carried their advance as far as in the first, the perfection of their fire discipline enabling them to beat back even the Irish brigade for a time.[14]

---

11   J. P. Leonard, *Historical notes on the services of the Irish officers in the French army: addressed to the National Assembly* ([Reprod.]) / by general Arthur Dillon; transl. from the French by J. P. Leonard (Dublin: Duffy, 1870s?).

12   Russ, A. Pritchard Jr., *The Irish Brigade: A Pictorial History of the Famed Civil War Fighters* (New York: Skyhorse, 2020).

13   Duc de Broglie, *La Journée de Fontenoy* (Paris: Paul Reveilhac, 1897).

14   John William Fortescue, *A History of the British Army* (London: MacMillan & Company, 1899), vol.2, p.118.

As the Boer War broke out at the very end of the nineteenth century, it illustrated again the ambivalence of the Irish attitude towards Britain's forces. A minority of Irish colonists living in South Africa joined so called 'Irish Brigades' in the service of the Boer republics while a large number of British troops sent against them came from Ireland. The island had multiplied gestures of good will in favour of fighting the war on behalf of Britain and, in the end, an Irish regiment was added to the Foot Guards in 1900 as a reward.

Between the French slowly forgetting any foreign help in their Second Hundred Years War against London and the British presenting the presence of Irish troops at Fontenoy as proof of their own military superiority, Irish nationalists felt the need to reaffirm the Irishness of the Brigade. In the early years of the twentieth century, the Irish Literary Society, eager to pursue the Irish cultural revival of the preceding decades, gathered enough interest and money from the Irish diaspora in New York, London and Dublin to set up a memorial commemorating the presence of the Brigade at Fontenoy. One of the Society's members, Barry O'Brien, wrote a booklet on the battle in which he mentioned two interesting anecdotes about the Irish involvement in the battle. According to him, while visiting the battlefield in 1905, he met an Englishman living in Belgium during the Boer War who learned about the 1745 battle and 'seemed to be [relieved]' when he discovered that Irishmen were the ones who had defeated Cumberland, saying: 'Well, it was some of ourselves, at all events, who beat us'.[15] O'Brien's own version of the battle included a story that could only inspire nationalist feelings. During a lull in the fighting between the Irish Brigade and the British regiments, one Irishman called Anthony Macdonough stepped out of the ranks to meet his opposite number from the British lines. Macdonough overpowered his adversary and brought him back to the Irish lines as a prisoner.[16] This episode was never mentioned before 1905 but obviously impressed people's imagination since the Society started to organise visits to the Belgian village which rapidly turned into semi regular pilgrimages. On the first of July 1907, a Celtic cross paid for by individual donations was inaugurated in Fontenoy itself where it still stands today.

By the time the First World War broke out, a moderate Irish nationalist like John Redmond could propose to Lord Kitchener the creation of an Irish Brigade directly referring the one that fought for France between 1691 and 1791:

> We have a right however to claim that Irish recruits for the Expeditionary Force should be kept together as units, officered as far as possible by Irishmen, composed if possible, of county battalions, to form, in fact, an 'Irish Brigade,' so that Ireland may gain national credit for their deeds, and feel, like other communities of the Empire, that she too has contributed an army bearing her name in this historic struggle.[17]

Meanwhile, Roger Casement, a radical nationalist, unsuccessfully tried to raise an Irish Brigade that would have served the German Empire during the war. Eventually, Redmond's

---

15   Richard Barry O'Brien, *In Memory of Fontenoy* (London: Irish Literary Society, 1905), p.11.
16   O'Brien, *In Memory of Fontenoy*, p.28.
17   PRONI, D1327/21/11, Statement by John Redmond, leader of the Irish Parliamentary Party, *The Freeman's Journal*, 17 September 1914.

volunteers joined the 16th (Irish) Division which fought valiantly throughout the Great War and found itself, in a weird twist of fate, near the Belgian town of Fontenoy when the hostilities officially ended on 11 November 1918.[18]

The archives of the Walsh–Serrant family contain a rare map of the British Isles on which several wax stains left by candles are still visible today. How many nights were spent pouring over every detail to either piece together the old estates lost after the Jacobite defeat or to prepare yet another pro-Stuart expedition will never be known, but it is obvious from the surviving documents left in these records and elsewhere in France that the members of the Irish community exiled on the continent did their utmost to make sure the memory of the Irish Brigade would endure. Their efforts were rewarded beyond their own expectations and though the Brigade never fulfilled its destiny as a weapon against Hanoverian Britain, it acquired a reputation for gallantry and nobility which still resonates today thanks to them and thanks to nineteenth century historians. Such an achievement perfectly illustrates how being on the losing side of a conflict is no preclusion for (re)writing history.

---

18   Thomas Bartlett, Keith Jeffery (eds.), *A Military History of Ireland* (Cambridge: Cambridge University Press, 1996), p.20.

Bibliography

Primary Sources

French Archives

Archives Départementales d'Indre et Loire (ADIL)
    ADIL, archives civiles, Canton d'Azay-le-Rideau, série E suppl. 5 (GG.5).
Archives Départementales d'Ille et Vilaine (ADIV)
    ADIV, Fonds Bourde de la Rogerie, 5J 72.
    ADIV, C943 1778-1780, Walsh's regiment, 'Status of the men in said regiment now in hospital, 19 December 1779'.
    ADIV, C1107, 1760-1787, Court martials in Dillon's regiment.
    ADIV, 1F 1204, Affaires militaires.
    ADIV, 8B550.
    ADIV, C1173, 'Etat des dispositions des troupes sur les vaisseaux du Roy et de la compagnie des Indes ci après', novembre 1756.
    ADIV, C3815, official marching orders, 1758, 1759.
Archives Départementales Loire-Atlantique (ADLA)
    ADLA, 1J art. 266, Paroisse Saint Nicolas, B.M.S., Grosse 45, folio 9, Grosse 27, fol.52, Grosse 28, fol. 3, Grosse 32, fol.17.
Archives Départementales Maine et Loire (ADML)
    ADML, Walsh-Serrant Archives, Correspondence, bundles n°40, 47, 181, 187, 189.
Archives Départementales du Nord (ADN)
    ADN, Série 9 B 276 175.
    ADN, Parlement de Flandres, série 8 B, affaire Barrett, 1730.
Archives Municipales d'Angers (AMA)
    AMA, EE 11, pp.111, 112, 115, 116.
    AMA, BB99, folio 70.
Archives du Ministère des Affaires Etrangères (AMAE)
    AMAE *Suppléments Correspondance politique*, Documents Divers, 1676-1696.
    AMAE, *Correspondance politique*, pamphlet inciting desertion dating from 1693 (article 271 in volume 272).
    AMAE, *Correspondance politique*. Traité de paix entre la France et l'Angleterre conclu à Ryswick le 20 septembre 1697 (Paris, 1697), article IV, pp.172–173.
Archives Municipales de Marseille (AMM)
    AMM Series EE 127/2, affaires militaires, 13 February 1756.
Archives Municipales de Reims (AMR)
    AMR Fonds Tarbé, carton xv, n° 293, *Relation anonyme de la bataille de Malplaquet, rédigée au camp de Ruesne le 13 septembre 1709 par un militaire qui servit à l'aile gauche de l'armée française.*

Archives Municipales de Troyes (AMT)
AMT, Anon., *Essai épique sur les Irlandois, dédié à son altesse sérénissime, Eduard Stuard [sic] Prince de Galles* (no known publisher, no date).
Archives Nationales Outre–Mer (ANOM)
ANOM, COL E 390, ark:/61561/up424kemfjgx, Walsh, comte, major du régiment de Walsh à l'île de France, 1788.
Bibliothèque des Champs Libres, Rennes
Hommage des Irlandais Unis de *** [sic] au corps législatif de la République française (Paris, Imprimerie Nationale, Messidor An VI, 1 July 1798).
Bibliothèque Nationale de France (BNF)
BNF, Département des Manuscrits, réf. Français 7666, Louis de Courcillon, abbé de Dangeau, *Journal des bienfaits du Roi*, vol. 9, February 1690.
BNF, Département des Manuscrits. réf. Français 22710, Louis de Courcillon, abbé de Dangeau, *Collection de l'abbé Dangeau sur l'état de la France au temps de Louis XIV*. Series CLXX foreign regiments – Irish regiments 1690-1704.
Service Historique de la Défense (SHD)
SHD Louvois to Bouridal, 11 May 1690, D.G. (Dépôt de la Guerre) n°960.
SHD, A1 1896, n°255.
SHD, Archives administratives, Section Ancienne, Dossiers personnels, Ancien Régime, Brennan; Jeanne Creagh; O'Connor; Colomb O'Donnell, Jean; Thomas Hackett, Thomas; Skiddy.
SHD, Archives administratives, Section Ancienne, infanterie, régiments réformés ou incorporés avant 1715, série XB 1 (p.249), régiment de Fitzgerald.
SHD, Archives de la guerre, document copied by Mrs Kerney Walsh, O'Fiaich Library. *Estat des noms et service des officiers tant en pied que réformé du régiment irlandois de Fitzgerald au camp de Moscolino [sic] ce 6 juin 1705.*
SHD, manuscript MR-2061 – 139. *Relation de la bataille de Fontenoy, gagnée par le Roy le 11 may 1745*, M. le Maréchal comte de Saxe commandant sous les ordres de Sa Majesté.
SHD, *Mémoire sur les catholiques irlandais*, série 75, n°173.
SHD, A1 vol. 1081, Lettres des commissaires des guerres, folio n°174.
SHD, A1 vol. 1896, folio n°255.
SHD, correspondance générale de la guerre, A1, vol. 1612, "mémoire d'un officier irlandois pour le recrutement d'un grand nombre d'Irlandois"
SHD, GR1 Yc 271, légion de Conflans, 1758-1776.
SHD, microfilm n°1236 series A111.
SHD, A1, vol. 1945, film n°352, pp.176–178.
SHD, Sous série GR XH 14-16 and XH 16b-d.

British Archives
British National Archives (TNA)
TNA, PC 1/2/238, *Extract from Minutes of the examination of Irish officers who quitted the French service*, dated 11 December 1713.
TNA, SP36/89.
TNA, State Papers Foreign, Marlborough, SP34/23/48, FF 93-94, Whitehall, 12 July 1714.
TNA, SP 36/33, 17 December 1734.
British Library (BL)
BL, Add MSS 21376 to 21381. 1 May 1727.
BL, Add MSS 21376 to 21381, Documents relating to the Irish Brigade chiefly consisting of soldiers' certificates and discharges, in 6 volumes.

BL, Anon., *A letter from a soldier, being some remarks upon a late scandalous pamphlet; entituled, An address of some Irish-folks to the House of Commons* (Publisher unknown, 1702), 16 pages.

Old Bailey Proceedings Online (OBPO)

OBPO, February 1737, trial of Philip Dwyer Bryan Macgrass (t17370216-31), *Old Bailey Proceedings Online* <http://www.oldbaileyonline.org> (accessed 20 May 2022).

Archives of Northern Ireland

Micheline Kerney Walsh Papers at Cardinal O'Fiaich's Library in Armagh (MKWP COFLA)

MKWP COFLA. Copy of SHD, Section Administrative, Dossier personnel, O'Callaghan.

MKWP COFLA, copy of Archives départementales de la Gironde (ADG), amirauté de Guyenne, 6B 46. 3 October 1720, "Passport for *Sieur* Bourck, captain alongside Beau and Cake his servants".

MKWP COFLA, copy of SHD Archives administratives, Section Ancienne, dossiers personnels Travail du Roi, Carton 3 (1740).

MKWP COFLA, copy of SHD, A1 vol. 1857, microfilm n°351, pp.692–695, Captain Butler from the camp at Wissembourg, 16 July 1705.

MKWP COFLA, copy of SHD, archives administratives, section ancienne, Ancien Régime Travail du Roy, carton 6 (1742) p.30.

MKWP COFLA, copy of SHD, Archives administratives, Section Ancienne, Dossiers personnels Travail du Roi, Carton 7, Paris, 28 June 1742.

MKWP COFLA, copy of SHD, document from O'Berne personal dossier. The underlined segments appeared in the original document.

MKWP COFLA, copy of SHD, facsimile, 4 January 1710 at Versailles.

MKWP COFLA, copy of SHD, section correspondance, A1, volume 2479, film n°353 (p.1168). Letter dated 29 July 1714.

MKWP, COFLA, copy of SHD, *Etat de la revue faite aux six compagnies irlandoises qui sont parties de lyon ce 4ème de May 1705, marchant en Italie.*

MKWP COFLA, copy from SHD, Archives Administratives, Section Ancienne, Dossiers personnels, Ancien Régime, Capitaine O'Hanlon. Letter from the Maréchal de Noailles, 26 October 1745.

MKWP COFLA, Copy of SHD, Archives Administratives, Section Ancienne, Dossiers personnels, Trésor Royal, Maurice O'Connell, letter to the Count de Saint Germain, 17 October 1775.

MKWP COFLA, copy of SHD, Archives Administratives, Section Ancienne, Dossier personnels, Charles O'Brien, n°228.

MKWP COFLA, Copy of SHD, Section Correspondance, A1, vol. 2089, microfilm n°352, p.993. 26 February 1708.

MKWP COFLA, copy of SHD, 2151, 3Yc 198 "NUGENT", 1723. 2152, 3Yc 199 "NUGENT", 1729. GR 1 Yc 407 "LEE" 1690-1728.

MKWP COFLA, copy of SHD, 2151, 3Yc 198 "NUGENT", 1723. 2152, 3Yc 199 "NUGENT", 1729. GR 1 Yc 407 "LEE" 1690-1728.

MKWP COFLA, copy of SHD, archives administratives, section ancienne, dossiers personnels, Ancien Régime, Edmond MacMahon.

MKWP COFLA, copy of SHD, archives administratives, section ancienne, dossiers personnels, O'Donnel.

MKWP COFLA, copy of SHD, archives anciennes, section correspondance, A1 volume 2515, film n°353, p.1357.

MKWP COFLA, copy of SHD, section correspondance, A1, vol. 2232, microfilm n°353, pp.421–427. Letter from Leblanc, 19 October 1710.

Public Records of Northern Ireland (PRONI)

PRONI, D1514/1/5/8, Draft memorandum by the Bishop of Derry on a Catholic oath, December 1770.

PRONI, D2707/A/2/3/45, 17 August 1777.

PRONI, letter from Duncannon, 24 June 1755.

PRONI, T2806 9840, Walpole correspondence.

PRONI, T2905/22/18, Portland to Henry Dillon, 7 October 1794.

PRONI, T2905/22/20 and T2905/22/20. 9 and 7 October 1794.

PRONI, T2905/22/21, Portland to Lord St. Helens about the re-constituting the Irish Brigade, 10 October 1794.

PRONI, T3019/110 and T3019/108. Dublin Castle correspondence.

PRONI, T3019/3085, Waite, Dublin Castle, to Wilmot. Kildare, 4 January 1757.

PRONI, T3019/690. Dublin Castle, John Potter, undersecretary, to Robert Wilmot, secretary to the Lord Lieutenant, 1 September 1745.

PRONI, T3158/1471, 13 December 1756, list of Popish and disaffected persons now in London.

PRONI, D638/12/115, letter from Ginkel, 29 December 1691.

PRONI, D1327/21/11, Statement by John Redmond, leader of the Irish Parliamentary Party, *The Freeman's Journal*, 17 September 1914.

Republic of Ireland Archives
National Library of Ireland (NLI)

NLI, negative microfilm n°1094.

NLI, positive microfilms n°98, 143, 146, 155, 183, 184.

American Archives
Newberry Collection (University of Chicago)

E 5 L92705 v. 03 no. 43. *Vers sur le Chevalier Dillon colonel d'un régiment irlandais tué à la bataille de Fontenoy, faits par un de ses amis* (Malta: à l'enseigne de l'Amitié, 1745), 2 pages.

Contemporary Sources

Francophone Sources
Anon., *Lettre à M. de Voltaire sur son Histoire de Louis XIV, par M.* *** (Paris: *Mercure de France*, June 1753).

Anon., *Lettre du Maréchal de Villeroi au Cardinal d'Estrées après la surprise de Crémone en 1702*, in M.D.L.P., *Pièces intéressantes et peu connues* (Maestricht: J. P. Roux, 1790).

Anon., *Lettres d'un officier Irlandois à un officier françois* (Paris: Publisher unknown, 1756).

Anon., *A l'auteur des Lettres à un provincial, sur la justice des motifs de la guerre, sur les conjonctures présentes de l'Europe* (Neuchatel: Publisher unknown, 1745).

Anon., *Campagne de monsieur le Marechal de Marsin en Allemagne l'an 1704* (Amsterdam: Marc Michel Rey, 1762).

Anon., *Du Quartier Général à Luzarra de l'Armée Impériale, Relation de l'action arrivée à Crémone, entre les troupes de sa majesté impériale & celles des alliés*, le 1 Février 1702 (The Hague: Adrian Moetjens, 1702).

Anon., *Extrait d'une lettre de la Haye, 30 August 1745* (The Hague: Balthazar Weins, 1745).

Anon., *La Guerre d'Italie, ou Mémoires du comte d**** (Cologne: Pierre Marteau, 1703).

Anon., *La vie du Prince Eugène de Savoie* (The Hague: Adrian Moetjens, 1702).

Anon., *La vie ou l'Histoire du Prince Eugene de Savoie* (Amsterdam: Henry Desbordes, 1703)

Anon., *Lettre d'un officier du régiment Royal Ecossois, à M. D. ancien capitaine irlandois. Sur la victoire remportée par le prince Edouard, régent d'Ecosse, sur l'armée angloise, commandée par le général Aweley près de Falkirk, le 28 janvier 1746* (Paris: Publisher unknown, 1746).

Anon., *Mémoires concernant la Campagne de trois rois faite en l'année 1692* (Cologne: Pierre Marteau, 1693).

Anon., *Mémoires de Mr D.F.L. touchant ce qui s'est passé en Italie entre Victor Amédée II Duc de Savoye et le Roy T. C.* (Aachen: Anthoine Steenhuysen, 1697).

Anon., *Récit du siège de la ville et citadelle de Tournay et de la bataille de Fontenoy par le sieur D**** (Tournai: Jovenau, no date).

Anon., *Relation de l'assassinat de M. Théobald Dillon, Maréchal-de-camp, commis à Lille, le 29 avril 1792, par un témoin oculaire* (Paris: Migneret, 1792).

Anon., *Relation de la bataille de Fontenoy, Et de la Victoire que l'armée du Roy, commandée par Sa Majesté, a remportée sur l'armée des Alliez* (Paris: Pierre Valfray, Imprimeur du Roy, 1745).

Anon., *Relation de la journée de Crémone, et de la défaite des troupes impériales, avec la suite des affaires d'Italie* (Paris: Michel Brunet, 1702).

Anon., *Révolutions d'Ecosse et d'Irlande en 1707, 1708 et 1709* (The Hague: Pierre Aillaud, 1767).

Artanville, Monsieur d', *Mémoires Pour Servir à L'Histoire du Prince Eugène de Savoie* (The Hague: Etienne Foulque, 1710).

Barre, Joseph, *Histoire générale d'Allemagne* (Paris: Charles J.B. Delespine, 1748).

Basnage de Beauval, Henri, *Lettres historiques (et politiques) contenant ce qui se passe de plus important en Europe; et les réflexions nécessaires sur ce sujet, July 1702* (The Hague: Adrian Moetjens, 1702).

Beauveset, Abbé de, *Epitre du Sieur Rabot, Maitre d'Ecole de Fontenoy, sur les victoires du Roi* (Fontenoy: Publisher unknown, 1745).

Berwick, Jacques Fitz-James duc de, *Mémoires du Maréchal de Berwick, écrits par lui-même* (Paris: Moutard, 1778).

Bulifon, Antonio, *Journal du voyage d'Italie de l'invincible & glorieux monarque Philippe V, roy d'Espagne et de Naples* (Naples: Nicolas Buliton, 1704).

Cavard, Abbé André, *Mémoires du comte de Vordac, général des armées de l'Empereur* (Paris: Veuve de Jean Cochart, 1702).

Chamillart, Michel, *Les ordonnances militaires du roy, réduites en pratique, et appliquées au détail du service* (Paris: Frédéric Léonard, 1710).

D'Estrées, Jacques d', *Le Controlleur du Parnasse* (Amsterdam: Wolf and Fleischmans, 1745).

Damiens de Gomicourt, Auguste Pierre, *L'Observateur Français à Londres* (Paris: Lacombe, 1770).

De Béthune, Dominique, *Le Persan en empire ou correspondance entre plusieurs voyageurs* (The Hague: Communauté des Libraires, 1745).

De Montandre-Lonchamps, François Edme, *Etat militaire de la France pour l'année 1768* (Paris: Guyllin, 1768).

Desmarets, Abbé, *Procez [sic] verbal de l'assemblée générale du clergé de France, tenue à Saint Germain en Laye au Chateau-Neuf* (Paris: François Hubert Muguet, 1703).

Desroches-Parthenay, Jean-Biaise, *Mémoires historiques pour le siècle courant, avec des réflexions & remarques politiques & critiques* (Amsterdam: Etienne Ledet, 1745).

Dillon, Arthur, *Lettre du Lieutenant-Général Arthur Dillon au ministre de la guerre* (Paris: Imprimerie nationale, 1792).

Dromgold, Jean, *Réflexions sur un imprimé intitulé: La Bataille de Fontenoy, poème: Dédiées à Monsieur de Voltaire, Historiographe de France* (Paris: Pancoucke, 1745).

Dugas Quinsonas, François, *Apologie du poème de M. de V**** sur la bataille de Fontenoy* (Paris: Publisher unknown, 1745).

Dujardain, Bada, *Apologie du Sieur Bada Dujardain imprimée par ordre de Philippe de Hesse, son maître* (The Hague: Gillis Van Limburg, 1702).

Espagnac, Baron d', *Relation de la campagne en Brabant et en Flandres, de l'an M.DCC.XLVII* (The Hague: Frederic Henri Scheurleer, 1748).

Espagnac, Damarzit de Sahuguet Jean Baptiste Joseph, baron d', *Journal des campagnes du Roi en 1744, 1745, 1746 & 1747* (Liege: Publisher unknown, 1748).

Expilly, Jean-Joseph, *Description historique-géographique des Isles britanniques ou des royaumes d'Angleterre, d'Ecosse et d'Irlande* (Paris: Prault, 1759).

Fréron, Elie-Catherine, *La journée de Fontenoy, Ode* (Publisher unknown, 1745).

Fréron, Elie-Catherine, *Lettres de Madame la Comtesse de ***, sur quelques écrits modernes* (Geneva: Philibert, 1746).

Grimoard, P.H. de, *Lettres et mémoires choisi parmi les papiers originaux du Maréchal de Saxe* (Paris: J. J. Smits & Cie, 1794).

Guérin, François-Nicolas, *La Victoire de Fontenoy, Poème au Roy* (Paris: Thiboust imprimeur du Roi, 1745).

Guyot Desfontaines, Pierre-François, Abbé, *Avis sincères à M. de Voltaire: au sujet de la sixième édition de son poëme sur la victoire de Fontenoy* (Paris: Publisher unknown, 1745).

Héricourt, Nicolas d', *Elemens de l'art militaire* (Paris: Gissey, 1753).

Lally Tollendal, Trophime Gérard, marquis de, *Mémoire produit au Conseil d'État du Roi par Trophime-Gérard, comte de Lally-Tolendal* (Rouen: Besongne, 1779).

Marchand, Jean-Henri, *La Bataille de Fontenoy, ou l'Apothéose moderne, opéra-tragédie en trois actes. Traduite du Grec par un Ciclopédiste* (Chambord: Panckoucke, 1768).

Mauvillon, Eléazar de *Histoire du Prince Eugène de Savoie* (Amsterdam: Arkstee & Merkus, 1740).

Monsieur D***, *Mémoires de la dernière guerre d'Italie, avec des remarques critiques & militaires* (Cologne: Aux dépens de l'Autheur, 1728).

Montandre-Longchamps, *Etat Militaire de la France pour l'année 1760* (Paris: Guillyn, 1760).

Palasne de Champeaux, Antoine-Julien-Pierre, *État militaire de l'Empire français pour l'an treize: dédié à l'Empereur, d'après son autorisation* (Paris: Leblanc, 1805).

Parlement de Paris, *Arrêt de la cour de parlement portant condamnation de mort contre Nicolas Moure dit More, complice de Cartouche* (Paris: Delatour & Simon, 1722).

Pierre Claude de Guignard, *L'Ecole de Mars: ou mémoires instructifs sur toutes les parties qui composent le corps militaire en France, avec leurs origines et les différentes manœuvres auxquelles elles sont employées* (Paris: Simart, 1725).

Quincy, Charles Sevin Marquis de, *Histoire militaire du règne de Louis-Le-Grand* (Paris: Denis Mariette, 1726).

Quincy, Marquis de, *Histoire militaire du règne de Louis Le Grand* (Paris: Denis Mariette, 1726).

Reboulet, Simon, *Histoire du règne de Louis XIV* (Avignon: François Girard, 1744).

Roussel, Jacques de, *Etat Militaire de la France pour l'année 1784* (Paris: Onfroy, 1784).

Sacy, Claude-Louis-Michel de, *L'honneur françois, ou histoire des vertus et des exploits de notre nation, depuis l'établissement de la monarchie jusqu'à nos jours* (Paris: Costard, 1772).

Spon, Jean-François de, *Mémoires pour servir à l'histoire de l'Europe, depuis 1740 jusqu'à la paix générale signée à Aix-la-Chapelle, le 18 octobre 1748* (Amsterdam: La Compagnie, 1749).

Thuillier, Dom Vincent, *Histoire de Polybe, avec un commentaire ou corps de science militaire par M. de Folard* (Paris: Pierre Gandouin & Cie, 1729).

Tressan, Louis-Élisabeth de La Vergne, *Réponse à M. de Voltaire sur son poème de "La Bataille de Fontenoy", par M. L. M. de Tr... [Tressan], Maréchal des camps et armées de Sa Majesté* (Paris: Gandouin, 1745).

Voltaire, *Histoire de la Guerre de 1741* (Amsterdam: Publisher unknown, 1755).

Voltaire, *La bataille de Fontenoy gagnée par Louis XV sur les alliées, le 11 May 1745* (Paris: Pancoucke, 1745).

Voltaire, *La bataille de Fontenoy* (Paris: Prault, 1745).

Voltaire, *Le Siècle de Louis XIV* (Berlin: Henning, 1751).

Voltaire, *Précis du Siècle De Louis XV* (Geneva: Publisher unknown, 1769).

Z***, *La conquête des Pays-Bas par le roy, dans la campagne de 1745, avec la prise de Bruxelles en 1746* (The Hague: Publisher unknown, 1747).

Anglophone Sources

'A Military Gentleman', *A New Military Dictionary: or, the Field of War* (London: J. Cooke, 1760).

'A Society of Military Gentlemen', *The Military History of Great Britain, from Julius Cæsar to the Conclusion of the Late War* (London: R. James, 1762).

Anon., *A True Dialogue Between Thomas Jones, a Trooper, Lately Return'd from Germany, and John Smith, a Serjeant in the First Regiment of Foot-guards* (London: B.C., Pater-Noster Row, 1743).

Anon., *Advice to a painter being a satyr upon the French King* (London: Randall Taylor, 1692).

Anon., *British Glory Reviv'd* (London: J. Roberts, 1743).

Anon., *Spain in 1739* (London: D. Henry and J. Robinson, 1747).

Anon., 'The Irish Absentees New Litany; and the Character of an Irish Absentee', in *The Pall-Mall Miscellany* (London: W. James, 1733).

Anon., *The Political Cabinet; or, an Impartial Review of the most remarkable Occurrences of the World, Particularly Europe* (London, J. Roberts, 1745).

Anon., *The Remembrancer, or Impartial repository of Public Events for the year 1782* (London: Debrett, 1782)

Anon., *The Triumphant Campaign* (London: J.M., 1743).

Biggs, William, *The Military History of Europe* (London: Baldwin, 1755).

Boyer, Abel, *The History of the Reign of Queen Anne, Digested into Annals* (London: M. Coggan, 1709).

Boyse, Samuel, *An Historical Review of the Transactions of Europe from the Commencement of the War with Spain in 1739 to the insurrection of Scotland in 1745 with occurrences during that period* (London: D. Henry, 1747).

Brooke, Henry, *The Tryal of Roman Catholics* (London: Faulkner, 1762).

Buchanan, James, *The Complete English Scholar. In Three Parts. Containing a New Method of Instructing Children and Perfecting Grown Persons in the English Tongue and of Learning Grammar in General Without the Help of Latin, Etc* (London: A. Millar, 1753).

Chaigneau, William, *The History of Jack Connor, now Conyers, part 2* (London: W. Johnson, 1753).

Corry, John, *The Adventures of Felix and Rosarito; Or, the Triumph of Love and Friendship. Containing an Account of Several Interesting Events During the Late War, Between France and Spain, in the Western Pyrenees* (London: Crosby & Co, 1782).

Cumberland, Richard, *The West Indian* (Belfast: Henry and Robert Joy, 1774).

Debrett, J., *The Parliamentary Register or History of the proceedings and debates of the House of Commons* (London: Debrett, 1796).

Dilworth, W.H., *The Life and Military History of the Celebrated Marshal Saxe* (London: G. Wright, 1758).

Ferrar, John, *An History of the City of Limerick* (Limerick: Andrew Welsh, 1767).

Finemore, William, *The Pretender's Exercise to his Irish Dragoons, and his Wild Geese* (London, Publisher unknown, c.1720s).

Forman, Charles, Esq., *A letter to the Right Honourable Sir Robert Sutton, for disbanding the Irish regiments in the service of France and Spain* (London: George Faulkner and James Hoey in Christ-Church-Yard, 1728).

Forman, Charles, *A Defence of the courage, honour and loyalty of the Irish Nation, in answer to the scandalous reflections of the Free–Briton and others* (London: J. Watson, 1735).

James, Charles, *An Universal Military Dictionary, in English and French* (London: Egerton, 1816), fourth edition.

Lempriere, William, *Practical observations on the diseases of the army in Jamaica* (London: Longman, 1799).

Mac O Bonniclabbero of Drogheda [sic], *The Irish Miscellany: Or Teagueland Jests: Being a Compleat Collection of the Most Profound Puns, Learned Bulls, Elaborate Quibbles of the Natives of Teagueland* (London: J. Perry, 1746).

Mandeville, Edward M., *Miscellaneous poems* (Waterford: John Veacock, 1798), p.151.

Plowden, Francis, *A Short History of the British Empire during the year 1794* (London: G.G. and J. Robinson, 1795).

Shebbeare, John, *An Answer to a Pamphlet, Called, A Second Letter to the People. In which the Subsidiary System is Fairly Stated, and Amply Considered* (London: M. Cooper, 1755).

Sheridan, Thomas, *The Brave Irishman, or Captain O'Blunder, a Farce* (Dublin: R. Watts, 1754).

Ordonnances and Regulations

Ordonnance du roi, pour défendre aux officiers des régimens Irlandois, qui à son service, de quitter leurs régimens pour passer en Ecosse, sur peine d'être cassés & privés de leurs charges (Paris: Imprimerie royale, 6 December 1715).

Ordonnance du Roy portant augmentation de troupes (Lyon: P. Valfray, 1 November 1733).

Ordonnance du Roy pour obliger les Anglois, Écossois et Irlandois qui sont en France de prendre parti dans les régimens irlandois qui sont au service de Sa Majesté (Paris: Imprimerie royale, 2 November 1734).

Ordonnance du Roy pour admettre les Irlandois qui ont déserté des troupes de Sa Majesté à profiter de la dernière amnistie, en s'engageant dans les régimens de leur nation (Paris: Imprimerie royale, 25 November 1734).

Ordonnance du Roy portant réduction des compagnies d'infanterie françoise et irlandoise, obliger les Anglois, Écossois et Irlandois qui sont en France de prendre parti dans les régimens irlandois qui sont au service de Sa Majesté (Paris: Imprimerie royale, 25 April 1736).

Ordonnance du Roy portant réduction des compagnies d'infanterie françoise et irlandoise (Lyon: Imprimerie de P. Valfray, 25 April 1736).

Ordonnance du roy, pour la nouvelle composition des cinq régiments irlandois; création d'un sixième régiment; & augmentation de solde aux sergens, haute-payes & soldats (Paris: Imprimerie royale, 1 October 1744).

Ordonnance du roy, portant réduction dans les régimens d'infanterie irlandoise & écossoise (Paris: Imprimerie du roi, 1749).

Ordonnance du roi, concernant les régimens irlandois (Paris: Imprimerie du roi, 1756).

Ordonnance du roi, portant augmentation dans les régimens irlandois & écossois (Paris: Imprimerie du roi, 1756).

Ordonnance du roi, pour proroger jusqu'au mois de décembre prochain, le complet des compagnies de fusiliers des régimens irlandois (Paris: Imprimerie royale, 1756)

Ordonnance du roi, pour proroger jusqu'à la revue du mois de juin prochain, le complet de l'augmentation réglée dans les régimens d'infanterie irlandoise & écossoise (Paris: Imprimerie royale, 1757).

Ordonnance du roi, concernant les régimens d'infanterie irlandoise (Paris: Imprimerie du roi, 1762).

Ordonnance du roi, concernant les régimens d'infanterie irlandoise (Paris: Imprimerie royale, 1775).

Ordonnance royale pour mettre la Légion corse sur le pied des autres légions françoises, sous le nom de Légion du Dauphiné (Paris: Imprimerie royale, 1775).

Ordonnance du roi, portant création d'un régiment d'infanterie irlandoise (Paris: Imprimerie royale, 1776).

Réglemens et Ordonnances du Roy, pour les gens de Guerre, vol. 14 (Paris: Léonard, 1706)

Réglement pour le traitement du régiment irlandois de Lally, destiné à passer aux Indes orientales (Paris: Imprimerie du roi, 1756).

Newspapers, Periodicals, and Journals

Courrier des Spectacles, 7 May 1805, n°3004.

Gazette (Paris) 1691 and 1745

Gazette de France, n°3235, Saturday 29 November 1806.

Gazette de Lyon, 'Relation de la bataille de Cassano', 18 September 1705

Journal de Paris, n°228, 8 May 1805.

Journal des Débats et Décrets, 7 May 1805.

Journal de l'Empire, 8 August 1807 and 18 August 1810.

Lettres Historiques contenant ce qui se passe de plus important en Europe (The Hague: Adrian Moetjens, August 1726), vol.70.

Lettres Historiques contenant ce qui se passe de plus important en Europe (The Hague: Adrian Moetjens, March 1702), vol.21.

Mercure Galant, 1701 and 1705.

Mercure Historique et Politique, vol. n° 119 (The Hague: Frederich-Henri Scheurleer, 1745).

Recueil des édits, déclarations, arrêts et ordonnances de l'année 1715 pour la Province de Languedoc, Ordonnance qui règle ce qui doit être fourni aux troupes qui sont en quartier dans la province, 27 décembre 1714 (Montpellier: Jean Martel, 1715).

Recueil des Gazettes, Nouvelles Ordinaires et Extraordinaires de l'Année 1702.

Recueil des Gazettes, Nouvelles Ordinaires et Extraordinaires de l'Année 1703.

Recueil des nouvelles ordonnances militaires (Metz: Collignon, 1767).

The Centinel, "Quid domini faciant?", 6 August 1757.

The Craftsman, 18 November 1730.

The Free Briton n°50, 2 December 1730.

The Gentleman's Magazine, 1745.

The Hibernian Magazine, 1779.

The Irish Monthly, vol.18.

The London Gazette, 1745.

The London Magazine, June 1745, vol.14.

The Monthly Review (London: T. Becket, 1795), vol.17.

The Scots Magazine, 1745 and 1746.

Printed Primary and Secondary Sources

Sources Published in the Nineteenth Century

Barbier, Edmond-Jean-François, *Journal de Barbier, Chronique de la régence et du règne de Louis XV: 1718-1763* (Paris: Charpentier, 1857).

Belhomme, Victor, *Histoire de l'Infanterie en France* (Paris: Charles Lavauzelle, 1893-1902).

Boislisle, A. de, *Lettres de M. de Marville, lieutenant général de police au ministre Maurepas (1742-1747)* (Paris: Champion, 1896).

Broglie, Duc de, *La Journée de Fontenoy* (Paris: Paul Reveilhac, 1897).

Byrne, Miles, Byrne, Fanny, *Memoirs of Miles Byrne, chef de bataillon in the service of France* (Paris: Bossange, 1863).

Dangeau, Philippe de Courcillon de, *Journal du Marquis de Dangeau* (Paris: Firmin Didot Frères, 1854).

Delisle, Léopold (ed.), *Les mémoires de Pierre Mangon, vicomte de Valognes* (Saint-Lô: Imprimerie Le Tual, 1891).

Bittard des Portes, René, *Histoire de l'armée de Condé* (Paris: Dentu, 1896).

Dussieux, L., Soulié, E. (eds.), *Mémoires du duc de Luynes sur la cour de Louis XV (1735-1758)* (Paris: Firmin Didot frères, 1861).

Fieffé, Eugène, *Histoire de Troupes étrangères au service de France* (Paris: Librairie Militaire, 1854).

Forman, Charles, *A Defence of the Courage, Honor, and Loyalty of the Irish Nation* (Dublin: Duffy, 1844).

Fortescue, John William, *A History of the British Army* (London: MacMillan and Co, 1899).

Guillon, Edouard Louis Maxime, *La France & l'Irlande pendant la Révolution: Hoche et Humbert, d'après les documents inédits des archives de France et d'Irlande* (Paris: Armand Colin, 1888).

Johnstone, Chevalier de, *Memoirs of the Rebellion in 1745 and 1746* (London: Longman, Hurst, Rees, Orme, and Brown, 1820).

Leonard, J. P., *Historical notes on the services of the Irish officers in the French army: addressed to the National Assembly* ([Reprod.]) / by general Arthur Dillon; translated from the French by J. P. Leonard (Dublin: Duffy, 1870s?).

Lescure, M. de (ed.), *Nouveaux mémoires du Maréchal duc de Richelieu, 1696-1788* (Paris: Dentu, 1869).

Malaguti, Charles-Joachim-Edgard, *Historique du 87e régiment d'infanterie de ligne, ex-12e Léger* (Saint Quentin: Moreau & fils, 1892).

Napoléon 1er, *Correspondance de Napoléon 1er* (Paris: Imprimerie impériale, 1856).

O'Callaghan, John Cornelius, *History of the Irish Brigades in the Service of France: From the Revolution in Great Britain and Ireland Under James II to the Revolution in France Under Louis XVI* (Glasgow: Cameron and Ferguson, 1870).

O'Callaghan, John Cornelius, *The Green Book, or Gleanings from the Writing-desk of a Literary Agitator* (Dublin: Duffy, 1845).

O'Conor, Matthew, *Military History of the Irish Nation: Comprising a Memoir of the Irish Brigade in the Service of France; with an Appendix of Official Papers Relative to the Brigade, from the Archives at Paris* (Dublin: Hodges & Smith, 1845).

O'Conor, Matthew, *The History of the Irish Catholics from the Settlement in 1691: With a View of the State of Ireland from the Invasion by Henry II to the Revolution* (Dublin: Stockdale, 1813).

Vault, François Eugène de, *Collection de documents inédits sur l'histoire de France, première série historique, mémoires militaires relatifs à la succession d'Espagne sous Louis XIV* (Paris: Imprimerie Nationale, 1854).

Vault, François Eugène de, Pelet, Jean Jacques Germain Baron, *Mémoires militaires relatifs à la Succession d'Espagne sous Louis XIV: 1702* (Paris: Imprimerie Nationale, 1836).

Voltaire, *Œuvres complètes de Voltaire, siècle de Louis XV* (Paris: Baudoin frères, 1828).

Sources Published in the Twentieth Century

Barry O'Brien, R. *In Memory of Fontenoy* (London: Irish Literary Society, 1905).

Bartlett, Thomas, Jeffery, Keith (eds.), *A Military History of Ireland* (Cambridge: Cambridge University Press, 1996).

Bois, Jean-Pierre, *Maurice de Saxe* (Paris: Fayard, 1992).

Boislisle, A. de, *Lettres de M. de Marville lieutenant général de police au ministre Maurepas (1742-1747)* (Paris: Champion, 1903).

Burrell, Sidney (ed.), *Amiable Renegade, the Memoirs of Peter Drake* (Palo Alto: Stanford University Press, 1960).

Corvisier, André, *La Bataille de Malplaquet, l'effondrement de la France évitée* (Paris: Economica, 1997).

Elliott, Marianne, *Partners in Revolution, the United Irishmen and France* (New Haven: Yale University Press, 1982).

Elliott-Wright, Philipp J.C., *The Officers of the Irish Brigade and the British Army, 1789-98* (PhD, University of Leeds, 1997).

Gallaher, John G., *Napoleon's Irish Legion* (Carbondale: Southern Illinois University Press, 1993).

Mulloy, Sheila (ed.), *Franco-Irish correspondence, December 1688-February 1692* (Dublin: Irish Manuscript Commission, 1983).

O'Connor Morris, William, *Memoirs of Gerald O'Connor of the princely house of the O'Connors of Offaly in the kingdom of Ireland* (London: Digby, Long & Co, 1903).

Sautay, Maurice, *La bataille de Malplaquet: d'après les correspondants du duc du Maine à l'armée de Flandre* (Paris: Service Historique des Armées, 1904).

Simms, J.G., *War and politics in Ireland, 1649-1730* (London: Hambleton Press, 1986).

Sources Published in the Twenty-first Century

Bamford, Andrew, *The Lilies and the Thistle: French troops in the Jacobite 45* (Warwick: Helion, 2018).

Beiner, Guy, *Remembering the year of the French, Irish folk history and Social Memory* (Madison: Wisconsin, 2007).

Bois, Jean-Pierre, *Fontenoy, Louis XV arbitre de l'Europe* (Paris: Economica, 2012).

Clarke de Dromantin, Patrick, *Les réfugiés jacobites dans la France du XVIIIe siècle* (Bordeaux: Presses Universitaires de Bordeaux, 2005).

Dagier, Patricia, *Les réfugiés irlandais au dix-septième siècle en Finistère* (Quimper: Généalogie Cornouaille, 1999).

Forray, Gilbert, Général, *Les débarquements en Angleterre de César à Hitler* (Paris: Economica, 2010).

Genet-Rouffiac, Nathalie, *Le Grand Exil, 1688-1715* (Paris: SHD, 2007).

Genet-Rouffiac, Nathalie, Murphy, David (eds.), *Franco-Irish military connections, 1590-1945* (Dublin: Four Courts Press, 2009).

Graham, D.P., *The Irish Brigade 1670-1745: the Wild Geese in French Service* (Barnsley: Pen & Sword Military, 2020).

McGarry, Stephen, *Irish Brigades Abroad: from the Wild Geese to the Napoleonic Wars* (Cheltenham: The History Press, 2013).

McNally, Michael, *Dettingen 1743, Miracle on the Main* (London: Osprey Publishing, 2020).

McNally, Michael, *Ramillies, 1706* (Oxford: Osprey Publishing, 2014).

Monod, Paul, Pittock, Murray, Szechi, Daniel (eds.), *Loyalty and Identity: Jacobites at Home and Abroad* (London: Palgrave Macmillan, 2010).

Murphy, David, *The Irish Brigades, 1685-2006, A gazetteer of Irish military service, past and present* (Dublin: Four Courts Press, 2007).

O'Connor Thomas, Lyons, Mary Ann (eds.), *Irish Communities in early-modern Europe* (Dublin: Four Courts Press, 2006).

O'Connor, Thomas, *Irish Voices from the Spanish Inquisition, Migrants, Converts and Brokers in Early Modern Iberia* (London: Palgrave Macmillan, 2016).

Russ, A. Pritchard Jr., *The Irish Brigade: a Pictorial History of the Famed Civil War Fighters* (New York, Skyhorse, 2020).

Verbeke, Demmy, Money, David, Deneire, Tom (eds.), *Ramillies, A commemoration in prose and verse of the 300th anniversary of the Battle of Ramillies, 1706* (Cambridge: Bringfield's Head Press, 2006).

Journal Articles

Atkinson, C.T., 'More Light On Almanza: From The Hawley Papers', *Journal of the Society for Army Historical Research*, vol.25, 104 (1947), pp.144–161.

Bracken, David, 'Irish migrants in Paris hospitals, 1702-1730: Extracts from the registers of Bicêtre, La Charité, la Pitié and la Salpetrière', *Archivium Hibernicum*, vol.55 (2001), pp.7–47.

Cooney, John, 'Two French Revolutionary Soldiers in Rebel Ireland', *Etudes Irlandaises*, vol.13–2 (1988), pp.101–07.

Denman, Terrence, '"Hibernia officina militum": Irish recruitment to the British regular army. 1660-1815', *The Irish Sword*, vol.20, 80 (1996), pp.148–166.

Binasco Matteo, 'Le migrazioni irlandesi in Francia fra il XVI secolo e i primi decenni del XIX secolo. Lo status quaestionis', *Studi Irlandesi, A Journal of Irish Studies*, vol.4 (2014), pp.163–182.

Gallaher, John G., 'Irish Patriot and Napoleonic Soldier: William Lawless', *The Irish Sword*, XVIII, vol.73 (1992), pp.255–263.

Gargett, Graham, 'Voltaire and Irish history', *Eighteenth century Ireland*, vol.5 (1990), p.117–141.

Gouhier, Pierre, 'Mercenaires irlandais au service de la France (1635-1664)', *Revue d'Histoire Moderne et Contemporaine*, vol.15-4 (1968), pp. 672–690.

Hamilton, Charles James, 'The Battle of Fontenoy- 11 May 1745', *Journal of the Society for Army Historical Research*, vol. 6, 24 (1927), pp. 94–96.

Heiss, Baron d', 'Détail de ce que j'ay vu de la bataille de Fontenoi donnée le 11 May 1745', *Revue Rétrospective* (1893), pp.66–71.

Joannon, Pierre, 'Les soldats perdus de l'armée d'Irlande', *Revue historique des armées*, vol.253 (2008), pp.43–54.

Jobit, Jean Louis, 'Journal de l'expédition d'Irlande', Nuala Costello, *Analecta Hibernica*, vol.11 (1941), pp.5, 7–9, 1–55.

Lenihan, Pádraig, 'The 'Irish Brigade' 1690-1715.' *Eighteenth-Century Ireland / Iris an Dá Chultúr*, vol.31 (2016), pp. 47–74.

McDonnell, Ciarán, 'A "Fair Chance"? The Catholic Irish Brigade in the British Service, 1793–1798', *War in History*, vol.23(2) (2016), pp.150–168.

Murphy, W.S., 'The Irish Brigade of France at the Siege of Savannah, 1779', *The Georgia Historical Quarterly* vol. 38, n°4 (1954), pp.307–321.

O Cuiv, Brian, 'The Wearing of the Green', *Studia Hibernica*, vol.17/18 (1977-78), pp.107–119.

Ó Hannracháin, Eoghan, 'An analysis of the Fitzjames Cavalry Regiment, 1737', *Irish Sword*, vol.19, 78 (1995), pp.253–276.

Parkhill, Trevor, 'The Wild Geese of 1798, émigrés of the Rebellion', *Seanchas Ardmhacha: Journal of the Armagh Diocesan Historical Society*, vol.19, 2 (2003), pp.118–135.

Petrie, Charles, 'Ireland in Spanish and French Strategy, 1558-1815', *The Irish Sword*, vol.6, 24 (1964), pp.154–165.

Reiter, Jacqueline, '"Day after day adds to our miseries": The private diary of a staff officer on the Walcheren expedition, 1809: Part 2', *Journal of the Society for Army Historical Research*, vol.96, 387 (2018), pp.231–250.

Rowlands, Guy, 'Foreign Service in the Age of Absolute Monarchy: Louis XIV and His 'Forces Étrangères', *War in History*, vol.17, 2 (2010), pp.141–165.

Skrine F.H., Esq., 'The Irish Brigade in the Service of France, 1691–1701', *Journal of Royal United Services Institution*, 58 (1914), p.477–500.

White, Barbara, 'The Criminal Confessions of Newgate's Irishmen', *Irish Studies Review*, vol.14, 3 (2011), p. 303–324.

Index

Abbeville 57
Aberdeen 135
Aiguillon, Duc de 144
Aix-La-Chapelle, Peace of 139, 190
Almanza, Battle of 40, 45, 195
American Civil War 182
Anne, Queen of England 47, 49, 69, 74, 79, 191
Argenson, Comte d' 59, 74, 83, 104-105
Aughrim, Battle of 21, 24, 81, 130-131, 181

Barbezieux, Marquis de viii, 29
Barcelona 32-33
Bellew, Col. Richard 28
Berwick, James Fitzjames, Duke of 27, 40, 42,
    44-45, 51, 61-62, 83, 96, 121, 133, 135-136, 140,
    143, 151, 157
Blenheim, Battle of (Second Höchstädt) 43-44
Bonhomme Richard 156
Boufflers, Duc de 34, 69
Boulogne 32, 100, 114, 141, 157
Bouridal, Jean-Baptiste Bachelier de 25-27, 29-30
Boyne, Battle of the 17, 22, 130-133, 151-152, 181
Brest 13, 17-18, 22, 24-28, 30-31, 51, 70, 133-134,
    142, 144, 170, 172-174
British Army, Regiments of: Bland's (3rd)
    Dragoons 117; Rich's (4th) Dragoons 117; 3rd
    Foot 44; 18th Foot 47; 76th Foot 147
Brittany 17-18, 25-26, 30, 66, 69, 74, 89, 140,
    142-144, 146-148, 155-157, 172
Bulkeley, François, Comte de 61-62, 95, 115

Calais 24, 31-32, 66, 72, 74, 114, 157
Camisards 48-49
Carabiniers 41, 105, 107-108, 112, 123, 152
'Cartouche' (Louis Dominique Garthausen) 86
Cassano, Battle of 44
Catalonia 32, 34
Catinat, Nicolas 18-19, 33

Cévennes 48-49
Chamillart, Michel 43, 67-68
Charles Edward Stuart, Prince 98, 112, 114-115,
    129, 133, 135-136, 138-139, 149, 165
Charles X, King of France 160
Cherbourg 142-143
Choiseul, Comte de 34
Choiseul, Duc de 149
Clare, County 21
Clare, Charles O'Brien, Viscount 42-44, 64, 66
Clare, Charles O'Brien de (Comte de Thomond)
    59, 110, 152
Clare, Daniel O'Brien, Viscount 33
Clarke, Henri-Jacques 175-176
Compagnies Franches de la Marine 144
Condé, Prince de 160, 163
Connaught 89, 171
Cork 23-24, 40, 66, 78, 89
Corsica 140, 149
Counter-insurgency 48
Cremona, Battle of 35, 37-41, 43, 69, 90, 98, 128,
    180
Culloden, Battle of 136-137, 139
Cumberland, Prince William Augustus, Duke
    of 98, 101, 105, 107, 109, 115, 117-118, 123, 136,
    151-152, 183

Desertion 16, 68-70, 70-71, 88, 90, 155, 166,
    174-175
Dettingen, Battle of 101, 115, 117, 131, 195
Dillon, Arthur (1670–1733) 33, 40, 44, 96
Dillon, Arthur (1750–1794) 159
Dillon, Edouard 156
Dillon, Edward 115
Dillon, Henry 168
Dillon, Jacques (James) 110-111, 113-114, 120, 127
Dillon, Théobald 160
Dinan 69, 71

Dorrington, William 34, 50
Douai 63-64, 70
Drake, Peter 32, 44, 194
Dublin 34, 57, 68, 74, 76, 81, 83, 89, 95, 165, 171, 183
Dunkirk 32, 50, 78, 82, 100, 134

Eugene of Savoy, Prince 35-36, 38, 42-43, 128

Falkirk, Battle of 135-136
Fitzgerald, Nicholas 50
Fitzjames, Comte de 62, 72
Fitzjames, Duc de 115
Fleury, Cardinal 82, 93
Flushing 174, 176
Fontenoy, Battle of 59, 97-98, 101, 103, 105, 109, 112-117, 119, 121, 124-126, 128, 131-133, 136, 138-139, 149, 151-153, 176, 178-184
French Army, Regiments of: Agenois 50; Berry 64; Boulonnois 50; Dauphiné 73; Eu 104, 126; Gardes Françaises 101, 104-105, 107-108; Gardes Suisses 19, 104-105; Légion du Dauphiné 154, 192; Normandie 98, 100, 104-105, 107-109, 113, 126; Ogilvy (Scottish) 146; Roy 47; Royal Ecossois (Scottish) 146, 188; Royal Italien 154; Royal-Vaisseaux 34, 98, 104-105, 107; Saintonge 64; Salm Salm 157; Solre 34, 105; Sourches 34; see also Carabiniers, Compagnies Franches de la Marine, Gendarmerie, Maison du Roi
French Revolution 13, 140, 153, 159-160, 164, 169-170, 174-175, 182

Galmoy, Pierce Butler, Viscount 34, 44, 50-51
George I, King of Great Britain 79, 82
George II, King of Great Britain 82, 98, 101, 117, 178
George III, King of Great Britain 164-165
Gendarmerie 105, 157

Harrington, Earl of 79-80, 82
Hennessy, Lieutenant Colonel 79, 82-83
Hoche, Lazarre 169-170
Höchstädt, First Battle of 42-43
Höchstädt, Second Battle of: see Blenheim, Battle of
Humbert, Jean Joseph Amable 170-171

Invalides, Hôtel des 27, 34, 40, 47, 72, 84-85, 87, 89, 114

Irish Brigade, Regiments of: Berwick's 44-45, 50-51, 61-62, 67, 73, 76, 121, 124, 135-136, 140, 143, 151, 154-155, 157, 159, 163, 166; Bourke's 35, 37-38, 40-41, 51; Bulkeley's 59, 84, 95, 108, 140, 146, 149, 154; Butler's 16-17; Clare's 17, 34, 42, 44, 56, 58-60, 71, 78, 94, 113, 121-122, 126, 134, 140, 142-143, 148, 154; Dillon's 16-17, 34-38, 40-42, 73, 99, 110-111, 115, 120-121, 127-128, 132, 140-141, 143, 153-154, 156-157, 159-162, 165-166, 168, 177, 182, 185; Dorrington's 44, 47, 71; Dublin Irlandois 34; Fielding's 16-17; Fitzgerald's 57; Fitzjames' 56, 74, 88, 107, 109, 115, 121, 127, 135, 137, 141, 148, 150; Galmoy's 48, 50-51, 156; Lally's 83, 99, 112, 121, 124, 140-142, 146; Lee's 43-44, 47, 50-51, 58, 66, 71-73, 79, 84, 87-89; Mountcashel's 16-17, 19-20, 22, 26, 29, 33; Nugent's 50, 57, 72, 74, 87-88; O'Brien's 16-17, 51, 64, 132, 183; O'Donnell's 47, 51, 73, 94; Roscommon's 149; Rothe's 83, 92, 124, 143-144, 148-149; Walsh's 154-157, 159
Irish Picquets 98, 135-137
Isle de France 157

James II, King of England 13, 16-17, 19, 27-29, 31-32, 34, 42, 45, 54, 56-57, 79, 121, 132-133, 147, 151, 162, 178
James III, King of England (Jacobite claimant) 49-50, 80, 100, 165

La Rochelle 70-71, 137, 170
Lally de Tollendal, Thomas Arthur 99, 112, 149, 152
Lauzun, Duc de 17-18
Lawfeld, Battle of 115, 131
Lawless, William 173, 176, 195
Lee, Andrew 19, 27, 33-34, 42, 69-70, 85, 96
Légion Irlandaise (later 3eme, finally 7eme Régiment Etranger) 171-173, 175-177
Leinster 89
Lille 58, 63, 66-67, 96, 137, 157, 160
Limerick, Treaty of 22, 66, 131
Limoges 66
Londonderry 13, 15, 54
Louis XIV, King of France 13-14, 16-19, 21-22, 28, 31-35, 37, 39-40, 42-44, 46, 49, 51-54, 56-57, 59, 65, 67-69, 82, 89-90, 95, 111, 128-131, 133, 152
Louis XV, King of France 98-101, 103-106, 109-115, 119, 126, 138, 140, 149, 182
Louis XVI, King of France 158-160

Louis XVIII, King of France 160, 177
Louvois, Marquis de 16-19, 29
Lucan, Earl of: see Sarsfield, Patrick
Luttrell, Simon 34
Lyon 70, 187, 192

Maison du Roi 98, 101, 104-105, 108, 112-113
Malplaquet, Battle of 46
Marburg, Siege of 148
Marlborough, John Churchill, Duke of 43-44, 46,
    68, 70
Marsaglia, Battle of 33
Maurepas, Comte de 65
Morlaix 172
Mountcashel, Justin MacCarthy, Viscount 16-17,
    19-20, 22, 26, 29, 33-34
Munster 84, 89

Nantes 18, 66-67, 71-72, 83, 99, 147
Neerwinden, Battle of 33
Newcastle, Duke of 79, 83, 117
Newtownbutler, Battle of 13, 54
Noailles, Duc de 99, 101
Normandy 30-31, 124, 140, 142, 152, 174

Paris 23, 27, 61-63, 65-67, 76, 90, 92-93, 95,
    101, 112, 114, 131, 145-146, 149, 151, 156, 162,
    169-171, 173, 177
Peninsular War 175, 182
Peterhead 135
Philip V, King of Spain 40, 42, 45, 69-70
Pitt, William (the younger) 125, 163-165
Pondicherry 142, 149
Pragmatic Army 97-98, 101, 117, 136
Prestonpans, Battle of 135

Quincy, Marquis de 41, 46, 190

Ramillies, Battle of 44, 195
Recruiting 26, 40, 45, 53, 58, 62, 68, 70-73, 78-79,
    80-84, 121, 125, 142, 147, 151, 156-157, 165-167, 173
Rennes 27
Richelieu, Duc de 110
Rochefort 24, 70, 157
Roscommon, Robert Dillon, Earl of 129, 149
Rosen, Conrad de 13, 16-17
Rossbach, Battle of 142, 148
Rothe (Rooth, Routh), Charles Edouard de 43, 46,
    96, 149

Roucoux, Battle of 115
Ryswick, Treaty of 32, 54

Saint Malo 70, 142, 147
Saint Omer 66
Saint-Germain-en-Laye 29, 32, 34, 52, 54, 56, 63,
    66-67, 90, 94, 137
Sarsfield, Patrick (Earl of Lucan) 21, 23, 28, 33, 52,
    130-131, 133, 155
Savannah 156
Saxe, Maurice de 98, 100-102, 105, 107-109,
    112-115, 117, 119-120, 124, 152, 182
Seven Years War 112, 115, 122-123, 125, 130,
    140-141, 143, 146-147
Sheldon, Dominick 27, 34, 50-51

Thomond, Charles O'Brien de Clare, Comte de:
    see Clare, Charles O'Brien de
Tournai 98, 119, 136
Tyrconnel, Richard Talbot, Duke of 13, 21, 42

United Irishmen 169-172, 175, 177
Utrecht, Treaty of 78

Valenciennes 66, 137
Vendôme, Louis Joseph de Bourbon, Duc de 34,
    41, 44, 51
Versailles 16, 18, 21, 25, 27, 39, 41, 49-51, 54, 57,
    59, 62, 70-71, 78-79, 81, 87, 90, 92, 94-95, 100,
    109-110, 133-134, 138-139, 143, 147, 150, 154
Villars, Claude Louis Hector de 46-47
Villeroy, Duc de 34-35, 39, 41
Voltaire 108-114, 120, 122-123, 127-130, 132,
    151-152, 182

Walsh, Antoine 135
Walsh-Serrant, Comte de 149-150, 153-157,
    159-160, 163, 166-168
War of American Independence 140
War of the Austrian Succession 74, 83, 88, 97, 115,
    124, 133, 138-140
War of the League of Augsburg 13, 16, 31, 33
War of the Polish Succession 98, 101
War of the Spanish Succession 42, 56, 61, 65, 67,
    69, 71, 73, 95, 97
West Indies 74, 156, 159, 163, 167
William III, King of England 13, 17, 21-23, 32-34,
    56, 125, 131
Wolfe Tone, Theobald 169-170

From Reason to Revolution – Warfare 1721-1815

http://www.helion.co.uk/series/from-reason-to-revolution-1721-1815.php

The 'From Reason to Revolution' series covers the period of military history 1721–1815, an era in which fortress-based strategy and linear battles gave way to the nation-in-arms and the beginnings of total war.

This era saw the evolution and growth of light troops of all arms, and of increasingly flexible command systems to cope with the growing armies fielded by nations able to mobilise far greater proportions of their manpower than ever before. Many of these developments were fired by the great political upheavals of the era, with revolutions in America and France bringing about social change which in turn fed back into the military sphere as whole nations readied themselves for war. Only in the closing years of the period, as the reactionary powers began to regain the upper hand, did a military synthesis of the best of the old and the new become possible.

The series will examine the military and naval history of the period in a greater degree of detail than has hitherto been attempted, and has a very wide brief, with the intention of covering all aspects from the battles, campaigns, logistics, and tactics, to the personalities, armies, uniforms, and equipment.

Submissions

The publishers would be pleased to receive submissions for this series. Please contact series editor Andrew Bamford via email (andrewbamford@helion.co.uk), or in writing to Helion & Company Limited, Unit 8 Amherst Business Centre, Budbrooke Road, Warwick, CV34 5WE

Titles

No 1 *Lobositz to Leuthen: Horace St Paul and the Campaigns of the Austrian Army in the Seven Years War 1756-57* (Neil Cogswell)

No 2 *Glories to Useless Heroism: The Seven Years War in North America from the French journals of Comte Maurés de Malartic, 1755-1760* (William Raffle (ed.))

No 3 *Reminiscences 1808-1815 Under Wellington: The Peninsular and Waterloo Memoirs of William Hay* (Andrew Bamford (ed.))

No 4 *Far Distant Ships: The Royal Navy and the Blockade of Brest 1793-1815* (Quintin Barry)

No 5 *Godoy's Army: Spanish Regiments and Uniforms from the Estado Militar of 1800* (Charles Esdaile and Alan Perry)

No 6 *On Gladsmuir Shall the Battle Be! The Battle of Prestonpans 1745* (Arran Johnston)

No 7 *The French Army of the Orient 1798-1801: Napoleon's Beloved 'Egyptians'* (Yves Martin)

No 8 *The Autobiography, or Narrative of a Soldier: The Peninsular War Memoirs of William Brown of the 45th Foot* (Steve Brown (ed.))

No 9 *Recollections from the Ranks: Three Russian Soldiers' Autobiographies from the Napoleonic Wars* (Darrin Boland)

No 10 *By Fire and Bayonet: Grey's West Indies Campaign of 1794* (Steve Brown)

No 11 *Olmütz to Torgau: Horace St Paul and the Campaigns of the Austrian Army in the Seven Years War 1758-60* (Neil Cogswell)

No 12 *Murat's Army: The Army of the Kingdom of Naples 1806-1815* (Digby Smith)

No 13 *The Veteran or 40 Years' Service in the British Army: The Scurrilous Recollections of Paymaster John Harley 47th Foot – 1798-1838* (Gareth Glover (ed.))

No 14 *Narrative of the Eventful Life of Thomas Jackson: Militiaman and Coldstream Sergeant, 1803-15* (Eamonn O'Keeffe (ed.))

No.15 *For Orange and the States: The Army of the Dutch Republic 1713-1772 Part I: Infantry* (Marc Geerdinck-Schaftenaar)

No 16 *Men Who Are Determined to be Free: The American Assault on Stony Point, 15 July 1779* (David C. Bonk)

No 17 *Next to Wellington: General Sir George Murray: The Story of a Scottish Soldier and Statesman, Wellington's Quartermaster General* (John Harding-Edgar)

No 18 *Between Scylla and Charybdis: The Army of Elector Friedrich August of Saxony 1733-1763 Part I: Staff and Cavalry* (Marco Pagan)

No 19 *The Secret Expedition: The Anglo-Russian Invasion of Holland 1799* (Geert van Uythoven)

No 20 *'We Are Accustomed to do our Duty': German Auxiliaries with the British Army 1793-95* (Paul Demet)

No 21 *With the Guards in Flanders: The Diary of Captain Roger Morris 1793-95* (Peter Harington (ed.))

No 22 *The British Army in Egypt 1801: An Underrated Army Comes of Age* (Carole Divall)

No 23 *Better is the Proud Plaid: The Clothing, Weapons, and Accoutrements of the Jacobites in the '45* (Jenn Scott)

No 24 *The Lilies and the Thistle: French Troops in the Jacobite '45* (Andrew Bamford)

No 25 *A Light Infantryman With Wellington: The Letters of Captain George Ulrich Barlow 52nd and 69th Foot 1808-15* (Gareth Glover (ed.))

No 26 *Swiss Regiments in the Service of France 1798-1815: Uniforms, Organisation, Campaigns* (Stephen Ede-Borrett)

No 27 *For Orange and the States! The Army of the Dutch Republic 1713-1772: Part II: Cavalry and Specialist Troops* (Marc Geerdinck-Schaftenaar)

No 28 *Fashioning Regulation, Regulating Fashion: Uniforms and Dress of the British Army 1800-1815 Volume I* (Ben Townsend)

No 29 *Riflemen: The History of the 5th Battalion 60th (Royal American) Regiment, 1797-1818* (Robert Griffith)

No 30 *The Key to Lisbon: The Third French Invasion of Portugal, 1810-11* (Kenton White)

No 31 *Command and Leadership: Proceedings of the 2018 Helion & Company 'From Reason to Revolution' Conference* (Andrew Bamford (ed.))

No 32 *Waterloo After the Glory: Hospital Sketches and Reports on the Wounded After the Battle* (Michael Crumplin and Gareth Glover)

No 33 *Fluxes, Fevers, and Fighting Men: War and Disease in Ancien Regime Europe 1648-1789* (Pádraig Lenihan)

No 34 *'They Were Good Soldiers': African-Americans Serving in the Continental Army, 1775-1783* (John U. Rees)

No 35 *A Redcoat in America: The Diaries of Lieutenant William Bamford, 1757-1765 and 1776* (John B. Hattendorf (ed.))

No 36 *Between Scylla and Charybdis: The Army of Friedrich August II of Saxony, 1733-1763: Part II: Infantry and Artillery* (Marco Pagan)

No 37 *Québec Under Siege: French Eye-Witness Accounts from the Campaign of 1759* (Charles A. Mayhood (ed.))

No 38 *King George's Hangman: Henry Hawley and the Battle of Falkirk 1746* (Jonathan D. Oates)

No 39 *Zweybrücken in Command: The Reichsarmee in the Campaign of 1758* (Neil Cogswell)

No 40 *So Bloody a Day: The 16th Light Dragoons in the Waterloo Campaign* (David J. Blackmore)

No 41 *Northern Tars in Southern Waters: The Russian Fleet in the Mediterranean 1806-1810* (Vladimir Bogdanovich Bronevskiy / Darrin Boland)

No 42 *Royal Navy Officers of the Seven Years War: A Biographical Dictionary of Commissioned Officers 1748-1763* (Cy Harrison)

No 43 *All at Sea: Naval Support for the British Army During the American Revolutionary War* (John Dillon)

No 44 *Glory is Fleeting: New Scholarship on the Napoleonic Wars* (Andrew Bamford (ed.))

No 45 *Fashioning Regulation, Regulating Fashion: Uniforms and Dress of the British Army 1800-1815 Vol. II* (Ben Townsend)

No 46 *Revenge in the Name of Honour: The Royal Navy's Quest for Vengeance in the Single Ship Actions of the War of 1812* (Nicholas James Kaizer)

No 47 *They Fought With Extraordinary Bravery: The III German (Saxon) Army Corps in the Southern Netherlands 1814* (Geert van Uythoven)

No 48 *The Danish Army of the Napoleonic Wars 1801-1814, Organisation, Uniforms & Equipment: Volume 1: High Command, Line and Light Infantry* (David Wilson)

No 49 *Neither Up Nor Down: The British Army and the Flanders Campaign 1793-1895* (Phillip Ball)

No 50 *Guerra Fantástica: The Portuguese Army and the Seven Years War* (António Barrento)

No 51 *From Across the Sea: North Americans in Nelson's Navy* (Sean M. Heuvel and John A. Rodgaard)

No 52 *Rebellious Scots to Crush: The Military Response to the Jacobite '45* (Andrew Bamford (ed.))

No 53 *The Army of George II 1727-1760: The Soldiers who Forged an Empire* (Peter Brown)

No 54 *Wellington at Bay: The Battle of Villamuriel, 25 October 1812* (Garry David Wills)

No 55 *Life in the Red Coat: The British Soldier 1721-1815* (Andrew Bamford (ed.))

No 56 *Wellington's Favourite Engineer. John Burgoyne: Operations, Engineering, and the Making of a Field Marshal* (Mark S. Thompson)

No 57 *Scharnhorst: The Formative Years, 1755-1801* (Charles Edward White)

No 58 *At the Point of the Bayonet: The Peninsular War Battles of Arroyomolinos and Almaraz 1811-1812* (Robert Griffith)

No 59 *Sieges of the '45: Siege Warfare during the Jacobite Rebellion of 1745-1746* (Jonathan D. Oates)

No 60 *Austrian Cavalry of the Revolutionary and Napoleonic Wars, 1792–1815* (Enrico Acerbi, András K. Molnár)

No 61 *The Danish Army of the Napoleonic Wars 1801-1814, Organisation, Uniforms & Equipment: Volume 2: Cavalry and Artillery* (David Wilson)

No 62 *Napoleon's Stolen Army: How the Royal Navy Rescued a Spanish Army in the Baltic* (John Marsden)

No 63 *Crisis at the Chesapeake: The Royal Navy and the Struggle for America 1775-1783* (Quintin Barry)

No 64 *Bullocks, Grain, and Good Madeira: The Maratha and Jat Campaigns 1803-1806 and the emergence of the Indian Army* (Joshua Provan)

No 65 *Sir James McGrigor: The Adventurous Life of Wellington's Chief Medical Officer* (Tom Scotland)

No 66 *Fashioning Regulation, Regulating Fashion: Uniforms and Dress of the British Army 1800-1815 Volume I* (Ben Townsend) (paperback edition)

No 67 *Fashioning Regulation, Regulating Fashion: Uniforms and Dress of the British Army 1800-1815 Volume II* (Ben Townsend) (paperback edition)

No 68 *The Secret Expedition: The Anglo-Russian Invasion of Holland 1799* (Geert van Uythoven) (paperback edition)

No 69 *The Sea is My Element: The Eventful Life of Admiral Sir Pulteney Malcolm 1768-1838* (Paul Martinovich)

No 70 *The Sword and the Spirit: Proceedings of the first 'War & Peace in the Age of Napoleon' Conference* (Zack White (ed.))

No 71 *Lobositz to Leuthen: Horace St Paul and the Campaigns of the Austrian Army in the Seven Years War 1756-57* (Neil Cogswell) (paperback edition)

No 72 *For God and King. A History of the Damas Legion 1793-1798: A Case Study of the Military Emigration during the French Revolution* (Hughes de Bazouges and Alistair Nichols)

No 73 *'Their Infantry and Guns Will Astonish You': The Army of Hindustan and European Mercenaries in Maratha service 1780-1803* (Andy Copestake)

No 74 *Like A Brazen Wall: The Battle of Minden, 1759, and its Place in the Seven Years War* (Ewan Carmichael)

No 75 *Wellington and the Lines of Torres Vedras: The Defence of Lisbon during the Peninsular War* (Mark Thompson)

No 76 *French Light Infantry 1784-1815: From the Chasseurs of Louis XVI to Napoleon's Grande Armée* (Terry Crowdy)

No 77 *Riflemen: The History of the 5th Battalion 60th (Royal American) Regiment, 1797-1818* (Robert Griffith) (paperback edition)

No 78 *Hastenbeck 1757: The French Army and the Opening Campaign of the Seven Years War* (Olivier Lapray)

No 79 *Napoleonic French Military Uniforms: As Depicted by Horace and Carle Vernet and Eugène Lami* (Guy Dempsey (trans. and ed.))

No 80 *These Distinguished Corps: British Grenadier and Light Infantry Battalions in the American Revolution* (Don N. Hagist)

No 81 *Rebellion, Invasion, and Occupation: The British Army in Ireland, 1793 -1815* (Wayne Stack)

No 82 *You Have to Die in Piedmont! The Battle of Assietta, 19 July 1747. The War of the Austrian Succession in the Alps* (Giovanni Cerino Badone)

No 83 *A Very Fine Regiment: the 47th Foot in the American War of Independence, 1773–1783* (Paul Knight)

No 84 *By Fire and Bayonet: Grey's West Indies Campaign of 1794* (Steve Brown) (paperback edition)

No 85 *No Want of Courage: The British Army in Flanders, 1793-1795* (R.N.W. Thomas)

No 86 *Far Distant Ships: The Royal Navy and the Blockade of Brest 1793-1815* (Quintin Barry) (paperback edition)

No 87 *Armies and Enemies of Napoleon 1789-1815: Proceedings of the 2021 Helion and Company 'From Reason to Revolution' Conference* (Robert Griffith (ed.))

No 88 *The Battle of Rossbach 1757: New Perspectives on the Battle and Campaign* (Alexander Querengässer (ed.))

No 89 *Waterloo After the Glory: Hospital Sketches and Reports on the Wounded After the Battle* (Michael Crumplin and Gareth Glover) (paperback edition)

No 90 *From Ushant to Gibraltar: The Channel Fleet 1778-1783* (Quintin Barry)

No 91 *'The Soldiers are Dressed in Red': The Quiberon Expedition of 1795 and the Counter-Revolution in Brittany* (Alistair Nichols)

No 92 *The Army of the Kingdom of Italy 1805-1814: Uniforms, Organisation, Campaigns* (Stephen Ede-Borrett)

No 93 *The Ottoman Army of the Napoleonic Wars 1798-1815: A Struggle for Survival from Egypt to the Balkans* (Bruno Mugnai)

No 94 *The Changing Face of Old Regime Warfare: Essays in Honour of Christopher Duffy* (Alexander S. Burns (ed.))

No 94 *The Changing Face of Old Regime Warfare: Essays in Honour of Christopher Duffy* (Alexander S. Burns (ed.)

No 95 *The Danish Army of the Napoleonic Wars 1801-1814, Organisation, Uniforms & Equipment: Volume 3: Norwegian Troops and Militia* (David Wilson)

No 96 *1805 – Tsar Alexander's First War with Napoleon* (Alexander Ivanovich Mikhailovsky-Danilevsky, trans. Peter G.A. Phillips)

No 97 *'More Furies then Men': The Irish Brigade in the service of France 1690-1792* (Pierre-Louis Coudray)

No 98 *'We Are Accustomed to do our Duty': German Auxiliaries with the British Army 1793-95* (Paul Demet) (paperback edition)

No 99 *Ladies, Wives and Women: British Army Wives in the Revolutionary and Napoleonic Wars 1793-1815* (David Clammer)